Mummy Knew

LISA JAMES

Mummy Knew

A terrifying step-father. A mother who refused to listen.
A little girl desperate to escape.

HARPER
element

HarperElement
An Imprint of HarperCollins*Publishers*
77–85 Fulham Palace Road,
Hammersmith, London W6 8JB

www.harpercollins.co.uk

element™

and *HarperElement* are trademarks
of HarperCollins*Publishers* Ltd

First published by HarperElement 2009

6

A catalogue record of this book is
available from the British Library

ISBN 978-0-00-732516-0

Printed and bound in Great Britain by
Clays Ltd, St Ives plc

Mixed Sources
Product group from well-managed
forests and other controlled sources
www.fsc.org Cert no. SW-COC-1806
© 1996 Forest Stewardship Council

FSC is a non-profit international organisation established to promote the
responsible management of the world's forests. Products carrying the FSC
label are independently certified to assure consumers that they come
from forests that are managed to meet the social, economic and
ecological needs of present and future generations.

Find out more about HarperCollins and the environment at
www.harpercollins.co.uk/green

To the little girl I used to be, and the many others like her.

Mummy
Knew

Prologue

The lady with the long black hair was coming to visit. Nanny said it would be nice to draw her a picture so she could take it away and stick it on her wall. 'You can show her what a clever girl you are,' she said.

She pulled out a chair at the kitchen table and I clambered up then she handed me my tin of crayons and a piece of grey cardboard from the back of a cornflakes box.

I drew a rainbow first, and Nanny suggested I draw a picture of the lady underneath it. I tried to remember what she looked like, but all I could manage was the straight curtain of black hair and a cigarette with an orange end clamped between her stick-like fingers. I didn't know what colour to make her eyes until Nanny handed me the brown. I added loads of thick black lines for the lashes and Nanny said they looked like spider legs. I was good at those. Finally, I rummaged through my tin and found a bit of red for the mouth. Nanny laughed a little and said I'd drawn it upside down. I watched as she took the tiny stub of crayon from me and turned the lady's mouth into a thick, upturned clown's smile instead.

'That's better, pet,' she said. 'Let's cheer her up a bit.'

Finally I drew a giant multicoloured flower, a few tufts of grass and a triangular yellow sun in the corner. Nanny said it was a work of art and took my hand in hers to write some words at the top in blue.

'To Mummy Love Lisa xxx.'

Nanny put the picture in pride of place on the mantelpiece and said I could give it to Mummy when she popped in at teatime. I was so excited I actually had a mummy, like all the other children at nursery, that I didn't want to go for my usual afternoon nap. I found my dummy and climbed onto Nanny's lap in the rocking chair instead. She held me close against her chest and I sucked my dummy in time to the beating of her heart as she sang nursery rhymes into my hair until I grew sleepy. Back and forth she rocked me. Images of Mary, Mary, Quite Contrary and Pretty Maids All In a Row with long black hair just like Mummy's filled my dreams.

When I woke up later that afternoon, I was in Nanny's bed. I reached for my dummy, which lay on the pillow beside me, and popped it into my mouth. It was then I heard a low, gravelly voice. Mummy had arrived and was sitting in the front room next door.

I kicked off the covers and opened the bedroom door to see Mummy sitting on the small brown sofa with Nanny opposite in her favourite armchair. They were both sipping tea from Nanny's best china tea-set. Mummy's black hair was a little bit longer than I remembered it and now she had a heavy fringe, and her eyes had big black circles drawn round them. She wore an orange dress with large hooped earrings and a long string of wooden beads.

2

'Here she is!' said Nanny, turning round in her chair to look at me before heaving herself up with a 'One, two, three … oop laa!' to reach for the picture I'd drawn earlier. She handed it to me and nodded towards the lady: 'Go on, give it to Mummy.'

I felt shy in front of Mummy because I'd only seen her a few times, but I was filled with pride as I walked towards her with my drawing held out in front of me. I thought she would be pleased.

'Bleedin' hell,' said the lady, making me jump. 'She's a bit too old for a dummy, ain't she, Mum? What is she – three? Four?'

'Don't you know how old your own child is, Donna?' said Nanny sharply as she plonked herself back down into her armchair.

Mummy snorted and snatched the picture from my hands. 'Christ! Is that meant to be me?' I noticed her mouth was turned down unhappily, just as I'd drawn it the first time. 'Makes me look like fucking Quasimodo.' She put it on the coffee table beside her.

'Mind your language,' said Nanny under her breath, and then 'Aren't you going give Mummy a kiss, Lisa?'

I looked at her, unsure what to do.

She rolled her eyes and said, 'How can she when she's got that bloody thing in her gob? Give us it here.' She snatched the dummy away, pointed at her cheek with a long pink fingernail and said, 'Come on, then. I haven't got all bleedin' day.'

Her long nails had scratched my lip as she snatched the dummy away and I stepped towards her with tears in my eyes.

Instinctively I moved to wrap my arms around her neck, just as I did when I kissed Nanny, but Mummy pushed me away angrily and said, 'Mind me make-up, Lisa. Jesus Christ Almighty.'

My tears spilled over then and I demanded my dummy back. I looked to Nanny for help but she was staring into her teacup and shaking her head as if I had done something wrong. I cried harder then.

'Fucking hell, Mum,' said Mummy. 'I don't know how you put up with it. Does she ever stop fucking whingeing?'

Mummy left shortly after. She didn't say goodbye. Nanny sighed and put my drawing back on the mantelpiece. It now it had a tea ring at the end of the rainbow.

I crept over to Nanny, my eyes still red with tears. 'Come here, pet,' she said and we snuggled up together on the sofa. Nanny put her arms around me. 'Don't you worry about Mummy,' she soothed, 'You've always got me.' I felt warm and secure and totally protected. I always did with Nanny. I had no idea that my life was about to change. It never occurred to me that we would be separated and I would never feel safe again.

Chapter One

Nanny and I lived in London's New Cross, an area just south of Tower Bridge, with my aunts Jenny and Freda and my Uncle Jimmy. Freda was the oldest of Nanny's eight children, and Jenny and Jimmy the two youngest. The family were very close, and the council flat was always filled with visiting relatives. I remember Nanny standing in the middle of the small steamy kitchen, one hand on the hip of her patterned apron, the other on her head as she said 'We'll have to put in for a transfer. We can't swing a cat in here.'

Uncle Jimmy, who was busy stuffing a cigarette paper with tobacco, said 'That's because it's like Piccadilly bleedin' Circus in here, what with all her kids in and out all the time. Bloody disgrace she is, that Donna. Always has been.' He bent down to me and added, 'You're a bleedin' nuisance, aren't you?' His face loomed large above mine and I immediately burst into tears.

Nanny quickly stepped forward to scoop me up in her soft comforting arms. 'He doesn't mean it, pet. He's only playing with you.'

I knew that Mummy, the lady with long black hair, lived somewhere nearby with my two sisters and my brother. They popped in and out regularly because Nanny looked after them while Mummy was at work, but I was much younger than them and they didn't pay any attention to me. By the time I was born on Nanny's kitchen floor in December 1966, Diane was eleven, Cheryl was nine, and my brother Davie was six. Their father had gone for a quick pint at the pub a few weeks before Davie was born and had never come back. Instead he got the boat back to Ireland and was never heard from again. After waiting years in the hope he would return, my mother was granted a divorce on the grounds of his desertion.

Six years later, at the age of thirty-four, she found herself in another unfortunate situation with my arrival on the scene. I never found out who my father was – my birth certificate lists him as 'Unknown' – although I did once overhear Nanny and Jenny saying I came from a quick five minutes round the back of a pub rather than an actual relationship. The arrival of a fourth baby must have made life very difficult for my mother at a time when divorce itself carried a huge stigma. Now she had an illegitimate child on her hands as well. Perhaps this is why I was left in the care of Nanny. Quite simply I was an accident – unplanned and definitely unwanted.

My Durham-born Nanny, on the other hand, adored me. I was her 'bonny lass'. Uncle Jimmy may have seen me as a bit of a nuisance, but he was largely indifferent – unless, that is, I got my toddler hands on his precious tobacco tin and emptied the contents down the loo, as was my habit for a time, and then he would get a bit cross. My aunts Jenny and Freda also made a huge fuss of me, as did my numerous other aunties and uncles. I couldn't have been in better hands. These early years were my best, a time when I was safe, loved and protected.

Jenny, Freda and Uncle Jimmy were out at work during the day, so it was just Nanny and me. In the mornings we'd sometimes get the bus along to Peckham High Street and do the rounds at the greengrocer's, the butcher's and the baker's, or else we'd walk to the park and I'd go on the swings. But these trips became less frequent because Nanny wasn't in the best of health. She was overweight and found it difficult to walk very far. Her thighs were covered in bulging purple veins, while her calves and ankles were swollen with open ulcers. Walking was painful, and she rocked from side to side with an exaggerated limp. It was Jenny's job to bathe the crusty red and yellow sores with warm salty water every evening, applying cream and a stretchy bandage to the wounds.

Most of the time Nanny and I stayed at home. I would ride my red tricycle up and down on the balcony that ran the length of our block while Nanny sat in a deckchair and dozed, with a scarf covering her white curls. She gave me a little silver Noddy bell for my trike and I used to drive the neighbours crazy, ringing it continuously until someone leaned out of a window and yelled at me to 'Pack it in!'

Another of my favourite games was 'fly away Peter, fly away Paul'. I'd sit on Nanny's lap as she fluttered torn strips of newspaper on her index fingers, making Peter fly away as Paul came back, over and over again, until I decided I wanted her to play 'little piggies' on my toes instead.

Despite Nanny's problems with her legs, she always kept the flat spick and span. Every day she tied an apron over her clothes and pottered about dusting and polishing with an old rag. She cleaned the kitchen window with newspaper and a bottle of vinegar so the room smelled like a fish and chip shop. She liked to keep the front step polished with red lacquer but one day, after getting down on all fours, she couldn't get up again. I had to knock on a neighbour's door, and between him and the man who came to read the electric meter, they managed to pull Nanny back to her feet. After that she didn't do the front step herself any more.

Every day after lunch, Nanny and I had a nap, but first we had to make sure I had a dummy and a 'picky bit', two items I was unable to sleep without. I liked to unpick anything woolly, and run the fibres through my fingers. After Jenny and Freda got fed up with finding several of their best jumpers ruined, Nanny had knitted me a drawer full of special multicoloured woollen squares, and these became my picky bits. She had broken my round-the-clock dummy habit with dire warnings of growing up with buck teeth, but I took to hiding dummies for safe-keeping, just in case she was ever tempted to take Uncle Jimmy's advice and 'chuck the filthy things away'. The problem was, I could never remember where I'd put them, so before our nap we'd have to go on a dummy hunt. Usually I'd give up after the first minute or so, full of tears and convinced we'd never find one. Nanny would continue the search accompanied by my background wailing until she finally caught a glimpse of pink plastic peeping up from the bottom of the coal bucket or somewhere obscure like

8

that. The only time she'd get exasperated would be when, after searching for a good ten minutes, I'd realise I'd had one in my pocket all along.

'Oh dear, pet, I'm getting too old for this,' she'd say, shaking her head.

Once we were both snuggled down in Nanny's soft bed, she'd tell me a story. I'd lie there, inhaling the sweet scent of her face cream, and listen transfixed. She would tell me about growing up in a little village near Durham where the fields were full of schoolbook-eating goats, and elves and fairies too. I can't remember the end of any of these stories because what with the comforts of my dummy, picky bit and Nanny's soft lilting voice, it wouldn't be long before I was in the land of nod.

When I was three and a half, I started going to the local nursery school every morning. Nanny would walk me there, waddling from side to side. We'd often have to stop for a few minutes because her legs were aching but she was always cheerful and we'd sing a song or two on the way. I didn't like nursery at first and would sob and cling to Nanny, at which point she'd let out a little cry and say 'Mind me legs, pet.' But it didn't take long before I started to enjoy it. There were so many toys to play with, so many things to do. I was in my element – up to my elbows in the sandpit or water-play tank, painting, drawing, gluing, sticking, and making friends. Just before home time we'd sing songs such as 'I'm a little teapot' and 'If you're happy and you know it'. The teacher, Mrs Paterson, would stand in front of us doing the actions. Then we'd gather up our things and spill out into the little playground to wait for whoever was collecting us.

Normally Nanny was one of the first to arrive. I'd often spot her from quite a way off as I recognised the way she walked. I'd jump up and down and wave, and when she managed to pick me out from all the other children, she'd wave back. We had a ritual in which once she reached the diamond-wire fence I'd run up to her and she'd bend down positioning her cheek for a kiss through the wire. I'd rush out through the school gate and thrust a painting or maybe a glitter-studded egg box at her. No matter how awful my offerings, Nanny always lavished praise on my artistic talents before reaching into her pocket and producing a little packet of my favourite Love Hearts sweeties.

Then one day I was waiting in the playground as usual, but Nanny didn't appear. I looked down the road but couldn't see her. Gradually the playground cleared of all the other boys and girls until there was only me and Mrs Paterson left. She stood shielding her eyes from the sun as she peered down the empty road.

'Oh dear, Lisa, Nan's a bit late today. Never mind. Come back inside and look at a book until she gets here.'

I sat on the blue square carpet in the reading corner, my legs crossed in front of me. The bright sun streamed in through the window, burning the top of my head. I shuffled over a bit into the shade, but found myself sitting in front of a huge cast-iron radiator which scorched my back through my coat. I was hot and hungry. Where was Nanny? Why hadn't she come?

I shrugged off my yellow plastic raincoat and pulled a book from the shelf in front of me. Mrs Paterson sat at the other end of the classroom with a paperback in one hand, a sandwich in the other. Her eyes remained firmly on her book and I wondered if she had forgotten about me. After a while the door opened. My heart lifted for a moment, but sank with my spirits when I saw it was only another teacher bringing a cup of tea for Mrs Paterson. They murmured together and the other teacher, someone I didn't recognise, looked over and said, 'Don't worry, love.'

I could hear the sound of the older children playing outside in the Junior playground. Some girls were playing a skipping game, the rope whacking the ground in regular beats as they sang about apples and pears. There was stinging behind my eyes, and soon the picture book on my lap was speckled with tear drops. I gave a loud sniff and wiped my nose on the sleeve of my jumper. Mrs Paterson turned to me. 'Don't worry, Lisa. It's all under control.' I didn't know what she meant.

The bell rang to start lunchtime lessons. I had been waiting for over an hour but it felt like days. I needed to use the loo, but didn't want to risk going in case I missed Nanny when she finally arrived. It was at times like this I needed my dummy and picky bit the most. Just when I felt a fresh wave of tears threatening to flow, Uncle Jimmy bustled in through the classroom door. A lady I recognised from the school office was with him. He looked out of breath and red in the face, as if he'd been running. He spoke to Mrs Paterson for a few minutes, both their faces very glum. I couldn't hear everything they were saying but at one point Mrs Paterson raised her eyebrows and said, 'Hospital?' Uncle Jimmy nodded and then shrugged his shoulders. I was still sitting on the carpet in the reading corner. I saw Mrs Paterson point over to me and Uncle Jimmy caught my eye and said 'Get your coat on, Lisa.'

I did as I was told, feeling more and more confused. Uncle Jimmy had never picked me up before. As Nanny had taught me, I clasped each of my sleeves with the tips of my fingers so they wouldn't bunch up, and slipped my arms into my coat. Outside Uncle Jimmy took my hand in his own, rough and scratchy from working on building sites, and led me off towards home. 'Where's Nanny gone?' I asked, but he didn't say anything, just kept striding on, his steel-capped boots tapping on the pavement with each step.

Later, I found out Nanny had been rushed to hospital after a fall. My aunts Jenny and Freda took me to visit her after dinner. Nanny looked her usual self, lying on a bed. I knew she had fresh bandages on her legs because they were bright white, not like the old yellow ones she had at home. I noticed she had a tube going into her arm and water was dripping into it from a bag hooked up beside her bed. It made it hard for her to give me a cuddle, but Freda lifted me up and I sat on the edge of the bed and began picking the blanket, running the wool through my fingers. Nanny stroked my hair for a minute and said sorry she hadn't been able to collect me from school but she was nearly better now and soon we'd be able to get back to normal.

'No, Mum,' said Freda. 'It's too much for you running up and down after a kid all day. The doctor reckons you need rest.'

'I'll talk to Donna,' said Jenny. 'It's about time she started taking responsibility. After all, she *is* her mother.'

Nanny stayed in hospital that night, and Jenny, Freda and Jimmy had a bit of an argument about who had time to take me to nursery in the morning. In the end, it was decided that Uncle Jimmy would do it. 'But I better not miss me bus,' he said, exhaling a big smoky cloud as he spoke.

It was dark when we set off the next morning and Uncle Jimmy kept snapping at me to keep up, while looking at his watch and muttering rude words under his breath. When we arrived the main school gate was padlocked shut. We were too early.

'Gordon Bennett!' he cried, smacking his hands on top of his head and pulling at his wiry black hair. 'What am I meant to do now? I'm definitely gonna miss me bleedin' bus!' He started rattling the gates and shouting 'Oi, Oi!' at the top of his voice. 'They're in there. Look – I can see 'em drinking bloody tea. Oi! Oi!'

I could just about make out Mrs Paterson and another teacher moving around in the classroom. The windows were brightly lit against the dark drizzly morning and I could see their shapes through the frosted glass. They were totally oblivious to Uncle Jimmy, who continued shouting and waving as he desperately tried to get their attention. Suddenly he stopped as if a thought had occurred to him. He began to smile as he examined the padlock. I watched as he dug deep into one pocket and then the other, his smile momentarily fading until he found what he was looking for. He pulled out a small metal pin, which he wiggled in the lock, saying 'This should do it.' After a moment or two, the padlock clicked open, and Uncle Jimmy let out a roar of triumphant laughter.

I laughed too, pleased to see him happy. 'Is that magic?' I asked.

'You could say that,' he chuckled, ushering me through the gate. He watched me walk halfway across the playground and then called after me, 'And tell them two deaf-aids in there to wash their bleedin' ears out.' With a final wave he sprinted off round the corner to catch his bus.

As I entered the classroom, I made Mrs Paterson jump in surprise and she dropped a pot of pencils. 'Lisa!' she cried. 'How on earth did you get through a locked gate?'

'My uncle let me in,' I replied, hanging my coat on a peg as my face burned bright red. Drawing on all my three-and-a-half-year-old's wisdom, I decided not to mention the ear-cleaning business.

Chapter Two

When I was four, my life changed drastically. Nanny's painfully ulcerated legs and deteriorating health meant she was housebound for much of the time. On good days, she could still get out to the local shops and do the cooking and cleaning she enjoyed so much, but she was totally ill-equipped to keep up with the energetic needs of a young child. So it was decided I should live with my mother from now on. Although Nanny did her best to make it all seem like a huge exciting adventure, carefully mopping up both our tears with a sweet-scented hankie, I was bewildered as she started to pack a battered red suitcase with my things.

'Don't cry, pet,' she sobbed over the jumpers she'd knitted for me. 'You'll always be my special little lamb.'

'But why do I have to go?' I asked. 'Why can't I stay here with you?'

'You know how poorly Nanny's legs are,' she explained, clicking the case shut. 'I just can't look after you properly any more, pet. It breaks my heart, but I'll see you all the time. And don't forget you'll have your mummy. You like her, don't you, pet?'

I popped my dummy in for comfort, as fresh tears ran down my cheeks.

'And then there's Diane and Cheryl. It's about time you got to know your sisters,' Nanny went on. 'And Davie, too.'

No matter what she said to make it better, I felt only confusion and fear. One day I was safe in the warmth and comfort of her arms, and the next I was rattling around in a strange flat with a family I hardly knew. Mummy didn't seem to want me there at all. I could tell by the way she pushed me off whenever I tried to cuddle her, and shouted whenever I wet the bed, which I started to do every night.

'What you pissing the bed for, you stupid girl?' she yelled. 'Now you're gonna have to sleep in it tonight, 'cos I ain't got any clean sheets.'

Mummy's flat was just off Peckham High Street, only fifteen minutes from Nanny's place, on the first floor of a huge red council block. I found the flat quite scary at first because it was dominated by a long dark hallway we called The Passage. There were three bedrooms. Diane and Cheryl, both teenagers now, shared one. I was put in with Davie, who was ten and long used to having a bedroom all of his own, where his little collections were arranged just so. It must have been quite a shock to find himself sharing with a whirlwind of a four-year-old sister he'd had little contact with before. This led to endless fights and squabbles. The more he warned me not to touch his ship in a bottle, the more I wanted to look at it from every angle as I wondered how it had got in there through such a small opening. His plastic English and German soldiers were carefully arranged, ready for battle, but

I couldn't help mixing them up – and the impulse to chew the ends of the rifles was impossible to resist. Davie didn't mind me looking at his *Beano* comics as long as I didn't tear, crumple or scribble on any of them. I tried my best not to but didn't always succeed. But it was the time he caught me playing dress-up with his prized Millwall hat and scarf that finally broke the camel's back. After that, Mummy squeezed my bed into the corner of the girls' room. I was pleased with this arrangement for a number of reasons. One, it meant that I didn't have to put up with a big brother who would pin me down and dribble spit into my face any more; two, I was away from the scary cupboard in his room with its resident monster; and three, Diane and Cheryl's room had much more interesting things for me to play with, such as high-heeled platform boots, spangly tops and make-up.

Our front room was L-shaped with an open fire where we burned coal, and it had a small balcony that overlooked a grassy square outside. Unfortunately we couldn't use the balcony because it was full of old junk, such as broken sinks and bits of wood. The kitchen was small with a narrow little window so high above the sink that nobody could see out of it. There was a separate toilet with a long metal chain that was so stiff I had to hang on to it to flush it. It was my least favourite place in the whole flat because every time I went in, the spider's web in the corner seemed to have grown. I even saw a dead fly in it once. The bathroom smelled of mould, and was always cold and damp. It had another of the tiny windows so characteristic of the flat, high up near the ceiling, but this one was filled with rippled frosted glass. Mummy's bedroom was closest to the front door, and smelled of a mixture of Youth Dew perfume and cigarette smoke. The flat was often untidy and furnished with an odd assortment of furniture that had seen better days, but it was homely and clean enough. I quickly settled in, and pretty soon I felt as though I'd lived there forever.

Just after I'd moved in with Mummy, the council offered Nanny and my aunts a transfer to a lovely new maisonette over the road from our place. Their block sat atop a row of shops, and their flat was right on the end above the newsagent's. Nanny, Jenny and Freda moved in, and Uncle Jimmy stayed a while before moving in with Uncle Roy and Auntie Brenda in Essex. So although I didn't actually live with Nanny any more, I didn't have a chance to miss her much because her flat was like a second home. I would visit every day, often having meals there, and whenever I came in and out of our block, I could look over and see her windows. On sunny days, winter and summer, Nanny and Freda would sit out on their balcony watching the world go by so we were always waving and blowing kisses. Mummy was a barmaid at Uncle Bob's pub, often working double shifts at lunchtime and in the evening, so having Nanny so close by was ideal for her. She never had to worry about childcare arrangements because Nanny, Jenny and Freda were always on hand, dependable as ever.

Mummy wasn't the cuddly type like Nanny, and at first I was quite shy around her. She always seemed to be out working and if she was at home she would be too busy to stop and play or read me stories. One morning, I crept into her room to watch as she got ready for work. She was sitting on the edge of her bed, cigarette balanced in the ashtray beside her, brushing her thick and unruly black hair with hard, noisy strokes.

'What's that at the front of your hair?' I asked, pointing to a triangle shape that became visible when she pulled her hair back.

'It's called a widow's peak.'

I didn't know what that was but thought it was very pretty. 'What's that mark on the end of your nose?' I asked next.

'It's a beauty spot,' she told me, adding that it had flown up there all on it's own. 'It used to be on my cheek, like Liz Taylor's, but one night while I was asleep it flew onto my nose.'

I believed her totally, and from then on I'd always think of it as Mummy's magic beauty spot. She laughed when she saw my wide-eyed expression and helped me check up and down my arms and legs to see if we could find any on me.

'Is this one?' I asked, pointing at a freckle, and she agreed that it probably was.

'Now bugger off, I'm busy,' she said, pushing me away as if she'd suddenly had enough of me. 'I ain't got time for nicey-nicey chit-chat.'

Mummy had the same chocolate-brown eyes and dark complexion as Diane and Davie. Cheryl and I were the opposite with our rosy complexions, blue eyes and chestnut-brown hair. I'd often wish I was dark like Mummy. I liked to watch her lining her eyes in black so they looked double the size, and then slicking on a coat of rosy brown lipstick and rubbing her lips together before turning her face this way and that as she peered at herself in the hand mirror. Every few minutes she'd reach for her cigarette, hold it to her lips and squint her eyes as she took a long deep drag. Seconds later a massive stream of smoke emerged from her mouth and nostrils. Sometimes the ash would drop on her clothes and she'd quickly rub at it until it disappeared. The brown tips left in the ashtray would be coated with rosy brown lip marks. I didn't like the smell of the smoke, and on the rare occasion when she hugged me, I'd hold my breath until she let me go.

Before leaving for work, she'd reach into her bag and pull out a bottle of perfume to squirt behind her ears. Sometimes she even squirted it up her skirt. Once I copied her with a pretend bottle and everybody laughed, except Davie who went bright red. I'd ask if I could have some of Mummy's real perfume but most of the time she'd say, 'No, keep your sticky mitts off it.' One time she sprayed a bit under my chin but it made me feel sick and gave me a headache, and she said 'There you are, I told you it wasn't for you.'

At the weekends I'd often sleep over at Nanny's, but during the week it was Diane or Cheryl's job to put me to bed while Mummy was at work. They weren't as patient as Nanny had been when it came to the dummy hunt, and on the nights they couldn't find one, they just let me stay up and fall asleep on the sofa in front of whatever programme they were watching.

Mummy didn't usually get home from work until around midnight after the pub had shut, and was often tired in the mornings, but after she'd had a cup of tea and a cigarette she'd have woken up sufficiently to help me get washed and dressed. She wasn't as organised as Nanny when it came to doing the laundry and other household chores. It was alright for Cheryl and Diane, who were old enough to go to the launderette with their own clothes and bedding, but often Davie and I had to ask her to change our sheets or find us something clean to wear. 'I never get any bloody time to meself,' she'd grumble, but usually something would be done.

I don't recall ever going to the launderette with Mummy, but I often went on Sundays with Cheryl. One day we popped into Nanny's on the way and Nanny mentioned that Jenny was working overtime and hadn't been able to take their usual weekly wash. This had left Nanny and Freda a bit short 'in the underwear department'. Cheryl volunteered to take a few things to keep them going until Jenny got a chance to do the rest in the week. When Nanny handed the blue laundry bag over, it was stuffed to the gills with what can only be described as the biggest bloomers I'd ever seen. Cheryl and I exchanged a little giggle.

The bag was quite heavy, and as Cheryl was already carrying her own washing bag, I made an effort to be helpful. 'You carry one handle, Cher, and I'll have the other,' I said, hauling my side up to my shoulder with both my hands. Of course the difference in our heights and my relative lack of strength made it very awkward, especially as we battled against a near gale force wind that day. Cheryl was around fourteen and going through a stage where she coloured beetroot red easily. I could see a group of boys up ahead leaning against the huge arch that led through to the high street. We had to pass them to get to the launderette. 'Oh, no. It's that Kenny Fisher,' said Cheryl, her face beginning to flush pink.

Head down, she quickened her pace, almost dragging me along behind her.

As we drew level with the boys, a fierce gust of wind knocked me off my feet, causing me to drop my side of the bag and to Cheryl's great embarrassment, Nanny's underwear spilled out onto the pavement. The boys could barely contain their amusement at the sight of Nanny's bloomers, which were now blowing along like tumbleweed.

'Fuck me, look at the size of them drawers!' shouted one of the boys as the wind twirled them round.

Cheryl's face had turned puce. She was mortified. It wasn't until later that evening that she saw the funny side. I heard her telling the story to Diane and Mummy, and they all laughed until they cried.

One morning I woke up to hear Diane and Cheryl talking. Diane was getting dressed and Cheryl was sitting up in bed, a pillow propped behind her.

'Mum's got some geezer in there,' said Diane, lifting her long dark hair out of the back of her jumper. 'Made a right racket when they came in last night.'

'I know,' said Cheryl, blushing.

'What geezer?' I asked, suddenly embarrassed and self-conscious because I'd never said the word 'geezer' before. I knew it was a grown-up word, but I didn't have a clue what it meant.

Diane laughed, but Cheryl looked a bit panicked and said, 'Shush, Lisa.'

We sat still for a few minutes, nobody speaking. Diane walked over to the window and stared down at the grass below where I could hear dogs barking. Cheryl lay back down in her bed and pulled the blankets up to her chin. Then the noises started – a squeaking and rhythmic tapping, which seemed to get faster and louder. They were coming from Mummy's room next door. Diane's and Cheryl's expressions were a mirror of each other's, with wide eyes and mouths.

'What's that noise, Diane?' I asked, confused. I could hear whimpering noises now. 'Has Mummy hurt herself?'

'Look, just be quiet, Lisa!' Diane snapped. And then, to Cheryl, 'I can't believe they're at it again!'

Then the noises stopped and the momentary silence was punctuated by a loud male groan.

'Is that Uncle Jimmy?' I asked.

'I should bloody well hope not!' said Diane, making Cheryl burst into a fit of giggles that she attempted to silence by pressing her hands to her face.

It must have been the weekend because there was no school that day. Mummy was acting strangely. She remained in her bedroom for most of the day, with the door firmly shut. I could hear someone talking and laughing. It was a man. I'd seen a leather coat hanging on the back of the kitchen door with a newspaper rolled up in the pocket. It had a photo of a racehorse on the front.

Diane and Cheryl went out with their friends, and Davie went to play outside. I felt lonely and decided to knock on Mummy's bedroom door, but before I had a chance to ask her anything, she shouted at me to go and watch telly or something. When I knocked for the third or fourth time to ask if I could go over to Nanny's, she lost her temper.

'For fuck's sake, Lisa,' she shouted through the door, 'You know you're not to cross the bloody road on your own. Go and play out the front if you want but stop being a bleedin' nuisance.'

I did go and play downstairs, walking along the edge of the pavement with my arms outstretched for balance, but I didn't stay long. A boy ran over, egged on by his friends, and pulled my knickers down to my ankles. I was so shocked that I stood there frozen for what seemed like the longest time, my arms still outstretched for balance. It was the first time in my life I felt a sense of shame. My face burned, just as Cheryl's did sometimes. I looked up towards Nanny and Freda's balcony and felt relieved they weren't sitting outside that day to witness my humiliation.

The man began to visit Mummy in her bedroom regularly, but I still hadn't actually seen him. Heard him yes, smelled him too – he was a heavy smoker, like Mummy – but I'd never set eyes on him. Everybody seemed to be creeping around the flat. Things felt different now.

One day I heard the man in the bathroom. He gave a deep rattling cough and then spat something out. I was just working out that he must have spat in the sink and not on the floor when Mummy came up behind me. Without a word she took my hand and led me into the bathroom. Suddenly frightened, I tried to pull away but she gripped my hand tighter and glared at me. Once inside the poky little room I tried to wriggle behind her legs to hide from the man who stood directly in front of her. I could see he was wearing the same leather coat I'd noticed hanging on the back of the kitchen door.

'Say hello to Frank, there's a good girl,' said Mummy trying to drag me out from behind her.

I daren't look up, overcome by shyness and, for some reason, fear. I felt the need to pee and crossed my legs to stop myself. I stared straight ahead resisting the urge to look up. My eyes were level with the man's hands. He was holding a cigarette the same way as Uncle Jimmy did, between a yellow-stained thumb and index finger, cupped inside his palm.

'She's shy,' Mummy explained, an underlying note of annoyance in her voice.

Suddenly the man sank down to my level, so his face was inches from mine. I stepped back slightly and felt a trickle of wee slide down my leg. I looked into his face for the first time and saw that he had light brown hair that hung down over his collar. Two giant strips of hair ran down in front of his ears to meet the dark stubble on his chin. He smiled at me, showing a mouthful of bunched-up teeth, and his breath smelled all smokey and horrible.

'Hiding behind yer mum, are yer?' he asked. Not waiting for an answer, he stood up again and said to Mummy, 'I bet she'll break some hearts.'

They kissed then for a moment, making sounds as if they were chewing soft sticky toffees. They left their cigarettes to burn behind each other's backs as they wrapped arms around each other.

'Frank's coming to live with us,' said Mummy with a laugh as they parted. 'He's gonna be your new dad.'

I couldn't hold back any longer. I let my bladder go, and felt my red buckle shoes fill with warmth. Since I'd moved in with Mummy I'd started wetting the bed every night, but it had been ages since I'd had an accident during the day. I could tell she was very annoyed by the way she angrily threw her cigarette into the bath and yanked my arm so that I felt it click.

'Naughty girl! It's all in your shoes – look.' She turned to the man. 'Sorry, Frank, she's not normally like this.'

The man called Frank didn't seem to mind. He just laughed and pulled Mummy towards him for another noisy kiss.

Chapter Three

Although I was still only four, my new dad's arrival in my life made such an impact that the memories are burned indelibly into my mind. They play like short films complete with sound and colour, disjointed in places but vivid nonetheless. Before he came I was relatively carefree and settling into my new routines with Mummy and the family, adjusting to life without Nanny twenty-four hours a day – but that was all to change very quickly.

As 'Dad', as I was told to call him, made the sudden progression from simply being the stranger with the black leather coat who groaned in Mummy's bedroom a few nights a week into living with us permanently, he appeared, initially at least, to make an effort to be friendly, and we thought maybe things were going to be OK.

He brought us sweets and a kite, which he promised to help us fly on the green when it was windy enough. It sat in the packet in the corner for weeks and never got flown, but at least the thought was there. He also taught us loads of jokes, with naughty words in them. One was about a lady who gave birth to a head, which she kept on a red velvet pillow.

'The mother said, "Fuck me, I've just given birth to a head", and when it was the head's birthday, the mother said, "Guess what I've got for your birthday?" and the head said, "I don't care what it bleedin' is, as long as it's not another fucking hat!"'

Dad thought this was hilarious, and so did Davie, but when he repeated it to Nanny she got very annoyed.

'Fancy teaching that to a child!' she exclaimed. 'What sort of heathen has Donna moved in over there?'

One evening Dad splashed out on a meal of Kentucky Fried Chicken as a treat for everybody. I remember us all gathered in the front room. It was dark outside. The glow from the coal fire and the flickering TV provided the only light in the room. The fried chicken was laid out on a low coffee table in front of the sofa, where Mummy and Dad sat side by side. Davie, Cheryl and I sat on the floor. Diane wasn't there because she had gone to her boyfriend's. Dad was talking and laughing, and Mummy's adoring eyes never left his face. We were all smiling.

Suddenly Dad reached for a piece of chicken and realised that somebody had eaten the last drumstick. His face clouded over and his small dark eyes narrowed as he yelled at us.

'You greedy fuckers! Who the fuck has eaten all the chicken?'

We froze and looked round at each other, taken aback by the anger in his voice.

'Was it you?' he asked each of us in turn, jabbing with his finger.

I whispered 'No' when it was my turn, terrified of his aggressive tone of voice and the furious way he was staring at us. He looked as if he might murder the person who owned up, so no one did.

Mummy offered to make him an egg sandwich but he shouted 'Stuff your fucking egg sandwich up your arse,' and swept the remains of the meal onto the snowflake-patterned carpet. 'Greedy bastards!'

We cowered in the face of his mood, scared of setting him off again, and slipped off to bed shortly afterwards leaving Mummy to try and appease him.

A couple of days later Dad bought Davie and me a comic each and we settled onto the sofa happily flicking through them, glad to be in his good books. Then we heard Mummy and him rowing in the kitchen. Davie and I looked at each other nervously. We couldn't hear what they were arguing about but there was the crashing sound of cups breaking and then a yelp from our dog, Eddie. Dad stormed back into the room, snatched the comics from us, and ripped them to shreds. Only a few minutes before he had ruffled the hair on our heads; now we both got a whack round the ear because we were 'ungrateful fuckers'.

I soon learned not to trust Dad's moods. I knew that if I said or did anything he didn't like, he could flip. Davie called him 'Dr Jekyll and Mr Hyde' – behind his back, of course – and that's the way we all thought of him. He'd quite often be nice to me, playing at batting a balloon in the air or jiggling me on his knee, but the whole time I was bracing myself for a sudden change.

Mummy had never been much of a cook – she was always too busy – but on the rare occasions when she did have both the time and the inclination to cook anything other than something on toast, the food was delicious, almost as good as Nanny's. She would make Diane's favourite cheese and potato pie, or another crowd pleaser like toad in the hole with onion gravy, or shepherd's pie. But these times were few and far between, and we mostly ate simple food like eggs, beans, Heinz spaghetti and tomato soup. Even this level of choice ground to a halt after Dad's arrival. The cupboards were bare most of the time, except for the stuff she bought especially for him. Dad was the only person Mummy cooked for now, and she'd spend money she could ill afford making him his favourite steak and chips.

On the nights we didn't get any dinner, we'd either go without or Mummy would send us over to Nanny's for a meal there. Nanny, Jenny and Freda made it clear they didn't think much of Dad.

'He's a bad 'un,' I heard Nanny muttering.

'The sooner she gets rid of him, the better,' Jenny agreed. 'Says he's a window cleaner but I bet he's never done a day's work in his life. He's just sponging off her.'

Dad seemed to sense their opinion, or maybe someone had told him, because he decided to use me as an emotional pawn. 'If that old Geordie bitch thinks she's seeing her again,' he said, nodding towards me, 'she's got another think coming.'

He knew how much it would upset Nanny to be denied access to me, and whenever he was upset with them or in a bad mood, I would be banned from going over the road. His temper wasn't just taken out on Nanny, though. He'd punch walls, smash windows and rip cupboard doors off their hinges.

Then he moved on to precious family mementos like photographs, ornaments and our meagre record collection. He didn't care who the things belonged to, or what heartbreak he would cause by destroying them. The day he smashed Davie's ship in a bottle, Davie gave a heart-wrenching wail before running out of the flat and going to stay with Nanny for a few days.

'Go on, fuck off over there, you fucking nancy boy,' Dad shouted after him. 'How old's he meant to be? Eleven?'

Unbelievably, at times like this Mummy always sided with Dad. 'He should put his stuff away. Stupid boy,' she said, stooping down to pick up the thick shards of glass and the splintered wooden boat Davie had cherished for so long.

'Cunt!' said Dad, stalking back to his position on the sofa, a finger already poised to pull the ring on another can of extra-strength lager.

I couldn't understand why Mummy would let him do all these things, but she was different when he was around: giggly, and smiling, and always trying to catch his eye or get his attention. She never seemed to look at us any more.

'She's in love,' Cheryl told me, raising her eyebrows, and next time I saw Dad, I peered at him, trying to figure out what it was that Mummy loved. He was tall and slim, but had a pot belly which he seemed proud of – 'It takes ten pints a night to get a gut like this,' he used to boast – and his eyes were small and puffy above a long, sharp nose. Cheryl said he was fourteen years younger than Mummy, but he didn't look it.

'She thinks she's landed the jackpot, doesn't she?' she remarked to Diane. 'She didn't think she'd get anyone else, not with four kids in tow.'

'All my friends think he's quite dishy,' said Diane, 'but I can't see it myself. Have you seen the way he keeps scratching his arse? No thanks.'

Within a few weeks of Dad's arrival the flat's assorted wounds were patched up with duct tape, unsanded mounds of polyfilla and pieces of corrugated cardboard in lieu of glass. The shelves were devoid of the photo frames and various knick-knacks that had previously made the flat home. Diane, Cheryl and Davie, being older than me, were able to spend more and more time out of the way – but as the youngest, I was trapped.

I'd grown used to hearing the loud grunts and groans that came from Mummy's bedroom at all hours of the day and night, but now they were often joined by the sound of Mummy screaming in pain. I cowered under my bed or down in the dark corner beside the wardrobe, forming myself into the smallest ball I could, petrified that Dad would come for me next. I wrapped my arms around my knees, and tried to block out the sound of Mummy begging him to calm down. But on and on went the terrible crashes and thuds until I felt my heart would explode in my chest and ears.

Time and again the police were called by worried neighbours, but Mummy would simply go to the door, all indignant despite her battered face, and tell them to go away. 'I told 'em to sling their bleedin' hook. Interfering bastards.'

One day, after she had sent the police away yet again, she went into the kitchen to make a cup of tea. I watched her spoon the sugar into the cup and her hand was shaking so much that she was spilling as much on the counter as was going into the tea. I stood next to her and laid my head against her hip as the kettle boiled.

'What do you want?' she snapped.

'Are you alright, Mummy?' I asked, tears trickling down my cheeks and soaking into her dressing gown. 'Your eye looks sore.'

'Just go to your room or something,' she replied, pushing me away. 'You're always under my bloody feet.'

I knew by her reaction that she didn't want me to mention what Dad had done to her. It was almost as if she was embarrassed and couldn't meet my eye. So from then on whenever I saw her cut or bruised, or wearing her Polaroid sunglasses inside the house, I didn't say anything. In fact none of us did. I always felt very scared when I saw her bruises though. I was scared that he would hurt her really badly one time, and even more scared that he would hurt me. If he so much as raised his voice, I would find urine trickling down my leg. The more violent and unpredictable he became, the more I would wet myself, then I would panic that he would notice I'd had an accident and punish me with a slap or a kick. I crept round the flat like a little mouse, doing my best not to draw attention to myself.

I wished I could go back and live with Nanny again. But somehow I knew without asking that Dad would never let me.

Chapter Four

I started school when I was five. The nursery I'd attended when I lived with Nanny was based in the same Victorian building, so I was quite familiar with it already. I was looking forward to playing in the big girl's playground, where I could use the skipping ropes and hula hoops. Nanny knitted me a new hat and scarf, which I wore despite the late September heat, and Jenny and Freda bought me a pretty dress and long white socks from Woolworths. I felt really smart in my new outfit. Mummy couldn't walk me to school herself as she was having a lie-in with Dad, so Diane took me on the first day. It was a ten-minute walk away.

'I won't be able to walk you every day,' said Diane as she held my hand, 'so make sure you remember the way, just in case Mummy doesn't get up in time.'

'I should have brought a bit of bread to crumble, like Hansel and Gretel,' I said, and Diane laughed.

As we approached the gate, I was so nervous my insides were doing somersaults. But once I was inside I quickly settled in. The classrooms had proper desks with lids that lifted up and smashed back down on our fingers if we weren't careful.

I sat next to a girl called Claire Sullivan, and when we had to line up in twos we giggled as we held hands. I liked it at school, at least at first.

Mummy spent most of her waking hours at Dad's beck and call, catering to his every need, whether that meant running over the road to put his bets on, or spending hours in the bedroom with him whenever he announced 'Feel that, Donna. I've got the right horn.'

Mummy had plenty of time for him because since he had moved in, Dad had insisted on a few changes. Firstly, he stopped Mummy working for Uncle Bob in the pub because Dad believed it was 'whore's work' and besides, Uncle Bob was a 'no-good cunt'. Mummy could forget ever working there again – and another thing, she had better get used to the fact that she wouldn't be able to 'flash her tits all over the shop' any more.

'You're fucking everything that moves in that boozer,' he spat. 'What d'ya take me for, some kinda mug?'

'Why would you say that, Frank? I never look at anyone but you.'

'Cos you're a slag, that's why,' he replied with a sneer.

While he was at it, Dad also banned her from contact with any member of her extended family, especially 'the old bitch and two ugly sisters over the road'. Mummy accepted all this and even seemed pleased that he was so jealous and possessive of her, as if it was confirmation of his love.

'You just want me all to yourself, don't you?' she laughed.

The only time I remember her crying about any of his rule changes was when he trashed her make-up collection. He held her face in one hand, distorting her mouth so she looked like a fish, and then began to make her up like a clown with exaggerated red lips and large black crosses on her eyelids which smudged in her tears.

'Look at the state of you,' he said, roaring with laughter and twisting her face so she could look in the mirror. She began laughing then – laughing, coughing and crying all at the same time.

I was watching through a crack in the door, confused that Mummy could be happy and sad all at once.

With a clatter, Dad tipped Mummy's make-up into the tin wastebasket in the corner. Her best rosy brown lipstick fell onto the carpet and he stamped on it with a crunch.

'Could do with a new bit of carpet in here anyway,' mumbled Mummy, cigarette clamped between her circus-painted lips.

Once she had stopped working at the pub, the lack of money gave Dad yet another reason to lose his temper. Ever since he had taken up with Mummy she had provided for his every need and now that money was sparse Dad found things difficult.

'No booze, no fags, and I can't even have a fucking bet.'

In desperation, Mummy would send Diane or Cheryl over the road to Nanny's to ask if she could spare a few quid to tide us over. Since taking up with Dad she hadn't spoken to her family directly but she wasn't too proud to ask for cash. Nanny couldn't bear to think of us children going without the basics so she would always put a little money in an envelope and send it back to Mummy with her love. Little did she know that instead of buying food, Mummy would give the money straight to Dad who would quickly smoke, drink and gamble it away.

Sometimes I'd cry myself to sleep because I missed Nanny so much. I couldn't understand why I was sometimes allowed to visit her and other times I couldn't. I wanted to ask, but once I'd made the mistake of saying 'Nanny' in front of Dad and he'd smacked my bare legs so hard that I wore his red handprint for the rest of the day. It made me frightened to even think about her when Dad was around in case he could read my mind. If I saw Nanny and Freda sitting out on their balcony when I got home from school, they would wave and shout across the busy road, and even though I wanted to jump for joy and blow kisses, just as I used to in the old days when Nanny picked me up from nursery, I was worried that Dad might see me from our flat window, so I turned away and ran up the steps into our block as fast as I could.

Once Mummy whispered to me in the bathroom, warning me not to sneak over the road to see Nanny in case I got run over. She bent down until her frowning face was level with mine and her grip tightened painfully on my upper arms. I knew she wasn't really worried about me crossing roads because I walked to school on my own every day now and I was allowed to play in all sorts of dangerous places, such as the canal where a boy had drowned once and derelict houses with floors missing. I knew it was just that she didn't want me going over to Nanny's because Dad didn't want me to, and if he found out, he would be angry.

The thought of Dad's anger flipped my stomach. He quite often smacked my bare bottom if I didn't do what he asked straight away – and sometimes I didn't understand what it was he wanted me to do and got punished for it.

One day I was watching cartoons on TV when I heard him bellowing from the bedroom: 'Lisa, come here a minute.'

I ran through as quickly as I could, and when I got there I was surprised to see that he was lying on his bed completely naked. He was rubbing his ding-a-ling up and down and looking at the pictures in a magazine. I could see a naked lady on the front. She had blonde pigtails like Claire at school and was sucking her finger.

'Come and park your little arse over here,' he said. 'I want you to look at something.' He laughed and took a swig of lager before letting out a loud belch.

I didn't want to go over to him, but I was frightened not to. I climbed up onto the bed beside him, trying not to look at his ding-a-ling, which was sticking straight up in the air.

'What do you reckon, Lisa? Who's got the best tits out of these two – the blonde or the nig-nog?' He flicked the magazine with his middle finger. 'Get it right and it's tickle time, get it wrong and I might just have to bend you over my knee.'

My eyes filled with tears and I pointed at the black lady, hoping I'd got it right.

Just then we heard the front door opening and voices in the passage. It was Diane and Cheryl. Dad seemed annoyed and hurriedly covered himself with a sheet. He slammed the magazine shut and threw it on top of the tall pile of others beside his bed. The whoosh of air made a cloud of ash fly up from the ashtray and some of it settled on top of his drink.

'We'll have to play this game another time,' he said. 'Go on, piss off back to Scooby fucking doo or whatever shit you're watching.'

I ran back to the front room, my cheeks wet with tears.

'What's the matter with you?' asked Diane.

'Nothing,' I said quietly. I didn't even think about telling her what had happened, because already I was too scared of what Dad might do.

He was always telling me that I was his favourite, his special one, and in some ways that made me happy but it meant that he wanted me at his beck and call more than the others. When he was watching TV, he liked me to sit by the set so I could turn the dial to change channels when he wanted me to.

'It's like having one of the seven fucking dwarves as a slave,' he'd laugh. 'Which one are you?'

'Dopey,' I'd say, as he'd taught me to.

I didn't mind helping Dad because usually it made him friendlier towards me, but it wasn't always easy. When he was watching TV, I had to sit as still as I could because he hated me fidgeting.

'I'm trying to watch the film, here,' he'd shout, throwing a shoe at me when pins and needles finally forced me to shift position. I would have preferred to play in my room but I knew I'd have to wait until Dad told me I could leave.

During the ad breaks, he liked to play horsey with me. I had to climb up and straddle him as he bounced me up and down vigorously on his lap, and this made me giggle.

One day, he stopped in the middle of bouncing and said, 'You like sucking things, don't you, Lisa?'

I shrugged, unsure of what he meant, then blushed as I realised. Mummy had taken away my dummy ages ago and I'd started sucking my thumb as a substitute comforter. She kept telling me I'd end up with teeth like Goofy's so I had tried my best to stop but I was always forgetting.

'Would you like to suck mine?' asked Dad.

I looked at his thumb. It was stained brown from all the cigarettes he smoked and his nail was dirty and needed cutting. I couldn't imagine anyone wanting to suck a thumb like that.

'Well, would you?' he asked again.

I shook my head, and pressed my lips firmly together.

Dad laughed, and then licked his lips.

I knew I shouldn't but I started to wriggle off him. He grabbed me firmly with one hand, digging his nails into the top of my shoulder, and reached up to hold my nostrils closed with his other hand. He always did this when he wanted me to eat something nasty, like an old cigarette butt, for a joke. I held my breath for as long as I could, but eventually I had to gasp for breath. Before I knew it, he had rammed his dirty thumb into my mouth and was moving it back and forth really fast.

'Go on, suck it,' he said playfully. The taste was so bitter, I started to cough and splutter. I thought I was going to be sick.

'What's so funny?' asked Mummy, suddenly appearing in the doorway.

'Look at this, Donna,' he sniggered. 'She's good for a beginner but she'll have to go some to compete with you.'

Mummy thought it was hilarious. 'Oh, you do make me laugh,' she said.

40

I knew he was only trying to be funny, but I didn't like his jokes very much and I knew that he could suddenly turn from laughter to rage in a split second so I always had to be on my guard. Sometimes he would scare me with a sudden shout or move and I would have to cross my legs quickly to stop myself peeing. I wasn't always successful, though, and on occasion I'd let Eddie take the blame. I felt guilty about that but when I saw the beating Dad dished out in punishment, I didn't dare own up.

Mummy had got Eddie from Battersea Dogs' Home when I first moved in. He was a black, white and tan mongrel of labrador stock, always playful and boisterous but gentle with it. Like most dogs on council estates in the 1970s, Eddie used to take himself for a walk. He'd be let out in the morning and he'd be gone for hours until hunger and thirst forced him home. But once Dad had started beating him, he began to chase cars and cause a commotion down in the square, barking at everyone, especially men, so Mummy decided he wasn't allowed out on his own any more. The only trouble was that she didn't make arrangements for anyone to walk him on the lead either, which made Eddie's behaviour even more manic. He was desperate for the freedom he'd always known. Whenever somebody opened the front door he would attempt to charge through their legs. On the occasions when he did slip out, his behaviour was even more out of control, and the local kids, and some adults, would throw stones at him. I tried to take him out myself once but he was so strong on the lead that he pulled me the whole length of the road on my belly, grazing my face and knees, before I was forced to let go and watch as he nearly ran under the wheels of a bus.

So poor Eddie wasn't taken out much, and he had no choice but to leave puddles of his own alongside mine; puddles and mounds of poo as well. It wasn't unusual to step in it on the way to the bathroom as the passage was dark and even if you could smell it, you couldn't see it until it was too late. Unfortunately for Eddie, it was often Dad's bare foot that found it first.

One evening I was sitting on the floor behind the sofa in the front room. Dad was lying stretched out watching television. Eddie crept up, sniffed around and proceeded to urinate beside me. I wasn't shocked because I was used to seeing him do this, but it made me want to go too. I had been desperately crossing my legs for a while, unwilling to venture out from my place of relative peace and safety because earlier Dad had been in a bad mood and had put a foot through my dolls' house. I didn't want to have to walk between Dad and the TV and risk starting him off on another rant and maybe getting a smack on the bottom.

Eventually I could hold it in no longer. I slipped my knickers down to my knees, squatted and let it go, just on the spot where Eddie had done his wee, reckoning someone would have to clean there anyway. But as I did so, the sound on the television dipped for a moment and the hiss and splash I made on the floor could be heard clearly.

'What's that noise?' Dad demanded, pulling himself up into a sitting position. By the time he got up to investigate, I had just managed to pull up my knickers. Terrified at being discovered, I darted out in front of him and ran as fast as I could to try and find somewhere to hide.

I heard him bellow to Mummy, who was in the kitchen: ''Ere, Donna. The kid's pissed herself. Dirty little cunt.'

Mummy managed to find me first, hidden amongst the dirt and dog ends under her bed, but it didn't stop Dad rushing up behind her to give me a hard kick. I waited for Mummy to stop him as he dragged me back to the front room by the hair, but she did nothing.

'Please stop him, Mummy, please,' I sobbed.

She thrust her face into mine. 'Shut up crying!' she hissed. 'What do you expect me to do? It's not my fault.'

I thought I was going to pass out with fear. Holding me by the hair, Dad forced my nose down into the wet patch that Eddie and I had made and rubbed my nose back and forwards, calling me a 'piss-arse'. The shame was worse than the pain and I was inconsolable afterwards when Cheryl gave me a hug in our bedroom and tried to cheer me up by singing me a song.

I continued wetting the bed every night, too. If I didn't remember to draw back my sheets and blankets to dry off in the morning, I'd have to sleep with them wet the next night. Mummy had given up going to the launderette now, and the older girls were too busy trying to keep their own clothes clean without worrying about me. Soon I developed sores at the top of my legs where my thighs rubbed together and the urine burnt my skin. Sometimes Dad would see them as I sat cross-legged on the floor and he would tease me until I cried.

Early one morning I was lying in bed, halfway between sleep and wakefulness, when I felt a weight bearing down on top of me. I twisted and turned, trying to push it off because it was hurting. I could barely breathe, it was so heavy. I opened my eyes and squinted at a dark shape, relieved to realise it was only Eddie come to say good morning.

'Hello, boy,' I said, then I suddenly felt hot urine seeping through the covers onto me.

'Urgh, Lisa, what's that dog done?' Cheryl asked, lifting her head from the pillow to peer over at me.

'I think he's just weed on me,' I said, peeling off the covers. The frosty morning air made my wet pyjamas feel like ice.

'For God's sake! That's because he can smell your piss and he thinks it's where he's supposed to go,' she said.

I started to shiver, my teeth chattering, not knowing what to do next.

'Go and stand under the shower,' Cheryl instructed.

I stared at her blankly. I wet the bed every night and the most I did was wipe myself down with a wet flannel.

'Dog piss is stronger than ours,' she explained. 'You'll have to wash it off properly otherwise you'll have all the bitches after you on the way to school.'

I wasn't sure what she meant but I followed orders anyway. I picked my way down the dark passageway alert for any more of Eddie's deposits. I hated going into the damp bathroom, which smelled like a mix of mould, soap and wet ashtrays. The blue vinyl shower curtain was torn and fringed with mildew. I tugged it aside and heard it ping from another of the holding rings, so now it was only half attached and hung limply as if at half mast. I pushed it further aside so that I could inspect the bath for spiders. My body was beginning to itch in a way it didn't when I'd only slept in my own wet patch.

Cheryl appeared over my shoulder and turned on the tap for me. The rubber shower hose sprung into life, drenching the pair of us in freezing water.

'I'm not doing it!' I cried. 'It's freezing.'

'You dirty cow,' said Cheryl, disgusted. 'Get in there now.'

We stood looking at one another as the pipes gurgled and the bedsprings began to squeak in Mummy's bedroom opposite, then I gave in and let her lift me into the bath for a quick wash-down.

I usually got myself ready for school now, with a little help from Cheryl. Diane was usually staying with her boyfriend, Martin, so wasn't around much, and Davie had enough to contend with just trying to find something to eat. Mummy had started to slip even further behind with the washing so every day before school I had to either pull on the same clothes as the day before or set about finding something else. I'd often have to resort to rummaging through the dirty washing in the hope of finding something that I'd once considered too dirty to wear but which now looked Daz-fresh compared to the alternatives. Occasionally, when I had no other option, I'd raid my sisters' clothes but they were obviously too big and too grownup with their scooped necklines. Somehow I always seemed to be wearing T-shirts in winter and itchy sweaters in summer, but some things were constant regardless of season, such as my smelly knickers and odd grey socks.

We did P.E. in our underwear and I used to watch all the other children. Compared to me they looked like catalogue models. Everything matched: bright white vest tucked into knickers I just knew were clean on that morning. I had reached the age where I was self-aware enough to feel embarrassed about my own underwear. Some of the other kids would snigger and whisper about me behind my back and my friend Claire would tell them to shut up. I knew they had all noticed I was wearing the same knickers as last week, and I felt the odd one out. School wasn't as much fun as I'd thought it was going to be.

As I got a little older, I tried to help myself a bit more. I'd ask Mummy if she could give me some money so I could take my clothes to the launderette with Cheryl, but she would usually forget so I'd attempt to wash some things under the tap in the kitchen instead. If there was any washing-up liquid, I'd use a bit of that then spend ages trying to rinse the bubbles out. In the end, I'd give up and just squeeze the rest of the suds out before leaving the clothes in the airing cupboard. They'd dry stiff as a board and I'd have to crunch them up in my hand a few times before I could wear them.

Occasionally Nanny or Jenny would buy me some new clothes. For a few days I could pretend to be like one of the kids at school, with their coordinating outfits, but soon my lovely new blouse or trousers would be as grubby as everything else I owned.

I remember being particularly proud of a little woollen dress Jenny bought me from the market. It was pink with multicoloured flowers. After wearing it every day for a week,

I reluctantly took it off. Every few days I'd ask Mummy if she'd washed it yet, and she would say 'No, I bleedin' well haven't. Now bugger off out of it.' I came across it a few weeks later still buried at the bottom of the laundry bag. It had been there so long that the pretty flowers were blackened with mould. Mummy did eventually wash it, but not only did the black mould not wash out, but it also shrank so much that only my favourite dolly, Jemima, could wear it.

Around this time Aunt Freda had a heart attack and died. Mummy didn't bother to explain what had happened so it came as quite a shock to visit Nanny one day and find Aunt Freda's armchair empty.

'She's with the angels, pet,' said Nanny, dabbing her eyes with the edge of her apron.

Freda was the eldest of Nanny's four girls, and losing her so suddenly hit her hard. 'I can't believe Donna didn't even come to the funeral,' I heard her say to Jenny. 'How could she be so uncaring?'

'It's him, Mum,' said Jenny, trying to console her.

'I'm not sure it is,' Nanny replied. 'He's scum, there's no doubt about that, but Donna's always been a cold fish. Look how she left the little 'un like that.'

My visits to Nanny and Jenny remained intermittent but during the periods I was allowed to visit them, I'd spend most weekends there. In contrast to our flat, their place was always clean and tidy. Carpets were hoovered, floors swept and every surface dusted. The kitchen was pristine, without so much as a speck of dirt. Every night after dinner Jenny wouldn't sit down until every dish and pot was washed, dried and put away. I'd usually arrive on Friday evening in time for dinner. I especially loved Jenny's spaghetti bolognaise, which tasted a thousand times better than the orange tinned stuff I had at home. I used to laugh as I watched her throw a strand of spaghetti at the wall to test if it was cooked. If it stuck, it was ready to drain.

After dinner, Jenny would run me a lovely warm bubble bath. The carpet was pink and so soft I could wiggle my toes into it, in contrast to the slimy ripped lino at home. Soft clean towels hung on the rail. The spare toilet roll was covered by a dolly with a long skirt, whose name was Amanda. Jenny offered to let me take her home once but I refused because I couldn't bear to think of her sitting in our grimy toilet with the spiders. Besides, we never ever had a spare toilet roll; most of the time we had to use old pages from *The Sun*.

I wouldn't get out of the sweet-smelling bath until my fingers and toes were wrinkled like pink little prunes. At bedtime I'd squeeze in next to Jenny because I was bigger now and might hurt Nanny's legs in my sleep. I liked sleeping with Jenny. She was soft and fat, perfect for cuddling, and her made-up stories were just as magical as the ones Nanny used to tell me when I was younger.

On Saturday mornings Jenny would take me for a walk up to the High Street where we'd do some shopping. *The Generation Game* with Bruce Forsyth was on the television at the time and I'd make her laugh by doing an impression of Brucie's pose and saying 'Nice to see you, to see you nice.'

Nanny would be sitting out on the balcony when we got back. She was virtually housebound now, and the only fresh air she got was when she sat out on the balcony tending her geraniums and watching the world pass by. I'd go out and sit beside her. Sometimes we'd see Mummy and Dad walking in or out of our block but they didn't wave, and nor did we.

Sunday would start off nicely enough. Jenny was always trying to lose weight and had bought a yoga book so we'd clear a space in the front room and practise the Plough and the Cobra, the Bridge and the Bow. Usually we'd be in fits of giggles because neither of us could balance and we'd end up in all sorts of tangles, as if we were playing a game of Twister.

Sunday lunch would be delicious. Sometimes Davie and Cheryl would turn up to pile their plates with Nanny's special roast potatoes. But as the day wore on, my stomach would start to do little flips as I realised it would soon be time to go home. Home to the dirt, the disorganisation, the empty food cupboards, but worst of all, home to Mummy and Dad. Mummy who seemed to look straight through me most of the time when she wasn't complaining that I was in her way and driving her crazy, and Dad, who alternated between his special brand of hot and cold treatment – friendly one minute, hostile and violent the next.

At about seven o'clock the tears would start as I kissed Nanny goodbye. I'd lay my head against her chest and remember the times I used to fall asleep listening to her heart in the rocking chair when I was small. I revelled in her familiar warmth. I clung to her, not wanting to say goodbye because I never knew when I would see her again. It might be tomorrow or the day after, but Dad kept changing the rules and sometimes I wouldn't be allowed to visit for weeks.

'Now, now, pet,' she said. 'Don't you cry. We'll see you again soon and you can help me make a cake.'

With a last kiss, Jenny led me back over the road. She would wait outside our block until I ran upstairs and waved to her out of Davie's bedroom window to let her know I was safe. Except I never was, really. Not with Dad around.

Chapter Five

After a few weeks without Mummy bringing in a salary, the tension in the flat rose to pressure-cooker levels. At first Dad had relished having her at his beck and call twenty-four hours a day, but soon the reality of life without a steady income began to bite. He seemed stuck in permanent Mr Hyde mode because he could no longer indulge quite so freely in his three main hobbies of smoking, drinking and gambling.

Dad was obsessed with horseracing. He studied the form in *The Sun* and *The Sporting Life* and made sure to watch every televised race meeting. The only problem was that he wasn't very good at picking winners.

At the start of every race he'd perch on the edge of the sofa, restlessly shifting from side to side just like the horses that jostled for position behind the starting line. If he had placed a bet he would hold the ticket in front of him and begin to murmur under his breath. The small blue betting-shop pen would be lodged firmly behind one ear, a spare fag behind the other. As the horses galloped closer and closer to the finishing line, Dad would slide down onto his knees and edge closer and closer to the television, thrashing an imaginary

51

whip and roaring encouragement: 'Come on, my son. That's it, come on, you bastard.'

I'd hold my breath and cross my fingers and toes as I willed his horse to win. But my heart would sink and I'd start thinking of somewhere to hide as Dad's horse was overtaken in the final furlong, and his exhilaration gave way to bitter disappointment as it dawned on him that he'd just thrown more money down the drain.

'That's fucking bollocks, that is! Bastard fucking animal.' He'd rip the betting slip to shreds and let it flutter to the floor. 'You're fucking jinxed, you lot,' he'd yell and whoever was closest would be lucky to escape without a whack round the head.

One day he kicked the television over when the pundit in the pork-pie hat came on to heap praise on the winning horse. It made a loud bang, and smoke came out. We weren't without a television for long, though. Somehow, even though he didn't have a job, Dad always managed to get hold of things he wanted. Nobody knew exactly how, but it always seemed to be that he had a mate, who knew some bloke, who was friends with some geezer down the pub, and in exchange for a 'ton' or 'pony' Dad could get hold of anything.

I asked Davie if Dad had a real pony and he laughed, 'It's rhyming slang for twenty-five quid, stupid.'

So we might not have the basics like food and loo paper, but sometimes Dad would manage to get hold of things he needed, like cigarettes or, once, a case of ouzo, which Mummy said was like drinking 'fucking paint stripper'. The new telly he got was bigger and better than the last one, and it was colour, too. Me and Davie were so excited. When Dad was out or in an unusually good mood, we would watch our favourite cartoons on it. It was a whole different experience.

Meanwhile, the swearing, shouting and violence gathered pace and Dad was often heard threatening to leave Mummy for someone younger who didn't have such a 'baggy fanny'. I wondered long and hard about what that was but couldn't work it out. All I knew was that it didn't sound very nice and Mummy got upset whenever he said it.

It wasn't unusual to see the remnants of Dad's dinner sliding down the front room wall where he would aim his plate, frisbee-style. I would duck out of the way and Mummy would quickly try to salvage the food before the dog got to it, saying 'Oh, Frank, what you done that for?' as if gently chiding a tantrum-prone child who could never really do any wrong in her eyes. This attitude was the complete opposite to the way she would shriek at me if ever I dropped something by accident. 'For Christ's sake, Lisa. Why are you so bleedin' clumsy?'

The trigger for Dad losing his temper could be something as trivial as finding a lump in his gravy or the mere mention of Nanny's and Jenny's names, but more often than not the root cause always involved one of three things: his irrational jealousy, alcohol, or having backed the wrong horse at Kempton Park. Without money to keep him in booze, fags and betting slips, the arguments just kept getting worse.

Mummy started looking for a new job, but every classified ad she circled in the paper would meet with Dad's disapproval. He didn't want her working in an office because she might meet men and have an affair just like the slags on the

TV. He certainly didn't want her doing bar work again for much the same reason. Dad suggested cleaning, which was ironic because our flat was always in such a state. Mummy agreed to everything he said, even though I heard her tell Diane that it wasn't something she wanted to do – 'but at least it's cash in hand'. So that's why she started cleaning private houses for posh people in the West End.

While she was out at work, Dad and I got to spend more time together and he came up with a new job for me, which was scrubbing his back for him when he had a bath.

'You've got a lighter touch than your mother,' he said. 'She's like a fucking navvy.'

He used to like me to use my hands instead of a flannel. 'Get a good lather going,' he said. 'You could make a fortune in one of those massage parlours.'

I wasn't sure what a massage parlour was, but I was glad I seemed to be doing something right at last. One time he had pinched my thigh because I was 'doing it crap'.

I thought of Nanny and Jenny, and wondered what they would say if they knew Dad made me do things like this? They were both very careful not to let me see them undressed, and if anything rude ever came on the television while I was visiting, they would quickly turn it over. Once when Jenny took me up the high street to buy a Saturday morning custard tart, we saw a tramp in a shop doorway. His flies were undone and he was peeing in a big arc. Jenny was horrified and covered my eyes.

I didn't like seeing Dad naked but I was getting used to it because he was always parading round the place with no clothes on and even wiggling his privates in my face for a joke. Once he tried to make me believe his ding-a-ling was alive, like some sort of pet. 'Go on, give it a little stroke,' he urged.

I ran away and hid but I could hear him and Mummy laughing about it. She seemed to think it was all quite funny. She obviously didn't see anything odd in what he was doing.

'She probably thought it was a baby mouse,' Mummy joked.

'Watch it!' Dad said.

'Watch it? I can hardly fucking see it?' chuckled Mummy.

So if she thought it was OK, I supposed it must be. Maybe Nanny and Jenny were just too old-fashioned. That must be it.

One morning soon after Mummy started work, I woke up feeling sick. It was as if my stomach was full of butterflies desperate for a way out. I knew I wasn't ill in the true sense; it was just that the thought of having to go to school and sit opposite a girl called Susan Jackson was playing havoc with my insides. She had been moved into our class mid-term because she had been bullying a boy called William, who had a stutter. Finally his mother had marched into the head-mistress's office and demanded action so she'd been shifted from William's class into ours.

I had once seen Susan in the playground surrounded by a cackling gang of supporters, pressing her mean face into William's and making him cry. Her nastiness reminded me of Dad so I ran as quickly as I could and told the playground assistant what was happening.

Susan saw me pointing her out, so it was of little surprise that when she joined our class she swiftly targeted me as her new victim. Within a very short space of time she managed to convince my small circle of friends not to play with me any more because I was 'smelly' and a 'dirty tramp' and if they liked me, then they must be one, too. I wasn't frightened of Susan physically. Compared to the slaps, kicks and punches that were a way of life at home, her sly pinches and pokes barely made me flinch. Far worse, though, was her relentless teasing. I knew for a fact that sometimes names could hurt just as much as sticks and stones. I told our teacher about it but she rolled her eyes and said 'Just ignore her, Lisa.'

The day before, Susan had told everyone on our table that her mum didn't want her anywhere near the 'stinky one' in case she got nits. Everyone screamed in mock horror and screeched their chairs across the floor to get as far away from me as possible. Even Claire Sullivan, who only a few weeks before had linked pinkies with me and sworn we'd be best friends forever, was sucked into the vendetta.

Lying in my damp, urine-soaked bed, I imagined swinging Susan around by her long ginger plait, but I knew I would never do it in reality, no matter how much I wanted to.

My mind was made up. I didn't care if I had to take my chances at home with Dad, but there was no way I was going to school today. Mummy had been talking about having to go out on a special cleaning job and Dad had been suffering from a hangover all week after bingeing on ouzo, so I knew she would prefer not to leave me alone with him in case I got on his nerves. A plan began to form in my mind. I hadn't been able to see Nanny for some time because she had sent Mummy a letter begging her to 'see sense and kick that man out for everyone's sake'. Mummy had ripped it to shreds after Dad had demanded she read it aloud, and ceremoniously burnt it in the kitchen sink as he looked on approvingly.

'If that old bitch thinks she's seeing the kid again, she'll have a long fucking wait!' Dad declared, nodding over towards me where I was sucking my thumb in the corner. And his word was Law.

I hoped that today, Mummy would realise she had no option other than to send me over the road, where I could cuddle Nanny and eat cakes and sweets all day. I began to groan and pretend to be a lot sicker than I felt.

I heard Mummy take a cup of tea into Dad, who was still in bed with a bad headache and a sick bucket by his side. She was mumbling, then I heard his voice, gravelly from sleep, shouting 'I said no!'

Mummy emerged from the bedroom looking daggers at me. 'Trust you to be ill today. I'll have to take you to work with me now.'

It might not be Nanny's, I thought, but at least it was better than going to school.

Mummy went to quite a bit of trouble that day to find me something to wear that wasn't too badly crumpled or dirty. She also made me chew a fluffy junior aspirin she'd found at the back of the medicine cabinet. I was feeling much better now that I was no longer worrying about Susan Jackson, but I chewed the bittersweet pill in order to keep up the pretence I was ill.

Then Mummy stood behind me and attempted to sort out my rats' tails. She dragged the brush through my knotty hair, making me squeal in pain, and yanked it back into a ponytail so tight that I developed a genuine headache and was pleased she'd given me the aspirin.

She told me to put my anorak on and took a step back to look me up and down.

'No, you'll have to wear the tartan,' she said, delving into the back of the wardrobe to retrieve a coat that had already been a bit too small when she brought it back from a jumble sale the year before. I was seven now and the label inside said it was for a five-year-old. I had to take off my jumper in order to squeeze into it. Even then it was too tight and made my arms stick out stiffly to the side. It smelled funny too.

'Why do I have to wear this, Mummy?' I asked. 'Why can't I wear my anorak?'

'Because we're going somewhere posh and I don't want you showing me up,' she said, slinging her bag over her shoulder. 'Now get a move on or we'll miss the bus.'

We had to change buses a couple of times before we arrived in Chelsea. The street was a short walk from the King's Road and all the houses along it were massive, set back from the road with smart cars outside.

Mummy pointed to a large white house on the corner opposite. 'That's it,' she said, taking a last puff on her cigarette before grinding it into the pavement with her heel. 'If you think you're going to be sick, make sure it's not on the rugs. They're worth a fortune.'

A black limousine was parked outside with a liveried chauffeur reading a paper at the wheel. Just as we were about to open the ornate wrought-iron gate, four men emerged.

Mummy pulled back and stepped to one side, slightly bowing and nodding her head as she did so. The men were dressed in long white robes and wore what looked like red-checked tea towels on their heads, just as Alan Slaven had when he'd played Joseph in our school nativity play. I guessed they must be from Jerusalem or somewhere like that. The chauffeur threw his paper aside and sprang out of the car to open the door for them, then they all got in and drove off.

Another man, this one wearing a normal suit and tie, stood inside the front door. He had a posh voice and I noticed he was wearing heavy gold cufflinks. He led us up a curved flight of marble steps to the first floor, pulling a handkerchief out of his pocket and holding it over his nose and mouth. We walked down a long hallway towards a set of double doors and as we got closer I noticed a terrible smell. The man mumbled something behind his hankie, which sounded like 'Sorry about the mess' and then disappeared off down the corridor again.

'Cor blimey. Something stinks,' said Mummy, reaching for the ornate door handle.

As she opened the door, a huge room came into view. There was hardly any furniture, just a few chairs round the edges of the room.

'What the bleedin' hell's all this?' Mummy exclaimed.

The floor was covered with lots of beautiful rugs, but every square inch of them was strewn with food – mainly sticky grains of rice, but there were also chunks of meat and bones. Silver platters sat in the middle, some still piled high with food, which had rotted and was fit only for the giant bluebottles that flew from one dish to another. I pointed out what looked like a sheep's head to Mummy and she made a face.

'There's been some bleedin' party here,' she said, wrinkling her nose.

She gave me a black bag to fill and we worked side by side all afternoon. By the time we left, the room was as clean as it was going to get without the use of an industrial-strength hose. The man in the suit was very pleased and pressed a large wad of notes into Mummy's hand. All the way home she kept saying 'Oh my God' and looking into her bag to see if the money was still there.

When Dad saw how much the man had given her, he was suspicious. 'What did you have to do to get that?'

'They're sheikhs, Frank. This is small change to them. And I'd still be there shovelling sheeps' heads now if I hadn't had her to help me.' She jerked her thumb towards me.

Mummy thought I had done such a good job that she let me stay off school the next day too. She took me on another job in a place in Notting Hill and this time she let me polish the furniture with a yellow duster and a can of Mr Sheen.

'Is this alright, Mummy?' I asked, eager to please.

'That's it, Lisa. Give it some elbow grease,' she urged.

I felt so happy. Not only was I away from Susan Jackson, but it seemed Mummy was actually pleased with me for once.

When we'd finished, Mummy called up a narrow dark stairway, 'I'll be off now.' I had heard somebody using a type-writer up there while I'd been going around with my duster. The door opened at the top of the stairs and a man with greased-back grey hair came down. He wore baggy green corduroy trousers and a pair of small glasses hung on a cord around his neck. As he paid Mummy for the work, he looked at me and asked 'Shouldn't she be at school?'

'She's ill,' said Mummy.

'Is she now?' he said, bending down to look at me. 'She looks well enough to me. What's wrong with you, sweetheart?'

I didn't know what to say so I looked up at Mummy for help, and she nodded as if I should tell the truth. So I did. 'Nothing's wrong with me. Mummy needed a hand with the cleaning, that's all.'

He seemed surprised and took Mummy off to a corner, wagging his finger at her.

I could tell she was fuming when we got out on the street.

'What the fuck did you say that for?' she demanded. 'You trying to get me in trouble?'

'No, Mummy,' I replied, upset that I'd annoyed her.

'Nosey old bastard. What right has he got to lecture me, the cunt? He can stuff his fucking job.'

Whenever Mummy took me cleaning I tried my best to do a good job, and hoped that she and I would get closer once we were working together like this but she never said 'Well done' or 'Thanks' or 'Aren't you a good girl?' If anything, she acted as though it was a nuisance having me around. I would have done anything for a hug or a few words of praise but they were never forthcoming. She wasn't that kind of a mother, I supposed. She wasn't the cuddly type.

Chapter Six

By the time I was eight years old I had finally stopped wetting the bed at night but my bladder remained on a hair trigger, and sometimes when Dad was at his most threatening, he'd only need to make a sudden lunge towards me and I would wet myself before his slap had even connected. He'd been living with us for four years, almost as long as I could remember, and he was as volatile as ever. At various times, one or all of us would be ostracised. When it was your turn, you had to stay in your bedroom and nobody was allowed to talk to you while Dad was at home. Although the silent treatment had its benefits – Dad didn't scream in your face for a start – it also carried with it a great cloud of menace, which was somehow even more frightening.

Davie was almost always getting the big freeze treatment, but for some reason it seemed I had definitely become Dad's favourite girl and he took every opportunity to pull me onto his lap for cuddles. I didn't feel very comfortable with this affectionate behaviour, but if I pulled away even slightly from his scratchy kisses, his face would cloud over and a fierce look would descend to smother the smiles of a moment before.

'You know I love you like my own daughter, don't you, Lisa?'

I beamed a big smile at him then, because there was nothing I wanted more than for us all to be a normal family. I wanted him to stay as Dr Jekyll and bury Mr Hyde forever.

When Dad was in a good mood, he liked to play lots of jokes and games. He mostly played them with me, because more often than not he wasn't on speaking terms with Diane, Cheryl or Davie, and he didn't like them anyway.

'You're not like them other bastards, Lisa,' he said. 'They're all cunts.'

Some games I liked better than others. Bat the balloon was my favourite. Dad would lie in bed and I'd stand near his feet while we knocked the balloon back and forth between us. I never got bored with it, and could have played for hours, but Dad could only put up with it for a short time before he got fed up and burst the balloon with his cigarette.

My heart would sink because then it would be his turn to choose a game. I didn't like any of his favourites at all. Especially the ones that involved him taking my clothes off. I was eight now and becoming embarrassed. I'd try to cover myself with my arms but that would only make him tickle me, his fingers hurting as they dug in.

'Are you blushing?' he would tease, tweaking my chest and bottom. 'I've seen it all before, Lisa. Don't forget I used to wipe your arse when you were a baby.'

No matter what he said, I still didn't like it, and when he tied knots in the side of Mum's knickers and made me wear them I used to cry. I couldn't see the fun in it. Sometimes he'd wear a pair too.

'Can we play bat the balloon again after?' I'd sob as he slipped Mum's scratchy lace nightie over my head.

'Shut up about bat the fucking balloon, will ya?' he said. 'First we play this, then we *might* play that. But only if you give me a special kiss.'

I didn't like Dad's special kisses either. His whiskers scratched and his lips were all slobbery.

One day Mum came home from work earlier than expected, and he just had time to leap into bed and hide what he was wearing from her. He didn't seem bothered that I was almost naked and wearing her clothes.

'What's she doing with my fucking knickers on, Frank?' she asked.

Dad laughed. 'Leave her alone, you miserable cow. She's only fucking playing.'

'Get 'em off,' Mum shouted, slapping my legs.

'But Dad put them on me,' I said. 'I didn't want to.'

'Don't tell lies, you disgusting little cow,' shouted Mum, her face flushing with anger, 'or I'll slap your bleedin' face for you.'

I looked over at Dad, expecting him to explain about the game, but he only smirked.

'He's wearing some too,' I cried.

'Eh?' said Mum, pulling back the sheet to see Dad's ding-a-ling hanging out of her best silky pink pair.

Dad burst out laughing. 'What? Can't you take a joke?'

Mum sent me to my room, with a sharp poke in the back. Later I heard them arguing.

'I ain't fucking gay at all, you slag,' shouted Dad. 'It's just a stupid game. I'm only trying to entertain your fucking kid for ya.'

I don't think we played that game again for a while, though.

During the school summer holidays, Nanny and Jenny asked if they could take Davie and me to Canvey Island Caravan Park for a week's break. I begged Mum to let me go, whispering so Dad couldn't hear because we still weren't allowed to mention certain names in his presence. But Mum must have discussed it with him because he started to look at me in a frightening way, with a nasty tilt to one nostril.

I was amazed and delighted when Mum said we could go. We had a lovely time, running around the caravan park and making friends with the donkeys who lived on the other side of a ditch. Jenny would buy apples and carrots and we'd throw them over and watch while the donkeys chomped them down with their big yellow teeth. I felt as though a weight had been lifted from my shoulders for that week. It was like the old days when I was little. No anger, no violence, nothing to be wary or frightened of, only love and happiness. When it was time to go home I sobbed and cried, and not just because I had to say goodbye to the donkeys.

When I walked back into the flat, carrying my clothes in a bag, already washed and pressed by Nanny to save Mum the trouble, and clutching sticks of pink rock for everyone, the atmosphere was heavy. I found it harder to breathe somehow, and the thick fog of cigarette smoke that lingered in every room had little to do with it.

Mum and Dad were sitting on the sofa watching television. I went in to say hello, and they both just stared at me. I could see Mum was nervous, already worried I might try and tell them what a good time I'd had, therefore breaking the golden rule about not mentioning or alluding in any way to the people who lived over the road.

'Tell her to fuck off away from me,' said Dad, giving me my first clue that all was not well. He didn't talk to me again for weeks after that. He stared, snarled, sneered and even spat at me, but he never spoke to me once. On the whole I was pleased because it meant less shouting and swearing, less risk of plates, cups and ashtrays whizzing past my head, but I had an inkling that it wouldn't last.

During this time I noticed he was being a bit friendlier to Cheryl and Davie – especially Cheryl. One day when I was confined to the bedroom, she came bursting into the room crying wildly and clutching her dressing gown to her chest. I heard Mum shout, 'What's going on?' and Dad replied, 'Well, she's always flashing her tits.'

A massive row began with Mum shouting at Dad, and Dad shouting at Mum. But it wasn't long before Dad turned to violence and Mum stopped answering back.

Cheryl and I wrapped our arms around each other and sat crying in the corner, flinching as we heard crashing and banging all over the flat.

'I never touched her, the slag,' shouted Dad. 'But I fucking will if she ever comes near me again. I'll stab her, the fucking bitch.'

Later when Dad went to the pub, Mum came into the bedroom with a bleeding lip and stared long and hard at Cheryl.

'You satisfied, are ya?' she asked.

'Mum, it's him,' said Cheryl. 'Ask Diane. He's always leering. I can't stand it much longer.'

'Well, you know where the fucking door is,' snarled Mum.

Cheryl burst into fresh tears and began to stuff some of her clothes into a plastic bag. 'I'm going over to Nanny's for a few days.'

'That's right,' said Mum. 'You always did like to stir the shit. What's the matter, you jealous?'

'How can you say that to your own daughter?' asked Cheryl, shaking her head. 'It's sick.'

I couldn't quite work out what it was all about, but I suspected Dad had been rude with Cheryl. The thought frightened me.

Cheryl left and went to stay with Nanny later that afternoon. The atmosphere in the flat got even worse. Davie and I were the only ones left, and we didn't know which way to turn. We spoke in whispers and spent most of our time in our rooms. We never knew when another row between Mum and Dad would erupt. But we didn't have long to wait.

'I ain't no fucking pervert,' shouted Dad, followed by the sound of something smashing against the wall.

'When have I ever said that?' protested Mum, more than a hint of appeasement in her voice. 'I love you, Frank. Just calm down.'

The shouting went on for what seemed like hours. I occupied myself by playing schools with my dollies, trying my best to block out the screams and shouts in the room next door. One of the neighbours rang the front doorbell to see if Mum was alright, and she shouted at them to 'mind your own fucking business'.

Shortly after that it went quiet for a while, and just when I thought it was all over, Dad yelled, 'I've had enough of you and this shit-hole, you fucking whore. I'm going.'

'Please, Frank,' Mum sobbed. 'Please don't leave me.'

I heard the front door nearly slam off its hinges then Dad's voice shouting through the letterbox: 'And don't think I'm ever coming back. You were a shit fuck anyway.'

I was over the moon that Dad had left, but Davie told me not to count my chickens.

'He'll probably be back later,' he predicted miserably, 'off his head on drink.'

I was worried Davie was right, but I kept my fingers and toes crossed anyway.

The flat looked as though a tornado had sped through it, with broken cups and upturned furniture strewn about. It was a couple of days before we began to believe that Dad wouldn't be back, but then we gradually reappeared one by one, as if we'd been taking shelter from a storm. In a way we had been. Diane came back from her boyfriend's, Cheryl came home from Nanny's and Davie and I emerged from our bedrooms, just in time to see Mum slam the door to her own. She didn't want to be a part of the family reunion.

'Just leave me alone, will you?' she shouted if any of us tapped on her door.

It was a shame Mum was so upset. I thought she would have been pleased to get rid of him. Grown-ups were too complicated for me.

The flat felt different without Dad. It was bliss to be able to walk around without fear and watch TV and use the kitchen when we wanted to. When Dad was at home he dominated every room. If he was in the front room we'd all be too frightened to go in unless we knew for sure he was in one of his better moods, and even then we had to remain on guard for a change in the wind. If he was slouched over the kitchen table, we'd go and get a drink from the bathroom tap rather than show up on his radar. It just wasn't worth the risk of upsetting him. But all that had changed now. It was like being released from some sort of prison, and best of all, now that he had gone, I didn't have to be careful of accidentally mentioning Nanny's or Jenny's names. I was free to pop across the road and visit them any time I wanted to.

Everyone, apart from Mum, seemed happier than they'd been for a long time, including Eddie the dog. Poor Eddie had suffered so much. Dad had taken to kicking and cursing him every day. Now that Dad wasn't around to torment him, he was like he was a different dog, almost reverting to a playful puppy again.

Mum remained in her room. I often heard her crying and muttering things into her pillow. When Diane and I took her in a cup of tea and some jam sandwiches, she was lying on her bed, a roll of loo paper resting on her tummy, and a cigarette burning between her fingers with an inch-high tower of ash. She lay perfectly still, staring at the ceiling with puffy, red-rimmed eyes.

'Here, Mum,' said Diane, making a space on the bedside table. 'You've got to eat.'

'I don't want anything,' said Mum, pulling herself up to stub out her cigarette. 'Just leave me alone.'

'Come on, it's not the end of the world,' said Diane.

'It might not be for you,' said Mum angrily. 'But I love him, Di, and I deserve a bit of happiness.' Her eyes welled up, and she pulled off a length of loo roll to blot away her tears.

'What about us?' asked Diane, a slight edge creeping into her voice. 'Don't you love us?'

Mum ignored her question and lit another cigarette. After she had blown out a long stream of smoke she said, 'I'm over fucking forty. This is my last chance, and none of you wants me to be happy – not you lot, not me mum, no one. I'm gonna end up on me own forever.'

'Don't be silly,' said Diane.

'I bet they're having a right laugh over the road, aren't they?' said Mum, referring to Nanny and Jenny.

'They're just worried, that's all,' said Diane. 'They can't work out why you haven't spoken to them for the past four years.'

'I bet she's going, "Oh, that Donna, she's always picking the wrong men,"' Mum said, imitating Nanny's Geordie accent.

Even though I was only eight, I knew that Mum had definitely picked the wrong man in Dad, and I vowed to be a lot more careful when I grew up. I remember wondering why she couldn't just find someone else, someone nicer who wasn't rude all the time. Why wasn't she happy that Dad had gone? He hit her and yelled at her even more than he did to the rest of us. What did she love about him? But instead she moped around, gazing out of the window as if waiting for him to return and smoking endless cigarettes.

Our happiness and Mum's misery were short-lived. I got home from school a couple of days later to see the familiar leather coat on the kitchen door and heard grunting noises from the bedroom and I stopped dead, feeling as if there was a lead weight in my chest. He was back.

Mum and Dad spent the first few days in bed together, then Mum gathered us all into the front room. She said they had an announcement to make, that they were getting married. Cheryl and Davie both cried. Cheryl's tears slid down slowly, but Davie let out huge wracking sobs and cried in a way I'd never seen him cry before, even worse than when Dad smashed his ship-in-a-bottle.

'What you crying about?' Mum asked, her head cocked to one side, as if genuinely baffled by his reaction.

'We won't be able to go over Nanny's any more,' he said, and I saw Dad bristle slightly.

'But we'll be a proper family,' Mum said gaily. 'Won't that be nice?'

They had a bring-a-bottle party to celebrate and invited everyone in Dad's large extended family, including his brother Keith, his sister Lesley and various other relatives we'd never met, as well as his numerous drinking buddies. It was as if Dad had invited everyone he'd ever met but Mum, on the other hand, invited nobody. It went without saying that she hadn't invited Nanny and her many brothers and sisters because she hadn't spoken to any of them since meeting Dad, and she didn't have any friends of her own because she wasn't allowed out without Dad. But it was quite a shock when Mum told us that none of us children could attend.

'I'm not having you winding him up, not tonight,' she said. 'I can just fucking see it now, shown up in front of all his family. Not on your fucking nelly.'

By this time Diane had moved back out again, so Cheryl went to stay with her. That left me and Davie.

'Can we go over Nanny's?' I asked.

'No, you fucking can't,' Mum snapped. 'I'm sick of them knowing all my fucking business.'

Davie and I were locked in a bedroom. Mum gave us a bottle of coke, some crisps and a packet of peanuts and instructed us to stay put until everybody had gone. She even left a bucket in case we needed the loo. The music was blaring into the early hours and our flat sounded like the pub on the corner did on special nights like New Year's Eve. We could hear other children playing with our toys out in the passageway, but it seemed that Mum was ashamed of us because we weren't allowed to join in.

Mum and Dad got married at a registry office one day when I was at school and, as with their 'engagement party', none of us was invited. I had always wanted a proper family with a mum and a dad, and I would have loved to go to their wedding and maybe even be a flower girl, but it was made very clear to me that as far as I was concerned nothing had changed.

Life continued pretty much as it always had, except that over the weeks and months I noticed Mum's belly was getting bigger. At first I thought she must have been eating too much, but then I worked out that she was having a baby and I waited for the day when she would tell me. I would have asked her myself but I was shy. Talking about babies would mean talking about sex in a roundabout way and I was far too embarrassed to do that. Even though I had grown up hearing every grunt and groan Mum and Dad made in their bedroom and seeing Dad's pornographic magazines lying around, I was still embarrassed about such things. My face reddened as I imagined the moment Mum would sit me down and tell me I was going to have a little brother or sister. But in the end, I was saved the embarrassment because it was Cheryl who finally said the words, straight after Mum had been carted off in an ambulance, screaming and clutching her huge distended belly.

'Lisa, do you know Mum's having a baby?'

Of course I knew! I had turned nine years old two months before.

The baby was a little girl and they named her Katrina. I thought she looked like a perfect little doll. She was so tiny her veins showed through her paper-thin skin and I remember staring at her for ages in her little Perspex cot, which was parked at the side of Mum's bed. I adored her straight away and couldn't wait for Mum to bring her home, but the hospital insisted on keeping them both in for a while. At the age of forty-three, Mum was classed as an older mother, so the hospital wanted to take special care of her for a few days, and she had smoked through the pregnancy so Katrina was born on the small side.

While they were away, Dad wasn't at home much because he was either out celebrating in the pub or else up at the hospital breathing gin fumes all over little Katrina's sleepy head. With him out of the way, Cheryl felt safe enough to bring

Jenny over to the flat. It was her first visit since Dad had moved in with us five years before, and I remember her walking around from room to room, her mouth slack with horror as she saw how we were living. As usual the flat was a mess, but Jenny seemed particularly upset to see the various dents and holes in walls and windows.

'What on earth's been going on over here?' she kept asking.

I tried not to think about how angry Dad would be if he came back and found her there. I was terrified, jumping at every sound, but filled with excitement too as I dragged Jenny around showing her things like my special cupboard where I kept some brightly coloured plastic carrier bags stuffed with everything from elastic bands to felt-tip pens.

'Come and look at my collections, Jenny,' I cried and she duly admired them, telling me that everything looked very useful and I was clever to have collected them.

She must have been sick with worry when she went back across the road to report to Nanny what she had seen but they were powerless, especially now that Mum was married to Dad. There was nothing they could do.

For the first few weeks after Mum brought Katrina home from the hospital, the atmosphere in the flat was calmer. Dad seemed to curb his drinking and gambling, and the fits and rages that I had grown so used to became less frequent. However, the violence was replaced with psychological cruelty. He would use Katrina as a weapon. Sometimes Cheryl and I would be allowed to hold her, and at other times he yelled at us to 'Fuck off away from her.' It was sad to see

Katrina's gummy smiles turn into startled cries as we hastily pulled our fingers from her tiny grasp.

When Mum and Dad wanted to go to bed in the afternoon, Katrina would be left with whoever was around and more often than not it was me. I'd sit on the floor beside her in front of the television, constantly bouncing the baby chair to stop her from crying. Occasionally Cheryl and I were allowed to take her out in the pram, but more often than not there would be a massive row when we got back as Dad accused us of having taken the baby 'over the road to them cunts'. He was determined that none of Mum's family would ever meet her fifth child. But Nanny and Jenny were desperate to see the baby, so one day when we were sure Dad had gone out and wouldn't be back for a while, we sneaked Katrina over the road so they could give her a cuddle.

My heart was drumming because I imagined Dad would find out and break the door down any minute.

'Oh, look at her,' cooed Nanny tearfully. 'What an absolute angel.'

That was the only time Nanny saw her because we didn't dare risk it again.

By the time Kat, as everyone called her, was a few months old, Mum and Dad had secured the cleaning contracts for various media companies in the West End. Mum was out at all hours and run off her feet as she tried to juggle all the different jobs. She worked in the evenings, the early hours of the morning, and sometimes during the day as well when she had a special job in a private house. Dad brought in his older sister, Lesley, and a couple of other people he had rounded up from the pub to help out in return for a bit of cash in hand. Sometimes he would come along to check they were doing a good job, but mostly he stayed at home to watch the horse-racing on the telly and look after the baby.

Whenever Dad had a win on the horses, he'd usually do two things: number one, he'd take care of his first priority which was to stock up on gin, brandy and Special Brew; then, after studying the form for at least an hour, he'd put the rest of his winnings straight back onto a 'dead cert' at the bookies.

His wins were rare enough, and two in a row were unheard of. Everyone seemed to know this but Dad. So when the horse he'd picked so carefully fell at the first fence, or limped in last with the stragglers, he would be apoplectic with rage. For the next few hours he would storm about the flat fuelled by copious amounts of alcohol, trying to find people and things to blame for his bad luck. I'd try my best to hide with the dog.

His violence had almost become a way of life, but the thing that frightened me the most was how crude and lewd he would become after he'd exhausted himself smashing the place up. It was always the same pattern – violence first, crudity second. Maybe it was the drink, but he didn't seem to care I was in the room, and neither did Mum.

'Do you fancy it up the arse tonight, Donna?' he'd ask with a leer, as casually as if he were asking if she wanted a cup of tea.

Mum would laugh. I wasn't sure whether this was because she found it funny, or simply because she was relieved he had stopped his violent rampage. But sometimes he did things so repugnant that she seemed just as shocked as me.

One summer evening after Dad had been on a losing bender, *Coronation Street* was on the television. I was sitting with the dog on the floor by Dad's feet listening to him chomp and belch his way through a stack of egg and bacon sandwiches. He was drunker than I'd seen him in a long time, swaying from side to side. He was eating and smoking at the same time, as if he hadn't had food or cigarettes in a week and was making up for lost time. Egg yolk, ketchup and grease were smeared all over his face and vest, and bits of food littered his lap and the surrounding sofa. The dog, always desperate to supplement his meagre and haphazard rations, inched ever closer, long strands of drool hanging like jelly from his mouth.

'That dog's gonna have that in a minute,' said Mum from her armchair. 'Push him away, Lisa, don't just fucking sit there.'

No matter how hard I tried to move the dog, he wouldn't budge. Normally he stayed well away from Dad, so I knew he must have been desperately hungry.

'Can he have the crusts, Dad?' I asked timidly.

Dad tried to speak with his mouth full, but only managed to grunt and spray more food down his front. The dog edged nearer and when Dad raised his leg I thought he was in for a kick, but instead, Dad let off a loud fart.

'He can have that,' he said.

The revolting smell seemed to make Eddie more excited, and he moved closer until he was sitting between Dad's legs and dripping drool onto his trousers. Dad started teasing him, offering a piece of bacon and pulling it away at the last minute. Eddie gave little whimpers, which Dad thought were hilarious.

'Give him your crusts, you mean bastard,' Mum said.

Dad stuffed more bits of sandwich into his mouth and gave the dog his fingers to lick. 'Look at the fucking tongue on him, Donna,' he said.

'Now you know why he's always licking his balls,' Mum laughed.

'You know what I fancy after this, Lisa?' slurred Dad, popping open the top button of his jeans.

'A jam tart?' I suggested, knowing they were his favourites.

Dad considered this for a moment as he picked his teeth, and the dog hoovered the crumbs from his lap. 'Come to think of it, that ain't a bad idea. I could do with a *fucking* tart,' he said to Mum's whoop of laughter. 'But what I really want is a wet, sloppy blow job.'

I glanced over at Mum, my brows knitted in a frown. I didn't know what a blow job was but somehow it sounded rude.

Mum rolled her eyes, and gave Dad another indulgent chuckle. 'You make me die, you do,' she remarked.

I heard Dad unzip his flies. 'Here, watch this.'

Mum shouted, 'Oi, Frank! That's enough. Not in front of her.'

I heard licking noises and did a double take as I turned back to Dad. I couldn't believe my eyes. He had his thing out and was rubbing bits of egg yolk and bacon rind over it so that the dog would lick it off. 'Go on, son. Get your sausage.'

'Get out of it,' shouted Mum, kicking the dog in the ribs so that it gave a loud yelp.

Dad's eyes were rolling back in his head by now. 'I was enjoying that.'

Mum was shouting 'dirty fucking bastard' and I didn't know whether she meant Dad or the dog.

'Lisa, go to your fucking room,' she yelled, and I ran as fast as I could.

Unfortunately, the scene kept playing round and round in my head afterwards. A few days later, Mum let me visit Nanny and Jenny. Normally I didn't talk much about Dad and his rude ways because I didn't want to upset them, but on this occasion, I couldn't stop myself. I thought maybe they would find it funny – but Jenny and Nanny didn't find it funny at all.

They started asking me all sorts of questions about Dad. They asked me if he ever touched me in my private places. I said no because I didn't know if all the games we played, such as wrestling and tickling, counted. I was beginning to get frightened so I thought it best not to mention all the other rude things Dad did, like pulling his willy about. I didn't tell them about having to wash his back in the bath or pick whose titties were best in his magazines, or any of the other things because I thought they were probably just normal. Maybe all dads did this.

I stayed with Jenny and Nanny over the weekend and when I went home, Mum and Dad weren't speaking to me.

Dad had a big black eye, which was strange to see because it was usually Mum who had those. I quite liked being ignored. It meant I could play in my room, and I didn't have to sit near Dad any more. It was great because when he wasn't speaking he wasn't hitting either. If ever he walked into a room, I would slip out, trying to preserve the uneasy peace that had descended. Mum never really spoke to me much anyway, so it wasn't much different with her. But I could tell she was angry with me about something. She wouldn't let me go near the baby any more, and suddenly I had to go to school every day, which had both good and bad points.

A few weeks later I heard Diane and Cheryl talking. Apparently Uncle Bob, who owned the pub where Mum used to work, was so disgusted when he heard what Dad had done with the dog that he beat him up. Mum and Dad put in for a council transfer after that as they wanted to get away from the area.

One night I was sitting in the living room watching telly. Dad staggered in and before I could leave the room, he came and stood right in front of me. All I could see were the leather tassles on his brown shoes. I was too frightened to look up, although I could smell he had been drinking.

'Alright, Lisa?' he asked, slurring slightly.

I was so shocked to hear him speak to me after what seemed like such a long time, that I crawled between his legs and ran crying into my bedroom. I leapt into bed and pulled the covers over my head. I was petrified when I heard him stomping in after me.

'What, ain't I good enough for you any more, you little

cunt?' he said, reaching under the blankets and finding my ankle, which he yanked violently. He pulled me out of bed so that my head cracked hard on the floor. The impact made me see stars and throw up.

Mum said it was my own fault, as Dad was only trying to be friendly. 'I don't know why he's bothering to talk to you after you opened your big fucking trap and got him into trouble.'

But I was glad he'd got into trouble. It had made him think twice about being rude. I hoped he wouldn't start again now that Uncle Bob had given him a black eye.

I was still being bullied at school and took as many days off sick as I thought I could get away with. They sent a couple of letters but Mum screwed them up and chucked them in the bin. After a while, the teachers gave up asking me for letters explaining why I had been absent. They just accepted it. On the days off, I'd go cleaning with Mum but I was under strict instructions to really lay on the sickness act if anybody asked any questions like the old man had done that time in Notting Hill. I had it all planned. I would pretend to be sick in a bin. That should do it. Even though she didn't say it, I knew Mum liked taking me with her because I heard her telling Dad 'She comes in well handy, and it saves paying someone else.'

At first I found it fascinating to walk around the empty offices, black bin bag in hand, and imagine them crammed full of busy people during the day, people who worked in advertising and publishing and the music and film industries. Every desk said something about the people who sat at it during the day. I could tell which ones belonged to the bosses by their big leather chairs, calculators and executive toys, with silver balls which clicked back and forth for ages when I pushed them. The creative people had magic markers and huge drawing pads, but I liked the secretaries' desks best. Some of them had strips of photo-booth pictures on display, happy young girls laughing and poking out their tongues at the camera, and it was nice to put a face to the desk. I decided I wanted to be a secretary when I grew up, then I could fill my desk with assorted knick-knacks, make-up bags, and stuffed toys, just like theirs. They also had pots full of pens and pencils, and half-full coffee mugs with funny pictures or slogans like 'Kiss Me' on the side. I always knew what colour lipstick they wore because I'd have to scrub extra hard to remove the waxy imprint of their lips from the rims of the cups.

Although happy to live in squalor at home, Dad was fastidious at work. One day he arrived to do a spot-check, and found a glass I had just washed which still showed a faint red lipstick mark.

'Are you trying to get us the fucking sack?' he snarled, and stamped hard on my toes, making me cry out in pain. 'You're fucking useless, do you know that?'

I made sure I never made that mistake again.

I liked the electric typewriters in the offices. For months I resisted the urge to flick the power switch, but one day I did and nearly dropped an ashtray when it jumped to life, its loud hum shattering the silence that hung over the empty floor. It took me weeks to pluck up the courage to press a tentative finger to a key. It made a loud clacking sound and the type-writer shook a bit as the golf-ball mechanism hit and the carriage moved along a notch. After checking that nobody was around, I typed, 'the cat sat on the mat, the mat sat on the cat'. I hadn't thought to roll a piece of paper in and was horrified when I saw the shiny words glinting back at me from the matt black roller. I worried for days that the secretary would realise someone had been fiddling with her machine. Mum would lose the contract and, worst of all, Dad would go mad. But nothing happened, and I decided that the secretary had probably been too busy to spot my line about the cat. Besides, she looked too nice in her photo, with a Suzi Quatro hairdo and a glossy smile, to bother about getting cleaners the sack.

The novelty of being a new father seemed to wear off quite quickly, and Dad was soon back to his boozing and gambling. Mum was bringing home wads of cash every week, but no sooner had she stepped in the front door than he would pounce, write out a bet for her to take over the bookies and more often than not that would be the last we saw of that. The rest of the week would be an endless struggle with barely enough money for the basics.

Once, while Mum was at work, I ran out of milk and nappies for the baby. Dad was in a bad mood as he had just had another loss at the bookies. My stomach flipped as I realised I'd have to ask him for some money because Kat's nappy was leaking and smelly and she was crying for a feed.

'We've run out of nappies and milk, Dad,' I said, trying to soothe her cries by jiggling her up and down against my shoulder.

'What the fuck can I do about it?' he asked, jumping up to snatch Katrina from me and plonking her down on the sofa. 'It's your fucking fault.' His face was deep red with rage as he landed an almighty slap on the side of my head. I crossed my legs in a vain attempt to stem the inevitable flow of urine, but still it trickled down onto the nylon carpet.

'It's you who needs a nappy, dirty little fucker,' he jeered. I sobbed as much from humiliation as from the pain of his slap.

He went to the drawer in the sideboard where Mum saved her money-off coupons and I watched him sorting through to find a handful of ones she'd cut from packs of Paddy Pad nappies. He stuffed them into my hand and instructed me to run all the way to the chemist. I did as I was told.

The lady behind the counter looked baffled as I placed my coupons on the counter beside a pack of nappies. 'No, dear,' she said, frowning at my stupidity. 'You can only use one coupon at a time. It's ten pence off any one purchase.'

Dad was furious when I went back empty-handed. Katrina had to lie bare-bottomed on a newspaper with a bottle of weak tea until Mum came home later that day.

I noticed Mum was always cuddling Kat and cooing to her about what a pretty girl she was. I'd try to snuggle up beside them on the sofa, desperate for her to hug me as well, but all she did was stiffen and push me away. It was as if I was a stranger and she found the thought of touching me repulsive. I couldn't remember a time when she'd ever given me a spontaneous kiss and a cuddle. The most I got was a hard peck on the cheek. We didn't chat, laugh or hug as I had seen my friends do with their mothers. Mum was very cold towards me, no matter how hard I tried to please her, and I could never understand why. Every morning I'd do the washing-up from the previous night's dinner then I'd wash and dress Kat and give her a jar of baby breakfast before I went to school. I'd do any chores I was asked to without quibbling, but no matter how hard I tried, I never got the affection I craved from her. Before Kat was born, I used to tell myself that Mum wasn't a very cuddly person, but seeing her with the baby now, it was obvious that wasn't true. It was just me she didn't like to touch, at least not unless she absolutely had to, and that made me very sad.

It was great to have a baby to play with, though. I'd sit her in her bouncy chair and play 'Round and round the garden' on her plump little hands, and feed her a bottle or a cold jar of baby food. Mum wasn't very good at keeping her clean, so I'd wet a cloth and clean the dirt from between her toes, tickling her so she kicked and giggled, showing two tiny bottom teeth.

When Kat was a year old, and I had just turned ten, Mum and Dad got their transfer and we moved out of the flat and into a newly renovated council house in Nunhead. I cried when we left as I didn't want to move away from Nanny. Even though I wasn't allowed to see her very much it was such a comfort seeing her and Jenny sitting out on their balcony.

The house was part of an Edwardian terrace and it was like a mansion compared to the flat. All the original features had been stripped out and old fireplaces boarded up and replaced with a brand new central heating system. Everything smelled of paint and wallpaper paste; the house was pristine. I couldn't believe it was ours. It seemed so big.

On the ground floor there was a kitchen and dining room, which Dad quickly knocked through with his sledgehammer to create an uneven arch. On the first floor were the front room, the toilet and bathroom, then up another flight were three small bedrooms. Mum and Dad's room looked out over garden, and the other two looked over the street. Katrina, Cheryl and I were in one, my brother Davie in the other. Diane never moved in there with us because she stayed with her boyfriend full-time now. In fact, we had hardly seen her since Mum and Dad got married.

The great thing was that the top of the house seemed so far away from the bottom that when Dad was shouting at Mum or smashing things up, I could run up two floors to get away from him – much further than I had been able to do in the flat.

There was a garden out the back so when Mum and Dad went upstairs for a lie-down, I could take Kat outside so we didn't have to listen to their sex noises. The garden was full of broken glass and rocks, but when she was in a good mood one day Mum promised that we could plant some flowers and potatoes, just as I'd watched them do on *Blue Peter* once.

At first Eddie loved the garden too. It meant that he had somewhere to do his business and even though he cut his paws on the glass, he seemed happier now that he could get out from under Dad's feet and avoid the vicious kicks they often delivered. But eventually the long narrow garden became like a prison to him because he was hardly let inside any more. He would bark for hours on end and chase his own tail. Finally he found a way under the fence at the end, and from that point on he would roam the streets, only returning every couple of days to feed on the scraps I'd save from the dinner plates and put in his bowl.

One day Dad told me to go and say goodbye to Eddie. I asked why and he said they were going to put him down because he had fleas. I'd often asked Mum to get some flea spray but she never did. Soon Eddie was being driven mad, scratching so much that he'd clawed holes in his neck. Mum had Eddie on a lead outside the front door. I looked at his scruffy black white and tan coat and his big melting eyes and I wanted to throw my arms around his neck and sob, but Mum pushed me off.

'No, he's fucking riddled with them,' Mum said with a look of disgust on her face. 'They'll get on you, and then they might get on Kat.'

'Can't the vet do anything for him?' I asked with a heavy heart.

'He can do something, alright,' said Mum. 'He can put the bastard down. He's always been trouble, shitting all over.'

I watched Mum lead Eddie off and for some minutes I couldn't move or cry. I just stood there, rooted to the spot. I could hear Dad gloating from inside 'Good riddance to bad rubbish.'

Later I went to my room and cried into my pillow for my poor little dog, who I knew would be dead by now. He'd had a miserable life and he hadn't deserved it because he was really a very sweet-natured creature. I missed him a lot once he had gone.

When we first moved into the new house in Nunhead, there was a period of peace and calm between Dad and

Cheryl. I even saw them talking and laughing together on the sofa. But suddenly the atmosphere changed, and one day I heard Cheryl explaining to Mum that Dad was making her 'uncomfortable' again. Mum told her not to be so stupid.

From then on, Dad began giving Cheryl increasingly evil looks and frequently making her cry. Once I saw him smash a plate down on the table by her elbow, knocking over her mug of tea in the process. I didn't stay to find out what was going on, just ran as fast as I could to the top of the house. I tried to block my ears but I could hear Cheryl crying and Dad shouting 'Go on, show us your big tits, you fucking slag.' Mum gave a nervous chuckle, which I knew was her way of attempting to relieve the tension.

Crouching on the floor in my bedroom, I thought back to a few months before when Cheryl had taken me to visit one of her friends.

The friend wasn't like us. She was posh and wore hippy clothes with bare feet and rings on her toes. I'm not sure how Cheryl knew her but she wasn't like any of her other friends. Her name was Gail, and she lived in a small basement flat. The floor was covered in rugs. Giant bean bags were strewn about and a fine red scarf was draped over a lamp in the corner. Gail stood at the stove stirring a big pot of bubbling liquid. The smell made my eyes water, and she explained it was pepper soup.

'Haven't you eaten a pepper before?' She laughed when I admitted I hadn't, and I could see Cheryl blushing despite the red tinge of the light. When Gail handed me a bowlful, I felt quite sick. Not because of the soup, which was strangely tasty if a little bitter, but rather because her hair fell over one shoulder revealing a huge lovebite. I knew what lovebites were because Mum's neck used to be covered in them when Dad first moved in and Cheryl or Diane had explained it to me. It seemed to me that the words 'love' and 'bite' didn't really go together. Why would you bite someone you loved? To take my mind off the images of the painful-looking purple marks, I concentrated on blowing spoonfuls of the hot soup, and began to tune in to what Cheryl and Gail were discussing in hushed tones.

'He's always trying to touch me up,' Cheryl said. 'He's really lecherous, you know. It's disgusting.'

Gail, sitting with her legs crossed under a long floral skirt, nodded towards me, concern written all over her face. 'But not her, though?' she asked.

Cheryl spluttered on her soup as though Gail had suggested something too ridiculous for words. 'No, not her! She's only ten years old.'

I knew they were talking about Dad and although I didn't understand the word lecherous I had a pretty fair idea of what 'touching up' meant.

I'd seen him doing it to Mum a lot, shoving his hand up her skirt and down her top to feel her chest, and I wondered if he had gone that far with Cheryl. The idea made me feel sick. Maybe Uncle Bob could give him another black eye. Dad hadn't been as rude with me since then. In fact, he hadn't shaken his ding-a-ling in my face or tried to get me to stroke it for quite a while. He still liked to play horsey, wrestling and dress-up games though, and sometimes his hands would touch me in my private places by accident.

But that wasn't the same thing as *touching up*, was it?

A few days later, another big row started. I crouched down on the floor in my bedroom, holding my knees against my chest as I rocked to and fro. Then I heard the front door slam, and the front gate bounce off the wall. I jumped up to look out of the window and saw Cheryl running over the road in her high platform sandals, her coat flying behind her. I watched her sadly, wondering when I would see her again. Everybody kept disappearing from my life.

I never saw Nanny and Jenny any more since we had moved. I had been to visit Diane and her boyfriend in their flat once or twice, but when I got back Dad would always call me a 'betraying bastard' and be especially nasty to me, so it was clear I had to choose which camp I was in. Since I had to live with Dad day in, day out, it was almost a relief when Diane stopped visiting, but at night, as I said my 'God bless' prayers in the dark, I always kept her on the list of people I wanted him to bless.

Now Cheryl had gone as well, and I assumed she would stay at Diane's but I had no way of knowing. We didn't have a phone in the house – Dad wouldn't let us get one – but even if we did, I knew she wouldn't call in case he answered. She knew that if he found out we were in touch, he would make my life hell.

My brother Davie, who was nearly seventeen, was the last of the older ones left at home. He wasn't allowed to use the front room at all, and could only go into the kitchen when Dad wasn't using it. Consequently, he spent hardly any time at home. He often stayed with friends, and he went to Nanny and Jenny's back in Peckham once or twice a week.

One night I woke up to lots of shouting. Davie and Dad were having a row on the landing outside my bedroom door. This in itself was very unusual because since moving to the new house, Dad had gone out of his way never to utter a word to Davie, and Davie, like everyone else, was generally too petrified to do or say anything that might antagonise Dad.

Suddenly I heard Davie shouting, 'I'm going, and I'm taking Lisa with me.'

I jumped out of bed and opened my bedroom door to find Dad pushing him up against the landing wall.

Davie turned to face me and said, 'Who do you want to be with – them or me?'

I felt sick. How could I make that choice? Davie was too young to look after me and what would he do for money? But if I didn't go with him, I realised I was going to lose my brother just as surely as I had lost Nanny, Jenny, Freda, Diane and Cheryl.

Without giving me a chance to answer Dad shoved Davie into his room where he fell backwards onto his bed. 'If you ever take that kid out of this fucking house, I'll kill you, you cunt.'

Predictably, it wasn't long before Davie left for good. Where to, I had no idea.

I hadn't been allowed to mention Nanny's or Jenny's names for years now, and Dad added my brother's and sisters' names to the list. All the photographs of them he could find were ripped to shreds and I was told that if anyone asked me, I was to say I only had one sister, Katrina.

Life went on. Now it was just the four of us left and Dad had managed to isolate me from anyone else who cared about me. Sometimes at night, as I lay in my bed listening to the familiar grunts and groans emanating from the room next door, I'd think about how much I loved Nanny and Jenny and all those precious memories from the time when I lived with them. When I turned my thoughts to Diane, Cheryl and Davie, I felt bereft. It was almost as if they were dead – but this was worse. I knew they were out there in the world somewhere, living a life, and I wondered if they ever thought about me. Christmas came and went, and then my birthday, and I didn't get a card from any of them. All evidence that they had ever existed in my life was erased.

As time passed, I trained myself not to think about the family I had lost, even at night, because if I did, my heart felt heavy and my eyes filled with tears. The pain was too much. It became so ingrained in me not to mention my missing family members that they seemed part of another life altogether. Now if people at school asked me how many brothers and sisters I had, I wouldn't even hesitate to follow Dad's instructions. I just had one: Kat.

Chapter Seven

One day when I got home from school Dad wasn't there and Mum told me he had gone to prison. She gave no explanation other than to say, 'They done him up like a kipper. He's gone inside.' But I knew it was for drink-driving offences in friends' cars. He had been banned and fined quite a few times and I think he'd gone on to have an accident so the courts had lost patience with him. I was pleased because just like the last time he left home for a week or so, before he and Mum got married, the oppressive atmosphere in the house lifted.

He was gone for a few blissful months. It was as if a weight had been lifted from me, and from Mum. I skipped home from school every day, free of fear and worry. Mum was cheerful, a different person. The lines of worry that had characterised her face for so long began to soften. I wondered if my sisters or brother would visit now that Dad was safely out of the way.

'Can Cheryl come over, Mum?' I asked. It felt odd saying the name out loud.

'Shush!' she said urgently. 'We don't want Kat repeating that when he gets back.'

So that was it. She was concerned that Dad would find out so we couldn't get in touch with them.

Mum wrote to Dad every few days. She would sit at the dining-room table, black biro in one hand, cigarette in the other, and scribble away. She used to keep the letters he sent her in the bottom of the sideboard. I couldn't help sneaking a look at one. The paper was light blue and very thin and crinkly. I could barely read his handwriting, but the words I did make out were rude and full of the things he was going to do to her when he got back. I didn't understand most of them but they sounded harsh and terrifying, certainly not loving.

I knew he must be coming back soon when Mum sat down to cross off whole months' worth of days on the calendar. She obviously wanted him to think she had been pining for him and counting the days, when in reality I had never seen her so relaxed and happy.

Just as suddenly as he had disappeared, he came back, and the familiar black cloud settled once again. They spent the first few days locked in their bedroom. Mum would get up, go to work and then go back to bed with him, while I stayed off school and looked after Kat. Sometimes they would lock us out in the garden, which by now was overgrown with weeds. I never did get to plant the flower and vegetable garden I'd wanted.

After a couple of days of peace, the rows started again. Dad began shouting, swearing and smashing things, convinced Mum had been with other men while he was in prison, and she did her best to placate him. It was her habit to try and make light of things, hoping to appeal to whatever good sense he had left: 'You're being silly now,' she'd say. Sometimes this worked and Dad would run out of steam and accept a cup of tea and a cigarette she would light for him, but other times her attempts at reason failed miserably. A few days after he was released from prison, he beat her up very badly.

I came down to the kitchen the next day to find her standing there, her face bruised and the flesh around her mouth looking like a deflated Yorkshire pudding. She held her purse in shaking hands and asked me to go over to the shop.

'I want two packs of cigarettes, and two pounds of King Edwards,' she lisped. Her voice sounded funny. She couldn't pronounce the words properly, and it was then I noticed her two front teeth were missing.

My jaw hung open with shock and my eyes filled with tears, but neither of us commented on the state she was in. She hated it if I ever mentioned her injuries. I just took the money without a word and went to get them for her.

Later on, when I was hanging over the banisters, I heard Mum say, 'You've knocked me fucking teeth out, you bastard. That's nice, ain't it?'

'I've told you I'm sorry, Donna,' he said in his low, rasping voice. 'I'll never lay a hand on you again.'

The next day she went to the dentist, and by the end of the week she had two new front teeth, which looked much better than the old ones had done, except these were bright white and strangely at odds with her other nicotine-stained teeth.

Even though Mum had been through a terrible ordeal, she looked almost happy as Dad fussed over her for a few days.

95

He had hurt her badly in the past but she had never lost any teeth before and for the first time ever, Dad was contrite. It was as though the previous black eyes, split lips and bloodied noses meant nothing compared to this atrocity.

As far as I remember, apart from the odd shove here and there, he never hit her again. He didn't need to any more. The threat was always there. Dad only had to raise his voice and clench his fists to make Mum back down in an argument. Once beaten, twice shy and all that.

He may have stopped beating Mum, but it was around this time, when I was eleven, that he started lashing out at me a lot more than he ever had before. Now that I didn't have any other family members around to witness his cruelty, he was freer with his slaps, kicks and punches. He didn't have to worry about me telling anyone as I no longer had contact with anybody other than him and Mum – and Mum didn't count because she didn't seem to care what he did. He'd be careful not to mark my face, because it might get noticed at school, but I always had bruises over the rest of my body. Someone had to bear the brunt of his temper when his horse came in last, and it looked as though it was going to be me now.

At the same time as he was getting more violent towards me, Dad also started to become more affectionate. It was as if he liked to hurt me and make me cry as an excuse to pull me onto his lap and smother me in scratchy kisses.

'You know I love you, don't you, Lisa?' he'd say, stroking my forehead. 'You've always been my special girl, ain't ya? Have been ever since you were little.'

I knew this wasn't quite true because when I was younger he saw me as nothing more than a nuisance, not special at all. He was always calling me a 'useless spastic'. I remembered how he used to banish me to my bedroom and instruct everyone not to talk to me for weeks on end. It was only since we moved to Nunhead and away from the rest of the family that Dad had begun to show me anything approaching genuine affection. But I nodded in agreement anyway.

'I love you, too,' I said automatically, knowing it was what he expected me to say. If I appeared the slightest bit unfriendly it could set him off in a bad mood. Besides, when he was in a good mood, he could be nice. He was far from perfect but he was the only dad I'd ever known, and ironically, now that the rest of my family had gone, he was the only person to show me any affection whatsoever. Mum remained as cold and distant as ever.

Everyone knew that Dad was incapable of maintaining any one mood for long. He blew hot and cold with people. He was known for changing like the wind. Soft and warm one minute, a cold hard tornado the next. As I grew older, this hot and cold treatment became ever more pronounced. At times he treated me better than he ever had before. Everything I did was brilliant, everything I said made him laugh. He couldn't kiss and cuddle me enough and, much to Mum's obvious irritation, he would lavish me with praise.

'You're a fucking diamond you are, looking after your little sister, cleaning the offices and helping round the house. Ain't she a diamond, Donna?'

Mum would grunt something noncommittal without so much as looking at me.

'You're going to be a heartbreaker when you grow up. All the boys will be trying to get into your knickers,' he'd cackle, and he'd give my bum a sharp squeeze.

I knew that now we had moved, Dad wasn't worried about Uncle Bob beating him up again. He was starting to go back to his old ways. I didn't like it when he spoke about rude things, but I had to be careful not to react in the wrong way in case he got angry. It felt strange receiving all his attention and praise, not only because it made me feel uncomfortable a lot of the time, but also because I could sense it made Mum angry. Once I overheard her asking why he paid so much attention to me and ignored Kat. 'After all,' she said, 'she's your *own* daughter.'

'How can you be jealous of your fucking daughter?' Dad barked back. 'You're one twisted bitch.'

'I ain't jealous. It's just peculiar, that's all.'

'I tell you what's peculiar,' he snapped. 'My fucking fist'll be peculiar in a minute when it knocks you spark out.'

I couldn't work out why Mum didn't like Dad being nice to me, especially as she knew as well as I did that no matter how nice he was being, it wouldn't last and soon enough I'd be the odd one out again. I knew that I would eventually make a mistake, and cause Dad to lose his temper. I might forget to stir the sugar in his tea, or have the 'wrong look' on my face, and then all hell would break loose and his sharp slaps and kicks would knock me to the floor.

Mum would simply tut and roll her eyes and say 'What a fucking life!' She obviously blamed me for starting him off on one. 'You always do it, don't you?' she'd mutter through gritted teeth.

But I knew I hadn't done anything wrong. It was just Dad and his moods. My whole life became characterised by his hot and cold treatment. I never knew what to expect from one moment to the next.

Sometimes his punishments would be psychological. He would call me names, or ban me from using all rooms except my bedroom and the bathroom, just as he had done with Davie. In the past I'd felt relieved when I was on his exclusion list, but it didn't bring any real freedom. I couldn't slam the front door behind me and go off to the park for an hour or two, because Dad was watching my every move. I'd occupy myself in my room, maybe reading a book, but then he would seem to get extra mad and change tack. Sometimes he'd make me sit me on the floor in front of him with my hands on my head for ages. If I moved a muscle before he told me I could, I'd get a swift kick and obscenities would be screamed in my face.

The mental suffering was even harder than the physical. Only an hour or a day before, he would have been lavishing me with positive attention and praise, so the sudden reappearance of Mr Hyde was confusing and upsetting on many different levels. I felt lost and lonelier than ever, but at the same time unable to help myself by breaking free and occupying myself with friends or outside activities. I may have been excluded, but my every moment was accounted for. Eventually, after hours or maybe days of relentless mental and physical bullying, he'd look over at my swollen, tear-stained face and say 'Oi you! Come over here!'

As I shuffled towards him on my knees, I realised I was behaving just as Eddie used to do after he'd taken a few days of continual beatings. I was grateful my master was giving me another chance. As I knelt before him, Dad would take a few moments to blow smoke rings before saying, 'Give us a kiss, you silly little fucker.'

Relief would flood through me as I flung myself against him. I'd sob onto his chest and he'd rub his hands up and down my back and pull me tight in between his parted legs. I would sob and cry as if a dam had burst, all the pain and hurt flooding out.

'I'm sorry, Dad, I didn't mean it,' I'd say, unable to remember what it was I had done in the first place.

If Mum saw me crying, even though she knew what I'd been through, she'd say 'She's not boo-hooing again, is she?'

Dad would make a fuss of me for a short while afterwards, being extra nice, and I'd begin to dread the time he'd change again. Every time he put a bet on, I'd do a silent prayer and ask God to let him win so he wouldn't turn on me. And if I saw Mum polishing his best glass, filling the ice bucket and chopping lemons, which meant that Dad was starting on the gin and tonic, I'd get a pain in the tummy and have to rush to the toilet urgently, a stress reaction he often provoked in me. Whenever he sent Mum over to the shop for a couple of bottles of brandy we all knew it meant the next few days would be hell. Even Mum said that brandy made him vicious.

By now I was convinced Mum hated me. My very existence seemed to annoy her. She never talked to me directly any more, only speaking over my head to say something derogatory to Dad about me. I knew she loved Kat, because she was very loving towards her, always cuddling her and smiling and playing with her, and even though she had turned her back on Diane, Cheryl and Davie to please Dad, I felt intuitively that deep down she loved them in a way she had never loved me. One day, something happened that proved this to me without a shadow of a doubt.

Dad found a photograph of Diane hidden in the back of a kitchen cupboard and he went absolutely ballistic. It was an official confirmation photograph taken when Diane must have been about seven or eight years old. He held it up and I could see how cute she looked in her little white dress and matching shoes.

'What do you want this shit for?' shouted Dad, ripping the picture to shreds as he had done with all the others.

Mum fell to her knees and started crying. 'No, not my Diane. You bastard!'

Tears were streaming down her face and I could see Dad was momentarily taken aback by her dramatic reaction. I was too. It was the first time I had ever seen Mum cry over something like that. Usually she didn't show much emotion over anything to do with the family. She seemed to be able to sweep up the torn fragments of her past life and consign them to the rubbish bin without a backwards glance. She had been able to turn her back on everyone but Dad. But this time I was confused. She obviously valued that photo of Diane, and I got a glimpse for the first time of just what a huge sacrifice Mum was willing to pay to keep Dad happy. It didn't even occur to me that she might secretly keep in touch with the others. Surely there was no way she'd dare go behind Dad's back.

I felt jealous of the strength of Mum's feelings for Diane. Instinctively I knew she wouldn't ever weep over a torn photo of me. More and more she treated me with a kind of disdain, as though I was a waste of space, and I couldn't work out what I had done to deserve that. What had I done wrong? What was it about me?

The only visitors who ever came to the house were members of Dad's family. We used to see his sister Lesley because she worked for Mum and Dad as a cleaner, but sometimes she and Dad would have a row and we wouldn't see her again for months. Lesley had a son called Charlie who was about fourteen years old and he used to come over to ours at Christmas. Dad would make us both blush by teasing Charlie relentlessly about having a crush on me. A few times my stomach tied itself in knots when I saw a dangerous glint in Dad's eye. I could tell he didn't want Charlie anywhere near me, and neither did I. I wasn't interested in boys.

We also saw Dad's elder brother, Keith, and his family once a year. Keith had a daughter who was only a year younger than me. We used to play together in a way I wasn't allowed to do most of the rest of the year, because Dad wouldn't let me out to play with friends. We had lots of fun, and I'd be sad when it was time for them to go home and I knew I wouldn't see them again for another year.

Dad behaved like a normal dad when his brother was around. I once heard him telling Keith how he wanted to adopt me.

'I love her like me own daughter, Keith,' he said. 'I'd adopt her if I could.'

'I've always said, it takes more to be a dad than a quick bunk-up,' Keith replied. 'It's the love you show 'em every day, ain't it? You don't need a bit of paper to tell you she's one of your own.'

'You're right there,' agreed Dad.

I knew that Keith was aware of Dad's temper. In the past he'd had words with him for the way he'd knocked Mum about. I looked at him and wondered what he'd say if he knew I got knocked about as well, and always had a fresh bruise somewhere on my body? If that was an example of the love Dad showed me every day, I'd be happy to do without it. I didn't want him to adopt me. I couldn't wait to grow up and leave home, as my brother and sisters had done. Then I'd never have to see Dad ever again.

Chapter Eight

I'd started at a new school when we moved to Nunhead and I really liked it. There were no bullies in the class, I'd made some good friends and my attendance had been much better. But whenever Dad winked and said, 'Why don't you stay off and we can watch telly?' I didn't feel I had a choice. It was more of a command than a suggestion. I didn't want to fall behind in my school work, especially now we were doing fractions, but there was also a part of me that was elated that Dad wanted to be friends. The thought of making him angry by refusing to stay at home was too big a price to pay.

Once, I made the mistake of being honest with him. Dad had suggested I stay at home again.

'Come on, we can have a wrestle,' he said.

I refused, because we were doing the high jump in P.E. that day and, despite the fact I had never had any sporting prowess, I seemed to be really good at it. I had reached the final and might actually win something for the first time in my life. But the moment I started to explain this to Dad, I realised I had made a huge mistake. His face darkened and the smile slid off his face to be replaced by his distinctive snarl. It was as if he had morphed into a demon.

'Go on then, you cunt, fuck off with your mates.' He coughed up a ball of phlegm and spat it in my face. I knew what was coming next, but I didn't have time to brace myself before he landed a slap round the back of my head then grabbed me and forced my face down into the sofa.

In the end I didn't go to school that day. When Mum came in at lunchtime she was annoyed to find me at home.

'She's not off school again, is she?' she said, forgetting that she herself had kept me off school countless times whenever she needed an extra pair of hands cleaning. 'I've been up since four o'clock this morning. The least she could have done is the washing-up from last night.'

'I dunno what we're gonna do with her,' smirked Dad, over the top of page three of *The Sun*.

I wanted to tell her that I hadn't wanted to stay off at all. I was hoping to have come third or fourth in the high jump by now. I could have told her that I wasn't able to do the washing-up because Dad had made me sit in front of the telly with his legs draped over me, pinning me to the sofa, but of course I stayed silent. If ever I went to Mum for comfort, she'd mock me for crying. 'Oh my gawd, she's boo-hoping again. Someone turn the waterworks off.'

There was no point going to her for support as she would always agree with Dad's actions. She seemed to relish it when I was out of favour with him, because then he would be extra nice to her and Kat. It was just another tool to make me feel like an outsider in the household.

That's why I would always agree to stay at home if Dad suggested it. I had learned the hard way that to reject his friendship meant paying a huge price. I was conditioned to put a happy grin on my face to mask the sinking feeling inside. I tried to look at the bright side. At least I got to eat plenty of sweets. Dad would hand me a pound note and send me round the corner to Izzie's mouldy-smelling shop where the floor space was no more than five square feet of tattered lino. I would ask Izzie for forty fruit salads, forty blackjacks and forty toffee logs, just as Dad had instructed. Izzie would lumber off to the back shelf trailing ash from her king-size cigarette as she went. Then I'd watch and listen to the people in the queue tutting behind me as she counted out the sweets into a white paper bag with her fat arthritic fingers.

When I got back home, Dad would have queued up the programme we were going to watch on the new video recorder he had bought primarily to tape his race meetings. Then we'd settle down on the sofa together and Dad would divide the sweets, half each. He would lie down, head propped up with pillows, and I would sit in my usual place, pinned under his legs. It was the only place I was allowed to sit when we watched TV together because he liked me to stroke his bare feet. If I dared to sit in another chair or simply wanted to go up to my bedroom like any other kid, he would take umbrage and dish out punishment as he saw fit. Every time I stopped to unwrap a blackjack, he'd wiggle his foot urgently, and I'd have to rush to start stroking again, touching all his horrible cracked hard skin. The revolting cheesy smell coupled with his long yellow toenails made me feel sick. My arm used to ache because I had to keep it raised and moving for hours on end, but it was a small price to pay to keep Dad happy. Occasionally he'd give a little groan of pleasure and say, 'Yeah, do it like that,' and I'd be so pleased to make him happy. When he was happy he wasn't angry or violent, so I made sure to stroke him as best I could.

'You've got the lightest touch in the world,' he'd say, just as he used to when I washed his back when I was little, and I'd swell with pride.

Dad used to like *Columbo* and *Quincy*, but occasionally when he was being nice we watched *Little House on the Prairie*, which was my favourite. I'd often have tears streaming down my face by the end. Invariably Pa Ingalls would have shown what an amazing dad he was, and his little Laura with the red plaits would have learned an important lesson, one that filled her father with pride and caused him to well up with emotion. I felt curiously sad, and didn't fully understand it, except to wish I had a dad as nice and kind as Pa Ingalls.

Dad would laugh to see my tears, and usually he would open his legs and pull me up to lie on top of him on the sofa. I'd lay my head against his chest as he rocked me from side to side. Then I'd cry all the more, and wish he could be loving like this all the time. Sometimes as I lay there I would feel something hard sticking into my stomach. I wondered if it was his penis going hard like it used to back at the flat in Peckham when he used to touch himself in front of me. We'd recently had sex education lessons at school, so I knew what it meant now, and this made me feel guilty and dirty for suspecting such a thing about my own dad. I realised I must be mistaken, but much as I wanted to, I didn't dare pull away in case he guessed what I had been thinking.

When Mum wasn't at work, it was very rare for us all to sit together in one room and watch television. In the evenings, Mum and Kat would sit downstairs in the dining room to watch telly while Dad and I would be in the front room upstairs watching the very same programme. I can't remember why we got into this habit, but it soon became the norm and no one commented on it.

Sometimes Kat would come upstairs and want me to play a game with her, but Dad insisted that I continued stroking his feet, and he'd shout at her and tell her to 'go back downstairs with Mummy'.

Once while Dad went to the toilet, Kat toddled in with her tree-house toy and we started to play a game, just as we did every morning after breakfast. When Dad came back he kicked me hard in the ankle and growled, 'Who said you could stop doing my feet?' I leapt back into my position on the sofa, like a well-trained dog, and watched as Kat wandered off back downstairs, crying for Mum.

When I was eleven and Kat was two we both got scarlet fever and our bodies were covered with an itchy red rash. The doctor prescribed medicine and a bottle of calamine lotion to apply to the rash. I went into the bathroom, stripped off my clothes and covered my body the best I could but my back was particularly itchy and there were parts I simply couldn't reach. I didn't like to ask Mum but I felt I had no choice so I went into the front room where she sat smoking with Dad.

'Can you do my back please, Mum?' I asked, poking my head round the door, wrapped only in a towel.

'Do I have to?' she moaned, rolling her eyes up to the ceiling.

'Come here,' said Dad from his position on the sofa. 'I'll do it.'

Reluctantly I went and stood between his legs and watched as he filled his hand with a pool of the chalky pink lotion. I held my hair up with one hand and clasped the towel to my chest with the other as he smoothed the cooling lotion over my shoulders. Then I felt him tugging the back of the towel, so that he could reach lower. I loosened my grip just a little.

'Let the dog see the fucking rabbit,' he laughed, sweeping his hands down to the small of my back and skimming over the top of my buttocks.

I immediately tensed, embarrassed. Mum watched me from the other side of the room with a look of pure loathing on her face. I felt ill and wondered what I had done to upset her so.

'There you go, all done. I won't offer to do your fried eggs,' he said, referring to my chest.

Despite my burning fever, I felt myself blushing and was eager to leave the room. But before I could step away, Dad pulled me down onto his lap, and placed a hand across my brow. I shifted awkwardly, attempting to adjust the towel around me.

'Cor, she's burning hot, Donna,' he said.

'Yeah, so's Kat,' said Mum shortly. 'Come here, Kat, come sit with Mummy.'

'Yeah, but you wanna feel her head, poor kid. She's roasting,' he said, focussing all his attention on me. 'I'd better just take her up to bed.'

He stood up with an arm round me to support me and Mum glowered as we left the room.

He led me upstairs and waited outside the bedroom door while I slipped on a nightie and got into bed then he came in and knelt down beside me. As he kissed my hot forehead and held my hand, I began to drift off into a fitful sleep, vaguely aware that Dad had lain down beside me.

For a moment or two I sank into a dream before stirring into consciousness again. That's when I became aware that Dad had his hand down the front of his trousers and was moving it back and forth vigorously. I could feel it slapping into my own hand, which he held against his groin. My first reaction was of utter shock. What on earth was Dad doing? I knew it was wrong and rude, and I felt guilty that I had woken up and became aware of it. I realised he must think I was fast asleep and that he was doing things to himself in private. It made me feel almost like a Peeping Tom. I clamped my eyes shut and hardly dared to swallow in case he heard and realised I was awake. I knew Dad had a habit of being lewd and crude, but surely even he would be mortified if he knew I was aware of what he was doing to himself. My heart pounded in my ears and it felt like an eternity passed before he released my hand from his sweaty grip, and left the room.

It didn't even occur to me to talk to Mum about this incident and my increasing feelings of awkwardness around Dad. A lot of the time she could see for herself what was going on and the most she would do is laugh and say, 'Oh my Gawd, Frank,' as if it was all one big joke. She was as uninhibited as Dad when it came to things of a sexual nature. She routinely left a life-like vibrator on her bedside table beside the ashtray, and when Kat was a baby she used to pick it up and use it as a teething ring.

'Oh my Gawd, give us it, Kat,' she'd laugh.

Both Mum and Dad were careless or blasé about such things. Once when I had left my shoes in their bedroom, I knocked on the door and asked if I could come in to get them. When I went in, I was excruciatingly embarrassed to find them in the middle of sex. Mum was on her back with him on top, pumping away, and a sheet half covering them. As I stood frozen in the doorway, Dad continued to move back and forth. My face burned with embarrassment, but for the first time I felt a new emotion: I was angry with Mum that she could behave in such a way. I expected nothing else from Dad by now, but she was a mother, and mothers were supposed to protect their children, weren't they?

It was still routine to see Dad's penis on display. In summer he'd wear very short white swimming trunks and often his genitals would be hanging out of the side. He'd kick a balloon or ball to me and every time he raised his leg he'd expose himself. Either that or he'd sit with his legs apart blatantly scratching his scrotum, but Mum would never say 'Put it away, Frank. Everyone can see,' as a normal mother or wife would do.

It was around this time that he began instigating more and more physical games with me. Wrestling remained a favourite. He would pin me down with my arms above my head and lie on top of me, forcing my legs apart with his knees. Mum would be in and out of the room with cups of tea or cans of lager for Dad, and she often witnessed him grinding his hips between my open legs but she never said a word.

I was starting to wonder whether he was touching my bum and chest on purpose, but despite his previous lewd behaviour with pornography and nudity, and what he had done to himself in my bedroom when he thought I was asleep, a part of me couldn't quite believe he meant it in a rude way. He was my dad. We were only playing a wrestling game, and Mum was often in the room. Besides, I'd seen Giant Haystacks grip Big Daddy in a private place on the telly, but there was never any question that he was doing it on purpose, or being rude. Dad was my dad, and although I squirmed with embarrassment when he squeezed my buttocks or chest, I felt bad for having suspicions about his motives.

One day he had my face in a headlock between his thighs. My face was pressed into his groin and I felt the familiar hardness beneath his scruffy jeans. Mum was sitting in the armchair, flicking through the *Reader's Digest*. I couldn't breathe and just wanted to get away, so I screamed as loudly as I could. Dad released me quickly and rolled away, knocking his eye into the edge of the coffee table. A lump began to form. I braced myself for a smack but on this occasion it never came. Instead, he just looked at me with a shocked expression, as if my loud scream had surprised him somehow. He was used to getting his own way, and I could tell he didn't like the fact I'd resisted.

112

Most of Dad's games involved some sort of physical contact: playing horsy with me on his back, wheelbarrows where my skirt would fall over my head exposing my knickers, rugby tackling or drenching me with water in the garden so that my thin summer clothes became transparent. Although I felt uncomfortable at times, I was so grateful not to be on the receiving end of Dad's violence or bad temper that my over-riding emotion was one of relief. I tried to smile, blotting out the parts I didn't like, and pretended he was Pa Ingalls playing an innocent game in the sunshine with Half-Pint.

I was eleven and a half when an alarm bell rang in my head which I could no longer deny. I was lying on the floor on my tummy, in the classic children's pose, watching cartoons. The room was dark and Dad was lying at my feet. Usually we both sat on the sofa with his legs on top of me, so it felt like a special occasion for me to be lying free on the floor. In a strange role reversal, he began to stroke my feet, tickling one minute, massaging deep the next. It felt lovely, and I realised why he had become addicted to me stroking his.

After some time his hand moved up to my calf. I was wearing a very loose pair of grey corduroy trousers, which had once belonged to Mum. The television provided the only light in the room. Mum was downstairs with Kat, as usual, and Dad and I were alone. One minute he was stroking my leg and I was enjoying the feeling, then suddenly he reached his hand higher under my trousers and began to stroke the back of my thigh just beneath my bottom. I stiffened as I realised he couldn't possibly have run his fingertips under the elastic of my knickers by accident. It was as if a lightbulb had gone off in my head. I began to put everything together: all the lewd remarks, the touching and the rude behaviour. I knew then that when he exposed an erection, or played a pornographic video instead of *Quincy QC*, as he had done recently, it was on purpose. I remembered Cheryl complaining to her friend Gail about him always trying to touch her up and I felt a sense of paralysis come over me. For the first time ever, I understood about Dad and what he liked to do and I was shocked.

The fear came next. As soon as I could manage without upsetting him, I left the room and ran up to my bedroom where I lay on my bed and cried tears of confusion and hopelessness. What could I do? I knew without asking that Mum would be no help.

Over the next few days I began to think of finding Nanny and Jenny. I wondered if they thought about me and, if so, why they never wrote. I wondered where Diane, Cheryl and Davie had gone? If only I could contact them, they might let me go and live with them. Every time Dad stared at me now, I worried that he could read my mind and would know that I was being a 'betraying bastard'. I had seen in a letter that Nanny and Jenny had moved to Kent, to a place called Tunbridge Wells, but I couldn't remember their address apart from the number 10. I had been trained for so long to put all thoughts of them out of my mind that I couldn't think of the street name. Did it begin with an A or a C?

I felt sad when I realised that even if I could remember their address I wouldn't know what to do. It would be too embarrassing to talk to them about Dad and the rude things he was doing. All I knew was that I wanted to be with people who were clean, not dirty. I wanted people who loved me in a normal way, like the parents I saw walking with their children around the supermarket, but already I felt somehow contaminated. If I ever found Nanny again, she might look at me and see the shame and embarrassment that was beginning to leak from every pore. She might think I was dirty like Dad and not love me any more. It was better to remember her the way she had been in the past than to see her disappointed face now. I decided to forget about her and the rest of my family forever.

All I could do was try to keep away from Dad as much as possible, but it was very difficult because he became obsessed with knowing my every movement. He always wanted me near him. If I asked if I could go out with a friend from school, Dad made it clear that he would class it as an act of betrayal. He only had to spit in my cornflakes or call me a name like stupid prat, little piss-arsed fucker, ugly cunt or fat bitch, and I'd decide I didn't want to go out after all.

Mum was no comfort whatsoever. Her favourite expression was 'She's not boo-hooing again, is she? Does it ever stop?'

Dad wanted to control every aspect of my life: where I went, what I did, where I sat, yet because of his violent mood swings, I was still disproportionately grateful whenever he was nice to me. I tried hard not to do anything wrong as I lived in fear of his mood changing. He demanded that I spend every spare minute with him and this habit was well entrenched by now. The only respite I ever got was during the day at school, or if I volunteered to go cleaning with Mum. That's why, from the age of eleven and a half, I made sure I was doing a lot more cleaning. I knew she wouldn't take my side against Dad, but if I stayed close to her he wouldn't be able to do anything, would he?

Chapter Nine

The contacts Mum and Dad had made while cleaning for media companies in the West End had led to them securing the cleaning contract for a large new office building in Kensington, which had apparently cost millions to renovate. It was a mass of marble, smoked glass, chrome and shag-pile carpets. Every morning at 3.30am the alarm would go off and Mum would drag herself out of bed and get ready to catch the bus. If Dad was sober enough he would go with her, mainly to supervise the cash-in-hand cleaners they employed on a casual basis. Dad would come home at 8.30am, by which time I would have fed and dressed Kat and be ready to walk her to nursery. Mum wouldn't get back until noon, having spent the morning dispensing tea bags and toilet rolls to every floor of the huge building. In the evening she would be off out again to take care of another couple of cleaning jobs in an advertising agency and an insurance broker's. I often went with her to lend a hand on the evening jobs. Although I would have preferred to do my homework or watch telly, I knew that if I stayed at home I would be left with Dad and he might start to touch me again.

I began to look forward to going cleaning. I'd look at the people in the town centre, all finished work for the day, and I imagined the normal lives they were going home to. I knew by this time that my life was anything but normal.

Unfortunately, going cleaning with mum every evening wasn't enough to save me from Dad's attentions. When we got back around 9pm, he would usually be watching the little portable television in his bedroom upstairs. Kat would already be in bed asleep, and while Mum made herself a couple of tea, she would flick on the television in the dining room and settle down for a couple of hours until bed. Dad would call out for me, and I had no choice but to go up to his bedroom to see what he wanted.

'Come and sit beside me,' he'd say. 'You'll like this programme.'

Once when I said I would rather watch it downstairs, he launched himself out of bed naked and grabbed me by the hair. 'What am I, black or something, you cunt?'

Racism came as naturally to him as breathing. I'd had a Jamaican school friend called Janet for a while but when she came to pick me up at our front door, she heard Dad shouting 'Tell that coon to fuck off back to the jungle. Fucking golly-wog.' Understandably the friendship didn't last long after that, although her mother was still very friendly to me if we passed on the street.

There was never any way out of the situation, so I had to go upstairs and sit on top of the bedcovers watching telly with him, or playing a game like I-Spy. He could be so nice when he wanted to be that it was almost hard to reconcile the nice dad with the nasty dad. When he was nice, it was hard to believe he could ever be nasty, and when he was nasty it was almost worth it to have him be nice for a while after. But then things took another twist.

'Why not put your nightie on so you're nice and comfy?' he suggested. I didn't want to but rather than risk angering him, I pulled on my long blue nightie but kept on a T-shirt underneath so that I wasn't showing my bare arms or the 'V' that dipped at my chest.

Soon he began to insist that I wore my nightie every night and this became the new routine.

'Get under the covers or you'll get cold,' he said next.

Once I was lying beside him under the duvet, he stopped asking me to do his feet. Instead he would turn away from me onto his side and demand I 'do' his back. I would have to stroke him for ages and it was much worse than doing his feet. My arm would be shaking with the effort of keeping it raised and in motion. Periodically he'd bark out orders such as 'Lower!' or 'Over my ribs!' If I didn't do it right, he might grab my hand and guide it with his own, such an edge creeping into his voice that I'd try to make more of an effort. I'd have to sweep down low over the tops of his buttocks and up again around his ribs and chest. He'd shiver and get goosebumps, and that's how I knew I was doing it right. If my arm got tired or I was slap-dash and my touch wasn't light enough, he'd get really angry. He was fond of pinching me, giving a sharp little twist at the end that always left a nasty bruise.

But when I did the stroking right he'd compliment me on having the lightest touch he'd ever felt. He said nobody could stroke him as well as I could. I was happy to please him because it meant not getting hurt. I would have much rather been doing something else like any other child my age but, as always, I'd do anything so he wouldn't be angry.

When it was time for me to go to bed, I climbed out from under the covers and bent down to give him a kiss goodnight. I would pretend he was like any other dad, not violent or peculiar in any way, and when he gave me a kiss on the cheek and a big cuddle, I felt happy. But more often than not he would then pull me down on top of him, and without the jeans and the belt buckle to blame it on, it was obvious he had an erection. I was confused and distressed at first, but it soon became so common that I didn't think anything of it.

One night, just after my twelfth birthday, he pulled me on top of him, still above the duvet while he was naked underneath, and he ran his hands up and down my body in a way he'd never done before. It was almost frenzied, and as he cupped my buttocks in both his hands and pushed his erection into my stomach, his fingers pressed between my legs so hard that it hurt. I winced in pain, trying hard to disguise my discomfort. There was no way I could lie to myself and pretend it wasn't happening. Once he'd started this new thing, he began to do it every night.

Once Mum walked into the bedroom with a cup of tea while I was lying on top of him with his fingers between my legs, and I looked up, alarmed. What would she say? Surely she couldn't approve of him doing this? But as quickly as she'd come into the room, she backed out again, her face giving no clue about her feelings. By this time I knew she was aware of Dad's preoccupation with me, and rather than hit him over the head with a frying pan, as many women would be driven to do, she felt challenged. She seemed to feel that she and Kat were battling with me for Dad's attention and the thing she neglected to recognise was that I didn't *want* his attention – especially not the sort he was starting to give me.

Every night thereafter Dad would go through the same goodnight routine. It went on night after night with me stroking his back, and then the hands running up and down my body. It became more usual for Dad to 'accidentally' play a pornographic video in front of me. He would always laugh as he heard me gasp in embarrassment. Soon he started to stroke my legs under the duvet. At first it felt nice and it was a relief to be able to relax and not feel the pain in my arms, but as much as I tried to paint the situation in an innocent light to myself, I couldn't get away from the fact that it was odd to watch TV alone in bed with your dad.

I lay beside him in my nightie feeling very vulnerable. Tears stung my eyes as I felt his hands move up from the sides of my legs to the tops, and then circle their way down until he grabbed the inner sides of my thighs and lifted them apart. I was paralysed, unable to move. Before long, things took another, very frightening turn as, gradually, Dad began touching me between the legs. He would start by stroking the side of my leg. He'd do this for a few days and then the next time he would move to the inside of my leg. The next time he would part my legs to get better access to my inner thighs. All this would happen without any words being exchanged. And on it went very slowly so that by the time he actually made

121

contact with my genitals, it was as though the situation had crept up on me without my realising. But as soon as he first brushed my knickers with his little finger, as if by accident, I realised that this moment had been building up for what seemed like years, and the things I had secretly been worried about, feeling guilty and dirty for even thinking them, had finally happened. I wanted to pull away but I was too petrified to move, not only because I feared his violence but also because if I was wrong and it was all innocent, he'd know I had been thinking rude things. He would think I had a filthy mind.

By the time there was no question as to what he was doing, because he was using his whole hand to touch me firmly on the genitals, I felt it was too late to do anything. I felt complicit in some way and I was absolutely distraught and confused. The only way I could cope was to pretend it wasn't part of the 'real world'. It was like a dream that wasn't actually happening. I'd try and think of other things to keep my brain occupied.

The abuse was carried out in eery silence with the sound of the telly in the background and his occasional panting breaths. Soon, although things were still unspoken between us, he became more confident and rougher in the way he touched me. It used to hurt and I began to get very sore. I would lie there, hardly daring to breathe and certainly not brave enough to complain about the pain. I could feel the bed vibrating as he masturbated himself with his other hand. I imagined jumping up and saying goodnight before retreating to the safety of my room, but invariably I couldn't help imagining Dad running after me, and the beating that would follow, and that was enough to keep me pinned to the bed. I wanted to move and protest, but incredibly I was still hoping that it was innocent.

If Katrina wasn't already in bed, Mum would bring her up to say goodnight. She could see I was under the duvet with Dad, and that he was naked. I was often on the brink of tears but she would just tut and roll her eyes. I tried to catch her eye and make her understand that I didn't want to be there, that I hated it, but she'd never look at me directly. Despite the fact she had to get up in the early hours of the morning, she never asked me to go to bed so that she could take my place beside Dad. She always waited downstairs until she heard that he had let me go back to my room.

Sometimes the session would finish with Dad jerking and groaning, and at other times he would simply stop. That would be my cue to leave, without a backward glance or a word spoken. I'd simply go to my room and for the first few months I'd cry every night as I wondered what I had done to make this horrible thing happen to me.

Most nights after Dad had finished abusing me, I'd hear him and Mum having sex. There was no escaping the sound. It seemed as though Mum moaned and groaned especially loudly, as if she wanted me to hear her. I felt nauseous, because even at that age I had a very clear understanding that Dad's abuse of me had somehow made him excited and now he was releasing his excitement with Mum. It felt incestuous and wrong and horrible.

One night, Dad had been abusing me as usual and when I went to bed, I noticed blood had soaked my knickers. I had started my periods. Burning with embarrassment, I called Mum to my room and showed her my knickers.

She seemed just as awkward and embarrassed as me, and refused to make eye contact. 'Wait a minute while I get you some things,' she said to the floor, before disappearing and returning a minute later to chuck two sanitary towels on my bed.

For the next few days, Dad teased me mercilessly about how all the dogs would be sniffing round me. I blushed as he said 'She's a woman now.'

He began commenting regularly on my looks and developing body. He still liked kicking, punching or spitting at me, but the rest of the time he was telling me I looked beautiful and admiring the curve of my bottom in jeans. He would make me try on clothes and tell me to turn this way and that while he admired them.

'Doesn't she look beautiful, Donna?' he would say, and Mum would grunt and turn away. Once I caught the look in her eye and I could have sworn it was one of pure hatred.

Chapter Ten

y the time I started secondary school, Dad's abuse of me had been going on for months. I had almost grown used to it, and whenever his hand strayed between my legs I would tune out, and think about something else until it was over. It was this, and the fact we didn't speak about the abuse, that made it seem as though it wasn't really happening.

On my first day at school, I remember feeling like the odd one out for a number of reasons. It wasn't just that all the other girls had the official school blazers and were dropped off on their first day by one or other of their parents, but also because I felt tainted by the fact that Dad, the only dad I had ever known, was doing things to me most evenings that he shouldn't have been doing. I wasn't concerned that I was scruffy and lacking the required pencil case and geometry set listed in the school prospectus. These were minor considerations compared to what was going on at home.

Dad had taken me to the school shop in Victoria and made a great fuss about ordering me the whole uniform. 'I hope you know how much this shit is costing me,' he growled in my ear as the bespectacled sales assistant took my measurements. By the time the final balance was due a week before school started, he had blown the money on a horse race so I had to make do with a grey jumper and skirt from down the market. Things like that didn't really bother me. I had grown used to being the scruffiest kid in any class so it was all par for the course. It was the situation at home that caused me the most distress.

On that first day, I was half an hour late, and arrived red-faced and sweating, having run all the way. Mum was out at work so I had to waken Kat, get her washed and dressed and walk her to nursery as I always did. The only difference now was that my new school was much further away. This meant I had to sprint, puffing and panting, all the way up a hill to get to my school. When I arrived late I had to sign in at the office and was taken to my new classroom by the head of the first year, Mrs Jacobson. All the other girls were already labelling their work books and studying the timetable. Mrs Jacobson asked me why I was late and I muttered something about the alarm not going off. She gave me a look, as if deciding to herself that I was going to be one to keep an eye on.

Head down, I shuffled up the aisle and took the first available seat next to a girl called Karen Collins. She had incredibly long blonde hair, blue eyes and perfect peaches and cream skin. She also had a flair for fashion, and even though the school had a strict uniform policy, I noticed over the coming weeks that she always managed to wear something that was just a little bit different. She looked stylish and well-groomed whereas I was plain and scruffy.

I was surprised when Karen latched on to me because she was the archetypal popular girl, whereas I had no other friends. The thing that drew us together was a shared sense of humour and a love of mucking around, making each other laugh. We really clicked and for a few short hours during the school day, she would make it easier for me to put my problems on the back burner. But there was a sticking point. Every day after school, she would ask me to come out later. There was nothing I wanted more, just to be free and have fun like any other teenager, but I knew Dad wouldn't let me. Karen lived near me, and as we walked home together, picking up Kat from her after-school club, she'd keep trying to persuade me to come out. I didn't know how to explain about Dad and his strange ways, his violence and all the other more worrying things that were happening to me, so I'd have to make up excuses

'I just don't feel like it,' I said, struggling to think of a more plausible excuse.

I could see that she was puzzled by my refusal, especially as we had been having a laugh only minutes before. Sometimes, even though I told her not to, she'd come and knock for me. Dad would jump up to peek through the curtains and say 'It's that prat Karen. Tell her to fuck off.'

The friendship wasn't just about laughing and joking, though. As I grew to trust her, I told Karen a few things about my home life, such as the fact that I had to get Kat ready for school in the mornings, which was why I was always late. Karen was sympathetic. She had witnessed the trouble I got into when I arrived at school every morning and tried to find an excuse for my perpetual lateness.

'Why don't you just tell them you have to drop your little sister off first?' she asked.

'I don't want to get Mum in trouble with the school,' I said, meaning I didn't want to get myself into trouble with Dad for telling the truth.

Dad began insisting I stay off school more and more. I would have to walk Kat to school and then turn around and go back home again with a heavy heart. Sometimes he would send me out for sweets and we'd watch a programme he had taped, but more often than not he said he was tired and wanted us to go upstairs and watch the telly on the portable in his bedroom. I came to dread hearing him say, 'Let's go upstairs.'

'I really should be at school, Dad,' I told him one day. 'Mrs Jacobson has been asking me if there's anything wrong at home.'

'What the fuck you been telling her, you stupid bitch?' he snarled, throwing a spoon so hard at the wall above my head that it left a dent in the wallpaper.

'Nothing,' I said trying to calm the situation. 'I just said I haven't been feeling well, that's all.'

'Nosey fucking cunt,' he said, grinding out his cigarette in the remains of his fried egg sandwich.

When Mum came in at lunchtime, she didn't bat an eye at finding Dad in bed and me under the covers with him. It was a relief to see her because I knew that after she'd had a cup of tea she would get undressed and get into bed with him for a 'nap'. Then I would be free to go. I didn't have to collect Kat from school until 3.30pm, so I had a couple of hours to kill.

Usually I'd put the television on to mask the noise Mum and Dad were making upstairs, but there were never any good programmes at that time of day so there was nothing to distract me from thinking about all the things that were wrong in my life.

I hated the things Dad did to me. I felt utterly powerless. The only person who could have helped me was Mum, but she didn't seem to mind the way Dad treated me. Sometimes when he made a crude comment about my developing body, I would glance over at her as if to ask if she felt his behaviour was appropriate, but all she would do is make light of it by laughing, or saying 'Oh my gawd! Who's gonna look at you?' Most of the time she looked away, unable to meet my tearful eyes, and busied herself with lighting a cigarette or fiddling with her false teeth. I began to feel real resentment towards her for not rescuing me, which only added to the chasm that already existed where the mother/daughter bond should have been. At those moments, I felt unbearably lonely.

I wondered what Mum would say if I told her what Dad was doing to me as we watched television together, while she was downstairs watching the same programme in another room? She would have to be deaf, dumb and blind not to realise something wasn't right. The urge grew in me to mention it and get it out in the open.

One afternoon when I heard her getting out of bed and shuffling past the front room door on her way down to the kitchen, I stood up to follow her. I didn't know what I would say, but I knew I had to say something.

As I walked into the kitchen she said, 'You'd better go and get Kat. Time's getting on.'

'Mum,' I said, feeling tears welling up. 'Dad does things ...'

'What?' she snapped, her whole body stiffening. Her voice was low and threatening. 'What you on about?'

I could tell she knew what I was going to say but her voice, body language, and the angry expression on her face were all flashing a red warning not to proceed.

I carried on with sobs punctuating every word. 'He ... does ... it ... upstairs ... It's not ... my ... fault.'

She was quick to interrupt me, thrusting her face angrily into mine. 'Now don't you fucking start with all that bollocks.'

'All what bollocks?' Dad suddenly appeared behind me, a towel wrapped around his waist. 'What's going on here?'

'Nothing's going on,' said Mum, pouring boiling water into a couple of chipped mugs before spooning in heaps of sugar. 'She just wants all the fucking attention as per usual.'

'I'll give her attention,' said Dad, staring at me steadily. 'I'll have to smack her cute little arse in a minute.'

I stood rooted to the spot while I judged whether it was safe enough to leave the room. I kept my head down and stared at Dad's bare feet on the lino in front of me – feet on which I knew every corn and callous. After letting out a loud fart he turned and padded through to sit at the dining-room table.

'Oh, you dirty beast!' Mum called after him in mock revulsion, then she turned to me. 'Are you going to get your sister now or are you going to leave her standing in the playground on her own? Useless lump.'

After that brief conversation, she became even more cold and distant towards me. Everything I did seemed to irritate her and I had no idea why. I was only twelve and I just yearned for her to protect me, as I sensed other mothers did for their daughters. But she didn't love me the way they did. She didn't even like me.

A few days after our conversation, I was sitting on the floor in the front room, my geography exercise book spread out before me. I was trying to colour a picture of a volcano but Kat kept picking up my felt tips and scribbling on the side of my book. 'Kat, no!' I said again and again. 'Mum, please tell her.'

Mum sat in her chair saying nothing, just squinting at me through the haze of blue cigarette smoke that hung around her head. Then suddenly, from being so still and quiet, she seemed to explode. She rushed over to me, picked up my schoolbook and ripped it into pieces. She didn't say anything other than a jumbled mass of 'Fucking shit, fucking fed up, fucking little fucker,' all rolled into one sentence.

Her face red with rage, she turned on me, still swearing continuously. She pulled me up by the hair and dragged me out of the room then shoved me out of the door before slamming it behind me with a loud crash.

I sat on the landing in total shock, my hair tangled, my T-shirt ripped and my body trembling. Mum had never hit me like that before. I replayed the events of the last few minutes and struggled to make sense of what I had done to anger her so much. What was it all about? Instinctively I knew that ever since that day in the kitchen when I'd tried to tell her about Dad, she had been like a simmering pot. Now she had reached boiling point, and I was terrified about what she would tell Dad and what he might do to me when he got home.

I spent the rest of the day hiding under the bed in my room. When I heard Dad arrive I was shaking with fear. It didn't take long for me to hear raised voices but this time the main voice was Mum's, screeching and shouting in a way I had never heard before.

'Bastard!' she shouted.

I strained to hear but it was difficult from my position under the bed when they were two floors down in the kitchen. I didn't dare creep to the top of the stairs. I wasn't sure I really wanted to know what the row was about anyway. All I knew was that Mum seemed to hate me. She saw me as the enemy and I had no idea why.

I heard the door slam again and rushed to look out of the window. It was Dad, striding down the road. I jumped as the door opened behind me but it was only Kat. She looked frightened, with a dirty, tear-stained face and I felt really sorry for her. She was only four and Mum losing her temper like that must have been terrifying for her. I opened my arms and she ran into them and we cried together.

When Dad came back later that evening he was carrying two bottles of brandy, which was usually a sign of trouble to come. He walked into the kitchen and slammed them down onto the work top.

I slipped out of the room and ran upstairs, where I sat biting my nails down to the quick, dreading the moment I would hear his call – but it never came. The next morning I heard him snoring in the front room. He had obviously been

132

too drunk to go to work and Mum had left him to sleep it off. I didn't bother making any breakfast that day; I just rushed to get Kat dressed and out the door before he woke up and tried to stop me.

That afternoon, I was sitting in my classical studies class and Mrs Jones was telling us about Icarus and his waxen wings. Normally I loved to listen to old myths and fables but this day I found it hard to concentrate. I stared at the clock and willed it to stop. Every passing moment brought me closer to home time and Dad. I wanted the class to go on forever.

Suddenly the classroom door opened and our head of year, Mrs Jacobson, appeared. I watched her eyes scan the room briefly before settling on me. She whispered to Mrs Jones, who asked me to gather my things. My heart gave a frightened leap as I wondered what was happening.

Mrs Jacobson led me down to her office on the ground floor. 'Your mother's come to collect you, dear,' she said. When she ushered me into her office, Mum was sitting on a chair in front of the desk. She had a plastic carrier bag clutched to her lap, and I could make out the blue cotton of my nightdress through the thin white plastic.

I listened as Mum explained that there had been a family emergency. 'I don't want to go into details,' she said, 'but Lisa won't be in for a few days.'

'Yes, I've been meaning to contact you about her attendance,' said Mrs Jacobson, 'but under the circumstances, it can wait.'

'She's always been sickly, that's all,' said Mum, the irritation clear in her voice.

'Of course,' said Mrs Jacobson, looking me up and down with her sharp beady eyes. 'But in future we will need a note.'

'Well, I can't sit here all day,' said Mum, standing up abruptly. 'We've got to go. Come on, Lisa.'

My mind raced as I wondered what could possibly have happened. Had Dad gone away somewhere? My heart lifted at the possibility that he might have left us. But then if that was the case, where was she taking me with my nightdress in a plastic bag?

When we got outside, I kept asking what was happening, but she didn't say anything until we reached the bus stop. 'It's him, ain't it? He's finally gone mad,' she said sharply.

She seemed so angry that I wondered if they had had a row about me. I tried hard not to cry as I knew it was one of the main things that made her cross with me.

'Where are we going?' I asked.

'You're going to stay with Diane for a few days.'

'Who?' I asked in shock. I couldn't believe I had just heard her say my oldest sister's name out loud.

'Diane.' She pulled a crumpled piece of paper out of her coat pocket. 'She's living up Hackney way.'

I couldn't stop the tears then. I hadn't seen Diane in four years, since I was eight, but it felt like an eternity to me. I was overwhelmed by feelings, crying and smiling all at the same time, but gradually a terrible cold fear descended on me. If Mum knew for sure about Dad abusing me and that's what their big row was about, then she would surely tell Diane. And Diane would tell Cheryl and Davie, and Nanny and

Jenny. The thought of everybody looking at me as if I were dirty made it hard to breathe. I was frightened.

'Can you stop that wailing?' asked Mum. 'You're showing me right up. What you got to cry about anyway?'

When our bus came along, she pinched off the lit end of her cigarette and put it in the pocket of her brown sheepskin coat for later.

We sat in silence for a while then Mum said, 'It's your fault, just like it was Cheryl's.'

At first I didn't understand what she was talking about.

'He's a man, for fuck's sake. What do you think's gonna happen if it's put on a plate for him?'

I felt as if she had just slapped me hard across the face. What was she saying? That I wanted Dad to do those vile things to me? I flushed bright red, and was glad we were both staring ahead out of the front window.

'Mum,' I sobbed, 'You don't understand. He hits me if I don't do as he says. It's not my fault.'

'Well it ain't fucking mine.'

We didn't talk after that. I pressed my forehead against the window, closed my eyes and wished I'd never been born. How could she blame me? What could I possibly have done differently?

After we got off the bus at the other end, we walked along a busy main road. Mum looked at the piece of paper to check the address and we stopped outside a dilapidated house set back from the road behind a dense, overgrown garden. Lots of the windows were smashed, and black bin liners used as curtains fluttered in the breeze.

'This can't be it,' said Mum. 'What the fuck's she doing living here?'

She pushed open the rusty front gate and we picked our way up the front path, careful to avoid the broken glass and empty lager cans. We had to climb some steps to get to the front door, which had FUCK OFF scrawled on the front in black felt tip. Mum hesitated but before she could knock at the door, it opened to reveal a youth in his early twenties. He had curly ginger hair, spots around his protruding jaw, and bad teeth.

'Is Diane in?'

'Diane be here soon,' he said nodding. He had a strange manner about him and when he led us through to the front room, Mum whispered to me that he must be 'a bit simple'.

The room had an old brown sofa and a gas fire in the corner. I recognised a couple of Diane's ornately beaded handbags hanging on the wall as decoration. A friend at her first job had brought them back from a trip to India. I remembered holding them when I was a little girl.

Mum asked the boy, who had introduced himself as Ewan, if she could use the toilet. He pointed to an open doorway, which led to the back of the house. It was then I noticed the word BOG scrawled at the top of the doorway in the same handwriting as the FUCK OFF on the front door. Mum noticed too, and her mouth fell open for a moment.

Ewan began to laugh. 'Bog, bog,' he kept saying.

It wasn't long before Diane arrived home. I flew into her arms, tears streaming down my face. She looked just the same as I remembered her: long dark hair, parted in the middle, the same colour eyes and skin as Mum. She was even wearing the same Afghan coat she had on when I last saw her. I sat glued to her side and ran the soft white trim through my fingers.

It wasn't until Diane shrugged off her coat that I noticed she was expecting a baby. She had just been for a scan and she spent a while explaining in detail to Mum what position the baby was in. Watching the two of them together, it was as though they had never been parted. I could tell from the conversation that they hadn't kept in touch but even so, their bond was so strong they seemed to pick up where they had left off. I didn't know how Mum had Diane's address but guessed someone must have passed it to her behind Dad's back.

Diane explained they were only staying at the house until they found somewhere else.

'I should bloody well hope so, too,' said Mum. 'It's a right dump. Who's Ewan, when he's at home?'

'He came with the house,' Diane laughed. 'He's alright though.'

When Diane suggested I go and put my bag upstairs in her bedroom, I knew they were going to be talking about Dad and me. I planned to listen to what they said outside the door but the floorboards creaked, and besides, I didn't think I could bear to hear them talk about it. I felt too ashamed.

I walked up the stairs and found Diane's bedroom on the left. It was pretty, and there were more things I recognised from years ago – knick-knacks and framed photographs that showed Diane and Cheryl standing beside Mum, who was wearing three-quarter-length Capri pants and a scarf over a small beehive. It must have been taken in the early 60s.

'Hello, Lisa.'

I spun round to see Diane's boyfriend Martin standing in the doorway. 'Christ, you were only this high when I last saw you,' he said, holding his hand at waist height.

'Hello, Martin.'

'What's Frank been up to this time, eh?'

I just stared at the floor and felt my face burn bright red.

When I went back downstairs, Mum and Diane were still talking over a cup of tea.

'Anyway, I thought it best to bring her here for a while, 'cos he said if I take her home he's gonna fucking kill her.'

Diane shook her head in disbelief. 'You'll be alright here with us for a while, won't you, Lisa?'

I covered my face with my hands, so sick of crying. I was confused. I didn't understand who knew what, and because I didn't want to be judged as dirty, I couldn't bring myself to speak about the things that were tearing me apart inside.

When Mum stood up to go, she gave me a casual wave of the hand, but I flew across the room and hugged her tight. It felt odd to rest against her softness and breathe in her smell. She never hugged me herself, just stood with her hands held awkwardly to the side. I wished with all my heart that she would love me the way I loved her. No matter how cold she was, how abruptly she treated me, or how many times she let Dad take me up to his bed, I couldn't stop the love I felt. I knew she was a bad mother, but I still yearned for her love and would have done just about anything to please her.

'I'll come and get you when he's calmed down,' she said.

I nodded and Diane passed me a bit of toilet roll to blow my nose. I wanted to ask why Dad wanted to kill me but I was frightened of the answer, so instead I stood with Diane at the front door and waved Mum off back down the glass-strewn path.

'Simple Ewan' turned out to be really nice. We played Monopoly and card games together. Every day I'd ask Diane if Cheryl and Davie might come to visit, or whether we could go and visit Nanny and Jenny, and she promised we'd see them all soon.

The house may have been ramshackle, with broken doors and windows, but I noticed it was very clean – much cleaner than at home – and cosy in its own way too. Every morning I'd wake up in my sleeping bag on the sofa and the first thing I'd notice was an absence of fear. Each day that passed brought a lightness of feeling. I wasn't weighed down with the thought of Dad. I didn't have to worry about the filthy things he did to me in the bedroom, and I didn't have to worry about his violence.

It was like being on holiday. If I walked in front of the television while someone was watching a favourite programme, there wouldn't be a kick on the back of my legs as punishment, or if I accidentally knocked over a glass of water there would be no slap to the head. But most importantly, my private places were my own. I began to dread Mum arriving to take me home.

'Can't I stay here with you, Diane?' I asked.

'Don't be silly, Lisa. You belong with Mum.'

'Mum wouldn't mind,' I said, thinking to myself that she might actually be pleased with the idea.

'No,' Diane said, and I realised I shouldn't have asked. She had her own life to lead. 'It's just, you know, what with the baby coming.'

'It's alright,' I said. 'I understand.'

I began to resign myself to the fact I would have to go back to Dad, although I felt sick to the pit of my stomach. A small part of me hoped that Mum would simply forget about me – but she didn't. I had been with Diane exactly a week when I saw Mum walking back up the path towards the house and my heart plummetted. It was time to go home.

Diane walked us to the bus stop. By the time the bus arrived I had run out of tears, and I felt as though I was wearing a tight salt mask.

'What's wrong with you?' said Diane softly. 'You cried when you got here and you're crying when you're going home. What is it? Why are you so upset?'

I realised then that she didn't know about what I had to put up with at home. Mum held my arm and I felt her grip tighten as she manoeuvred me onto the bus.

'It hurts,' I said, then called over my shoulder. 'I'll miss you.'

'We'll visit. Promise,' shouted Diane as the bus started to pull away, but I knew she wouldn't. I stood on the open platform clinging on to the white pole and watched Diane waving goodbye.

'Could I go and stay with Nanny and Jenny instead?' I asked Mum on the way home.

She gave a nasty laugh. 'You must be bleedin' joking. They wouldn't have you.'

I didn't want to believe her, but a niggling voice at the back of my mind reminded me that nobody ever came to see if I was alright, and a sharp pain jabbed inside. I knew that everybody was scared of Dad, but he was only one person and they were a group of adults. I imagined them all turning up with burning torches like they did in films when they wanted to drive the baddie out of the village. If only they would do that, life would be so different. We could all be together, happy again.

Chapter Eleven

When we arrived home, my stomach flipped in fear as Mum put her key in the lock. The house was very quiet because Kat was still at school.

'You better go up and say hello to him,' said Mum before I had even taken my coat off.

'I don't want to,' I mumbled, afraid he might hear.

'You get up there,' she commanded. 'Don't you start him off again. My nerves can't take it.'

I dragged my feet up to the first floor, where I heard the faint mumble of the television. He was sitting on the sofa in the front room wearing a short towelling dressing gown. He flicked the TV off as I came in.

'Alright, Dad,' I said, sitting opposite him in the armchair. This felt odd in itself because normally I had to sit at his feet.

He didn't say anything to me, only stared, the expression on his face close to absolute hatred. I couldn't believe Mum had sent me up to see him knowing he was still in his 'gone mad' mood. I sat in the chair and stared at my lap, occasionally looking up in the hope that his expression had softened but it remained the same. I remembered all the times in the past when he'd given me the hot and cold treatment, and I knew eventually he would call me over to him. I didn't want to be sitting there in a stuffy room, not knowing if I was going to be hit or pawed and slobbered over. But I knew if I got up and said 'See ya, I'm sick of all this,' I wouldn't even make it to the door.

True to form it wasn't much longer before he stood up, flashing his genitals as he tightened the belt on his dressing gown, and said, 'I'll be in the bedroom.' I understood that he meant me to follow him and, with a heavy heart, I obeyed.

'Get your clothes off and get your nightie on then,' he instructed as I walked in the door.

I obeyed slowly, without looking at him.

'Hurry up!' he urged cheerfully. 'I haven't got all day.'

The next morning I woke up to find that overnight I had become a pariah. Dad, Mum and little Kat were in their bedroom having a cup of tea and he was screaming obscenities through at me.

'Little cunt features', 'shit-face', 'piss-arse' and 'Fuck off out of it with the other cunts', he yelled.

I sat and sobbed, wishing there was a way I *could* fuck off out of it.

As Dad shouted his insults through the thin bedroom walls, I heard Mum chuckling and making light-hearted comments. Maybe she was trying to calm him down, but a part of me knew she was pleased when I was out of favour because Dad paid more attention to Kat and her.

I felt as though my head was going to explode. I had to get out. I would run away and live under an arch somewhere. It couldn't be any worse than this.

As quickly as I could, I pulled on my clothes from the day before and pushed my bare feet into my plimsolls. I ran down the stairs two at a time, stopping briefly in the dining room for my anorak, which I'd last seen hanging on the back of a chair. I grabbed it and turned to leave but the way to the front door was blocked by Dad, wearing only a pair of Y-fronts. His chest heaved up and down as he tried to catch his breath. He had obviously run down the stairs after me.

'You're not going anywhere,' he said menacingly.

'I am,' I said, surprising myself with a tone of defiance I'd never used before. 'You hate me, and you're … you're always hurting me.' I wanted to say I didn't like the way he touched me between the legs and masturbated himself at the same time, but I wasn't quite that brave.

He sprang towards me and I braced myself for the usual blows. Instead, he caught me in a huge bear hug that hurt almost as much as a slap or a kick. I could hardly breathe. My face was buried in his right shoulder so I couldn't see the expression on his face. I wasn't sure if what he was doing was meant as a form of affection or punishment. When he put me down I saw that his eyes had misted over.

'You know I love you,' he said, 'but if you ever try to do anything stupid like run off somewhere, I'll fucking kill you, and you know that as well, don't you?'

I nodded. I knew it, alright. To me, Dad was all-powerful. I had never seen anybody stand up to him. Everybody was frightened of him. What chance did I have?

* * *

Anything I valued, Dad would, at one time or another, rip to shreds as punishment for some imagined misdemeanour – either before or after a slap, but never instead of. I tried not to show an attachment to any particular possession because I knew it would be the first thing Dad went for. He brought me a guitar once, which he said he had found in the bin at a recording studio where they had a cleaning contract, and insisted I learn how to play it. He sent me to the library for a how-to book and stood over me as I tried to learn the chords. The strings bit into my fingers and I hated every minute of it. One day he became angry when I couldn't stretch my fingers into the right position on the frets so he snatched it from me and booted it across to the other side of the room. It made a loud twang as the base splintered on the toe of his shoe. At least I didn't have to endure any more guitar lessons after that.

Although Dad had always drunk quite heavily, during this period he stepped it up a gear and began a particularly heavy phase of drinking spirits. He'd keep cans of chilled Special Brew as a chaser to wash down as much brandy or gin as he could guzzle, and every few days he would send Mum over to the off-licence to replenish his stock. She'd have to make sure there was a constant supply of sliced lemons and ice too. At Christmas he would fill the drinks cabinet with bottle after bottle of different spirits, even though he would be the only one drinking it. The most Mum would have is an occasional weak Martini and lemonade. She couldn't trust herself to drink because she had a very low tolerance for it, and in the early days of their relationship Dad had mistaken her giggles for flirtatiousness with other men. He had knocked her about so much over it that now she hardly dared touch the stuff.

During these periods Dad would spend all day drinking. More often than not he would be in no fit state to wake up for work at 3.30 in the morning, and when Mum was particularly under pressure, maybe with one of the other cleaners off sick, she'd come into my room and shake me awake so I could go and give her a hand. After a long night cleaning I would get the bus home on my own while Mum stayed on to do her extra duties, then I'd have to rush to get Kat ready and walk her to school. If I was lucky Dad would let me go to school where I'd spend all day yawning; if not he would insist I come home again.

Dad was very fussy about the glasses he drank out of. If it was gin, the glass would be long and tall, polished by Mum until it sparkled. Brandy was drunk in a balloon-shaped glass, in which he liked to swirl the amber-coloured liquid around like some sort of connoisseur. As fussy as he was about the shape and shine of his glasses, he didn't seem to notice that he himself looked like a tramp going through a rough patch. He wouldn't bother to shave or wash, and he'd wear the same food-stained clothes for days on end. The room in which he sat would often be overflowing with half-drunk mugs of tea, and ancient copies of *The Sporting Life* and *The Sun*.

From the minute he poured the first drink of the day, the house would go into 'batten down the hatches' mode. With any luck, after a few hours he would fall into a deep sleep, during which time we'd all creep about, freezing in our tracks if the floorboards creaked. On a few occasions either Mum or

I would have to rush and extinguish a cigarette he'd left to burn between his fingers. Once a cushion beside him began to smoulder and I had to extinguish it with the dregs of the ice bucket. Luckily he slept through the whole thing, filling the house with thundering snores.

If it didn't put him to sleep, drink seemed to fuel him with a supernatural energy, so that his rages went on for hour upon hour. Once I had to sit opposite him while he questioned me at length about whether I'd eaten his last jam tart. After about two hours of something akin to the Spanish Inquisition, I confessed I'd eaten it, even though I hadn't. I was just hoping to take my punishment and be allowed to go to bed. But instead he kept me up for another hour, flicking lighted cigarettes at my face and lecturing me on what a 'greedy bastard' I was.

Because he did most of his drinking at home rather than out in a pub, there was no respite. He would either drink in bed or lying flat out on the sofa, but wherever he was he would usually insist that I was there with him. There was no escape.

Drinking made him reckless in all respects. He gambled money away with careless abandon, not even bothering to study the form any more. He might as well have stuck a pin in the paper. It simply came down to whether he liked the name of the horse or not, or whether he could feel the psychic vibes. Occasionally he would win. Once he stood to win a few thousand pounds on some sort of multiple bet, but the final race in the series depended on a photo finish. Dad was pacing up and down, and swilling back his lager as he waited for the result. The tension in the house was palpable. I locked myself in the toilet and waited to hear Dad's roar of either jubilation or anger. I prayed it wouldn't be the latter. It wasn't. I could hear him jumping up and down and shouting 'Yes, fucking, yes!' Relief swept over me.

Although a lot of the money went straight back to the bookies he also spent quite a bit on the house. He wanted to create his own mini version of the offices where we cleaned. He ordered lots of shag-pile carpet and began stapling it to the walls in the living room. He also bought mirror tiles and stuck them absolutely everywhere. Leather sofas completed the look. I once saw a documentary about Hugh Hefner, the *Playboy* millionaire; by the time Dad had finished the renovation of our front room, it looked like a cheap imitation of Hefner's den. But he loved it.

My thirteenth birthday passed like any other day. Birthday cakes and parties had never been part of my world, but I was disappointed that I didn't at least have a card to open. I had long since given up hope that the lost members of my family would remember – after all, out of sight out of mind – but I did expect a card from Mum, and I felt quite disappointed not to get one. It was a Saturday morning, and usually I would have got up at 6am to go cleaning with Mum or Dad, but this week they had decided to have a lie-in, and I was grateful for that. My friends at school managed to do all sorts of interesting things at the weekend, like drama club or dancing lessons, but all I had to look forward to was a Mars bar and a packet of cheese and onion crisps during my break from pushing an industrial-size carpet cleaner or emptying bins. But the old saying that you don't miss what you never had is true. I was just grateful if Dad remained in a good mood for a whole day.

When Mum finally got up around 11am, I had already made Kat's toast and done the washing-up from the night before. As she stood waiting for the kettle to boil, Kat piped up: 'Mummy, it's Lisa's birthday today.'

'Oh, yeah,' she said. 'I'll get you something later, alright?'

It must have been one of those weeks when Dad had lost all the money at the bookies because when she went out later for a packet of cigarettes at the paper shop, she bought me a plastic necklace kit and handed it over to me unwrapped with the fifty pence price label still on. It consisted of a length of elasticated string and ten green plastic beads. The recommended age on the box was 6+.

I tried to hide my disappointment, but it was hard. I understood that Mum couldn't buy me something if she didn't have the money – there were many times we had all looked down the back of the sofa for lost change and felt as though we had struck gold if we found ten pence – but it was just the general lack of care I felt hurt by.

That's not what spoiled my birthday though. When Dad got up, he immediately started making lewd innuendos about me being a teenager now. He kept reciting a limerick, over and over again: 'When roses are red, they're ready for plucking; when girls are thirteen, they're ready for fucking.'

I would have traded all the birthday gifts in the world just to live my life without him sexually interfering with me. I knew what fucking was by now, and the thought terrified me. The words coming out of Dad's mouth sounded like a threat.

All day I tried to keep out of his way, fearful that he would try to fulfil the lyrics of the limerick this time. I wouldn't put anything past him.

Later that year, The Police brought out 'Don't Stand So Close To Me', a song about a schoolgirl with a crush on her teacher and the teacher's discomfort about it. Dad took to singing it to me at every opportunity. 'I'm the teacher and you're the saucy teenage tart,' he'd say, getting hard at the thought.

Dad had been sexually abusing me for over a year by this stage. Ironically, it had started during one of his short sober periods, so I knew that he was compos mentis and couldn't blame it on being out of his mind on drink. When he had been drinking heavily, he took the abuse to a new level, and there it would remain for months whether drunk or sober. It was during one of these hard drinking phases that he started removing my knickers for the first time. Previously he had touched my genitals over the top of my knickers while he masturbated himself. I felt much more vulnerable without knickers and it used to hurt a lot more afterwards because he'd try to shove his fingers inside me.

I was grateful that he never spoke on these occasions, or referred to them in any direct way in the real world. That way it was easy for me to detach myself somehow from what was happening. My mind would drift off and I'd think about school. Once I'd tried to think about Nanny and Jenny, but this was so painful that I trained myself never to do it again. I couldn't bear to think about people I loved while Dad was poking and prodding me between my legs. I felt dirty and the pain was too much to bear. So instead I'd think about a project I'd worked on at school or a programme on the television – casual things that didn't matter.

It usually took fifteen minutes or so before Dad groaned and thrust his hips up into the duvet. When he'd finished he would remove his hand, leaving me so sore that it hurt whenever I went to the toilet. I would slide out the side of the bed, careful not to make sudden movements for fear of making him angry. It was easier to pretend to myself that it hadn't happened if we didn't speak or make eye contact afterwards. There would be no prolonged goodnight routines where I'd have to endure him rubbing his hands up and down my body. I would simply leave the room without a backward glance. He was satisfied and peaceful, lighting up a cigarette and flicking over the telly with the remote.

I was grateful if I escaped his rages and violence. I'd lie in the dark in my bedroom afterwards and sometimes I'd cry but mostly I just felt numb. After a few minutes I'd hear Mum plodding up the stairs to bed and then the noises of them having sex would begin. How could she cope when she had to get up at 3.30am? Why didn't she ask me to get out of her bed sooner? It was in her power to save me but she never did. I was angry and incredibly sad all at the same time.

One night when Dad had been drinking brandy for most of the day, a beauty pageant came on the television. I was stroking his feet as he provided a running commentary on the girls' figures.

'Look at the arse on that!' and 'Cor, I'd love to give her one.'

My face burned in embarrassment and in a way I was glad that we were in the front room while Mum was sitting watching telly downstairs. I knew it was the brandy talking because he was being much cruder than normal.

When the programme finished, he grabbed his bottle and glass and stood up. He swayed from side to side for a few minutes.

'Let's go upstairs,' he said.

'I've got a belly ache,' I replied, desperately searching for a reason not to go upstairs with him.

'Wassa matter?' he slurred. 'Got a bloody cunt? I like my steaks rare.'

'I've got to do my homework,' I tried. 'It's got to be in tomorrow.'

'Fuck the fucking homework,' he said.

I was all too aware I had strayed into dangerous territory and he was becoming angry.

He slammed his foot down on my bare toes and I let out an agonised cry.

'What is it? Don't wanna be with me all of a sudden?'

'No, Dad,' I said, drawing my grazed feet beneath me.

'What am I? A fucking coon, like the wogs at school you wanna hang around with?'

I hated Dad with such a passion that day that I fantasised about smashing the big marble ashtray onto his head. My left foot was throbbing. I didn't want him to hurt me any more but when he insisted I go up to his room and lie down in the bed beside him, I didn't think I had any choice in the matter. I knew that after fifteen minutes of pain and humiliation, I would be allowed to go to my own room and get a good night's sleep. But on this occasion things were to get even worse than they had been before.

Fuelled by brandy, Dad escalated my abuse to another level. Instead of simply using his hand on me that night, he ripped my knickers off, crouched down on his knees and began to lick me between the legs. I was as shocked as the first time he touched me. I couldn't quite believe what was happening, except it was all too real. The more I squirmed away the more he dug his nails into my thighs and pulled me towards him. After a while, he stopped, looked down at his erect penis under the duvet and began to masturbate.

I had never cried openly while he abused me before, because somehow that would be breaking the spell of silence that existed between us. But now that he had taken it to another revolting level, one that was impossible to pretend wasn't happening, I couldn't stop crying. Whether it was because he was drunker than he had been for a long time or not, I don't know, but the sounds of my distress didn't seem to bother him. If anything they spurred him on.

I realised there was no point in holding back my cries. I wanted Mum to hear. I wanted her to help me. I was fed up with keeping quiet. Usually, when Dad touched me, whether we were in the bedroom or on the sofa in the front room, I didn't dare utter a sound in case Mum walked in on us. I was ashamed and I believed she would blame me because it was easier. Dad had never needed to instruct me to keep it as our little secret. The overwhelming guilt and shame I carried every day ensured I wouldn't tell a soul, and the very real threat of violence ensured my silence and cooperation.

Besides, who did I have to tell? I was completely isolated from anyone who could possibly have helped me. Mum was choosing to turn a blind eye and making things easy for him. I couldn't imagine any of my friends' mothers allowing their husbands to watch telly naked in bed with their daughters every night. All she had to do was sit in the front room with us each evening instead of watching the same programme downstairs on her own. As for seeking help from someone at school, or even the police, the possibility didn't even enter my consciousness. In a strange way, the last thing I wanted was for anyone else to find out. It was too shameful.

As if it wasn't bad enough that Dad was abusing me with his mouth between my legs, he also started talking about it for the first time, and the words he used were bewildering and distressing in the extreme.

'Lovely tight pussy,' he said as he came up for air. 'You've got such a pretty cunt. I love plating you.'

It wasn't until much later that I worked out that 'plating' was slang for licking the plate, a crude reference to oral sex.

I tried to go off in my head, thinking about what was happening in *Coronation Street* or *Crossroads*, but his assault on me was so direct and present that I found it impossible to be somewhere else. My life had just got a whole lot worse.

Soon licking wasn't enough and he started to bite me, savaging my private parts with his teeth, causing unbelievable pain. I screamed at the top of my voice and he suddenly stopped what he was doing, sat up and raised a hand as though he was going to punch me. I couldn't look him in the face so I shut my eyes against a vision no child should ever have to see. When he started again, I bit my lip until it bled to stop myself crying out.

At last he stopped and said, 'Have a wash and go to bed,' before collapsing between my parted legs. A drink-induced sleep had finally arrived to save me. I pulled myself out from under him and rushed to my room, where I lay hoping to die in my sleep.

When Dad sobered up the next day, he could hardly look me in the eye. He had temporarily lost his usual confident swagger, almost as though he had shocked himself the night before. But it didn't take long for him to do it again, and thereafter licking and biting me became his new habit.

He began to be increasingly rough. One night I couldn't stand it any more and, in a mad moment, I rolled off the bed and ran to my room, determined that I wouldn't let him put his mouth or hands between my legs ever again. My heart pounded hard in my chest. I reached my bedroom in only a few short steps along the landing, then time seemed to slip into slow motion as if I were in a nightmare and desperate to escape a frenzied serial killer. I stood with my back against the bedroom door feeling as though I was going to have a heart attack. Then absolute terror set in as I heard him coming after me, muttering the vilest of obscenities. I began to whimper as I felt him kick the door open behind me.

I was thrust forward onto the bed and in a moment he was on top of me, stark naked, his full weight making it hard for me to catch a breath. Reaching up with his right hand, he grabbed a handful of my hair and shook my head viciously from side to side until I felt the hair being ripped from my scalp. Then he tore the buttons from the front of my floral nightdress and exposed my bare chest. For some reason I found this more humiliating than anything else I had suffered so far. It felt too intimate. I didn't want his eyes on me.

Throughout he repeated the words 'fucking bitch' over and over again as if chanting some kind of mantra.

When he finally got off me, I was literally seeing stars. I barely felt his parting kick, but I knew I could never run away ever again. Not unless I was prepared to drive a stake through his heart first.

A new pattern was set. He finally felt free enough to roam all over my body, flipping me this way and that to derive his pleasure. Now when I went to bed I would often have to wipe his sperm from my face or buttocks. He also started to speak a lot, mainly to himself, as if narrating a porn film, like the ones he liked to play to me on his video recorder. He spoke about what he was going to do next, and throughout it all I might as well have been a dead body for all the reaction he got. I stopped crying quite so much, but inside I was a mass of turmoil. When I heard him spit onto his fingers to lubricate them before pushing them into me, it was all I could do to stop myself vomiting.

I was so sore that it burned when I peed. I kept getting a fever and a sick, dull pain in my lower back but Mum wouldn't let me go to the doctor's. She'd mix me a drink of bicarbonate of soda in warm water and that would usually clear it up until the next bout. But not always.

'Mum, please, it's so painful, that stuff hasn't worked,' I cried, doubled up on the floor one day. 'Why can't I go to the doctor's?'

'It's only cystitis, for Christ's sake,' she said. 'Anyone'd think you were dying. It's the "honeymooners' disease". I'm always getting it myself.'

'But I'm not a honeymooner,' I groaned. 'I shouldn't have it.'

'Which is precisely why you can't go to the fucking doctor's,' she said. 'Can you imagine what they'd say? If you think I'm gonna put my Kat at risk from the social services, you've got another thing coming. You've made your fucking bed, now you lie in it.'

Her words were at once cryptic and clear as day. She didn't care what happened to me. She was determined to pretend it wasn't happening.

I waited for the day she would face up to what Dad was doing to me. There were numerous occasions when she walked into a room and he wasn't quite quick enough to tuck his penis back into his trousers. She'd look away quickly, and continue as if she hadn't seen a thing. There was the fact that I spent most evenings in bed with him, and he kept grabbing me in full view of her.

Once he bit me on the chest through my nightdress, pulling away just as Mum walked into the room. We all noticed the dark saliva imprint in the shape of his teeth on the fabric and Mum's eyes widened before she set her face in its usual impassive expression.

He would openly grab my hand and make me feel his erection through his jeans. 'Look what you've done,' he'd say, leering at me, and Mum would quickly turn her face away. And now I had recurrent bouts of cystitis, and she didn't want to know.

See no evil, hear no evil, speak no evil – that was her policy. What she refused to acknowledge couldn't harm her.

Chapter Twelve

Mum had abandoned me to Dad, and since my abuse had got worse, she was having a much easier time of it. He was just as erratic and prone to fits of temper, smashing things and screaming the house down, but ever since he had knocked her teeth out he had remained true to his word and hadn't hit her again. Instead, I became the focus of his violent rages; except with me, he had to be very careful not to mark my face.

At this stage I was still going to school at least half the time, and if he had given me a traditional black eye or any visible injury, he must have known that the authorities would start taking a very close interest. Dad was many things but he wasn't stupid enough to bring down the whole house of cards when he could hurt me equally as much in places where the injuries stood little chance of being spotted. He found a plastic fly swot and took to smacking my bare bottom and back with it until I had red, raised welts all over the skin. There were many times when I literally found it hard to sit down, my bottom was so painful. He also used to bite me all over so that I was left with black and purple bruises in the shape of his teeth.

I knew Dad was looking forward to the day when I left school for good and there was little danger of outside agencies becoming involved in what he considered to be private family business. Then he would be able to relax, the master of his domain.

School was my only sanctuary, and I was heartsick on the days Dad wouldn't let me go. I loved to learn. English and drama were my favourite subjects. I used to enjoy reading aloud to the class and my teacher, Miss Connelly, often said I should be an actress. At lunchtimes I sometimes went to the school library and looked for books with scripts in. I read them to myself, doing all the voices, and dreamed of performing on stage one day. I found a book all about the National Youth Theatre but didn't dare dream I could ever attend one of their summer workshops. Drama was the only lesson where I could truly forget my problems at home. I hated myself for allowing bad things to happen to me. I was tainted, and it was a relief to pretend to be someone or something else for half an hour, even it it was only a tree swaying in the wind!

The drama studio in our school was painted red and had big floodlights hanging from the ceiling. When we were allowed to use them, the small space would heat up and the air would become acrid as months of dust burnt off. Everyone would cough and splutter, but to me the smell was pure theatre: greasepaint and alter egos.

Once the music and drama departments came together to stage a production of *The Boy Friend*, a musical set in the French Riviera in the 1920s. For some reason, despite my erratic school attendance, they wanted me for the part of Lady

Brockhurst, the domineering wife. For the first time in my life I felt special and part of something that didn't involve violence and a heavily weighted cloak of shame. But after my initial euphoria at being chosen wore off, I started to worry about the commitment. What if Dad wouldn't let me go to school? And how was I meant to attend the two evening performances when he never let me out after school?

As it turned out, rehearsals coincided with a phase when I was allowed to go to school more often than not. I only ended up missing a few in the end, and when it came to the two evening performances, Dad agreed I could go, probably aware that to refuse might open up a can of worms.

Karen played one of the flapper girls, glamorous to the end, and we had a laugh throughout the rehearsals. On the nights of the performance, the whole cast were peeking out through the curtain, trying to find their family in the audience. I was relieved that Mum and Dad weren't going to attend. I would have been worried all night about him picking fights with the other parents.

After the last show, Karen and I took off our make-up and followed the sixth formers over to the pub, where we stood outside and managed to get hold of a Babycham each. I felt alive and carefree. The alcohol made me feel happier than I had felt for years.

Karen was my only friend, the one person who could make me forget my troubles at home and have a laugh. With her, I could become someone else, someone free of sexual abuse and violence. I never gave her much information about what went on at home, so school was one long drama lesson where I pretended to be another person. She still couldn't understand why I wouldn't come out in the evenings. I wanted to, more than anything, but there was no way I could. Most nights I had to go with Mum on her early evening cleaning job, and then when I got home around nine o'clock, Dad would begin his nightly ritual of abuse before I was allowed to go to bed.

'Please, Lisa, it'll be such a laugh,' she would say. 'There's a disco on.'

'I can't, Karen,' I said again and again. 'I've got to go cleaning with my mum.'

Once I told her that I had to be at home in the evenings to stroke my Dad's back and feet. This was the closest I ever came to explaining what was happening to me.

'What? That's a bit weird, isn't it?' she said, frowning.

I wanted to tell her just how weird it was, but fear kept me quiet. I was frightened she would judge me, would think it was somehow my fault, just as I judged myself. What sort of girl was I to have let this terrible thing happen with my own father?

Sometimes, as I waited for the bus to go to the cleaning job with Mum, I would see Karen waving to me from over the road. It always hurt to see her out with her other friends. That's when I realised how much I was missing out on. I was fourteen by then and meant to be enjoying the best years of my life, but instead I was cleaning offices and being sexually abused.

Sometimes Karen came and knocked for me anyway, hoping to change my mind. I'd go to the door, careful to open it only a few inches, aware that Dad was listening to every word. She would stand on the doorstep, puzzled about how my personality had changed from only a couple of hours before at school, when I had been full of fun. I tried to flash her a message with my eyes that said 'Please, Karen, please go away. He's listening to us.' I could hear Dad mumbling in the background: 'Fucking little tart with her blonde hair. Who does she think she is?' and often I'd be forced to shut the door abruptly if he got up to come and intervene.

Sometimes Dad would send Mum to the door to get rid of Karen. She knew as well as I did that he demanded my contact with the outside world was kept to a bare minimum.

'She's busy.' Mum would say abruptly.

There was nothing I wanted more than to be free and have fun like any other teenager. After the two nights I had been allowed to take part in the school play, I developed a taste for freedom and I wanted more of it, so the next time Karen begged me to come out with her for the evening, I hesitated, considering whether there was a chance I could get away with it. She knew I wanted to, and wasn't accepting any of my usual excuses.

'Ask your Mum for a night off for once,' she said. 'Go on, Lisa, it'll be a right laugh.'

She kept pushing me for ages until I decided to risk it. Nothing ventured, nothing gained, I reasoned. Recklessly, like an innocent man signing a confession for a moment's peace, I said I'd call round for her later.

As soon as I left Karen at the corner of our road with a falsely jaunty 'See you later', the butterflies began to churn in my stomach. I walked home sick with nerves hoping that Dad might be in a drink-induced sleep and I could slip out without him noticing. The only time I'd been allowed out over the past year was on those two nights when I was in the school play. I didn't know how I could possibly walk in the door and announce I was going out later. It would be as alien as going home and asking my mum where my sisters and brother lived now. I knew Dad didn't like me out of his sight, unless I was cleaning with Mum and therefore still under his control. But as I remembered the thrill I'd felt during the school play when I'd just been another free young teenager, I grew more and more excited. I realised it had been a long time since I had tried to break free. Time had passed since the last time I had tried to get away from him, and as I was getting older I thought it may be worth another try. I'd recently read a book in the school library that said if you continue to act the same way then you have to expect the same results. I decided to act differently.

When I got home, I was disappointed to see that although Dad was drinking, he didn't look as though he'd be going to sleep any time soon. Mum had made dinner of hot dogs for us while Dad was having steak with mushrooms and his favourite Daddy's sauce. I was starving after not having eaten all day because no one had given me any lunch money, but was so worried about what I was about to say that I could barely swallow a bite.

In the end, I just came out with it and announced at the table that I was going out for a couple of hours.

Dad looked as if I had slapped him in the face. 'You what?' he demanded, his mouth full of steak.

'I'm going to knock for Karen,' I said, avoiding his gaze but hunching my shoulders against a possible onslaught of blows.

Mum got up from the table even though she hadn't finished and began hurriedly to clear the plates, obviously keen to distance herself from the hurricane brewing. Dad's expression was hard for me to read, but I noticed a slight, persistent nod, as if he were acknowledging a challenge.

Without looking back, I ran up to my bedroom, fully expecting Dad to follow, but when he didn't, my spirits soared and I began to chuckle 'Yes! Yes!' over and over again. Freedom had been as simple as that. Perhaps he didn't mind after all, and even if he did, he would have to learn how to lump it as I had done for the past two tortured years. I felt sick at the thought that all I had ever had to do to escape his clutches was assert myself.

I threw my school uniform onto the bed and stepped into a white skirt and shoes and burrowed in my drawer to find a crumpled blue striped top. It had a drip of ketchup down the front but it would have to do. When I was dressed I stood on my bed to try and see myself in the little mirror that was balanced on the drawers. I felt as free as a bird, excited at all the future nights out to come. I may not have enjoyed my teenage years so far, but I was determined to start.

I brushed my shoulder-length hair, wishing I'd washed it when I'd had a bath on Sunday, and smeared a bit of Vaseline onto my lips and eyelashes just as Brooke Shields had recommended in a magazine. Finally satisfied with my appearance, I flew down the stairs, keen to get out while the going was good. I was exalted at my sudden taste of freedom.

'Bye!' I shouted as I walked along the hallway.

I was just about to open the front door when Dad came thundering down the stairs. He grabbed me from behind and pushed my face up against the door, squashing my front teeth against my lips. I tasted blood. It all happened so quickly that at first I didn't feel the slaps, kicks and punches that followed.

'You want to go out with that prat Karen, do you?' he shouted in my ear. The next thing I heard was 'fucking-whore-bastard-cunt' – a long stream of expletives shouted with every whack, as though he was keeping time with a set of drums.

He punched my back so hard that I was winded, and shook my hair until I felt dizzy. I was aware of the noise my body made as it slammed into the thin walls in the hallway. I knew Mum was sitting in the next room listening, but she refused to show her face. If she had dared to venture out, she might have had to ask herself why my dad was behaving more like a psychotically jealous husband than a father.

Finally, just when I thought the onslaught was over, he reached up under my skirt, grabbed my knickers and shook me back and forth like a dog with a bone. I heard the sound of ripping fabric and felt the elastic cutting sharply into my flesh. He then chucked me out into the street with a final kick up the behind. I landed full force on my knees, and heard him slamming the front door behind me.

For a minute or two I was too shocked to move, then adrenaline forced me into action. I had to get away before he came out and dragged me back inside. I stood up and limped away, my head still spinning, hoping that nobody had seen. I may have been used to all sorts of terrible things, but I was still a self-conscious teenager who didn't want to be humiliated in front of the neighbours.

As I made my way towards Karen's flats, a few minutes' walk away, I kept looking over my shoulder, convinced that Dad would rear up like a monster at any moment. I had to use my wrists as a sort of brace to stop my torn knickers falling down as I walked and when I got into the stairwell of Karen's block, I had no choice but to remove them and chuck them in the rubbish chute. Obviously I was very upset inside, but I had learned to compartmentalise my feelings as a matter of survival. I had been through far worse in my time, so when I reached Karen's flat on the third floor, I put my anguish and pain into the same mental box that contained all the other dreadful experiences.

Despite my efforts to conceal what I had just been through, Karen looked at me and knew immediately that something was wrong.

'What's the matter, Lisa. You look upset,' she probed.

I shrugged off her concerns with laughter, giving no further clue that anything was wrong. We set out to make the most of our rare evening together, but I kept peeking over my shoulder every few minutes, terrified Dad would appear and drag me home.

We went to a youth club, and I couldn't help but envy all the kids who were free to go there every night and play table tennis or listen to Duran Duran on the cassette player. Karen bought me a coke and a bag of crisps and we went to sit near some slightly older boys who were in charge of the music.

'Alright, girls?' one said and we giggled into our crisps.

When I said goodnight to her on the corner, the sun was setting orange, low in the sky. I had really enjoyed myself, but I knew I wouldn't dare go out with her again. My stomach churned as I walked slowly up the path to our peeling front door, knowing that one way or another I would have to pay the price for my little taste of freedom.

And I was right. Dad was extra nasty to me for weeks after that. He would often remind me of my 'betrayal' and would lie with his forearm covering my throat so that I could barely breathe while he warned me not to be a whore and 'fuck him over'. He was so vicious and spiteful that I gave up all hope of ever going out after school again. Youth clubs were for other teenagers, not for the likes of me.

Chapter Thirteen

One day I came home from school to find Mum standing in the kitchen ripping a piece of paper to shreds. It looked like a letter. I wondered whether it was from my sisters, but when she dropped a scrap on the floor, I recognised Jenny's distinctive handwriting.

'Is that from Jenny?' I asked, almost making myself jump because I'd said her name out loud.

'Nanny's dead,' Mum said shortly, chucking the shredded letter into the bin and emptying an ashtray on top of it.

'No!' I felt as though I'd been punched in the pit of my stomach. I ran up to my room and cried and cried until I had no tears left. I was so used to smothering all thoughts of Nanny and the rest of my lost family that I struggled at first to summon up her image – of course there were no photos to look at round the house. But I would never forget how soft, warm and safe I felt when I used to sit on her lap and cuddle her. I was desolate that I hadn't been able to tell her how much I loved her one last time, and I hoped she hadn't buried all thoughts of me over the years, as I had had to do with my memories of her. Now there was no stopping the pain I felt. I was distraught. I had always hoped we'd be together again one day when I was old enough to break free from Mum and Dad. I'd fantasised about turning up on her doorstep, safe at last. But now she was gone forever, and so was a little piece of me.

Later I heard Dad laughing in the kitchen and singing 'Ding, dong, the witch is dead!' from *The Wizard of Oz*, and I wished I had the courage to kill him.

I began to wonder then if Mum was capable of ever feeling anything. The mother who had shown her nothing but love and support had been cruelly discarded many years before when Dad moved into her life. Now Nanny was dead and Mum hadn't shed a tear. What sort of woman was she to have turned her back on her own family for a man she now knew was abusing her daughter? It had been years since she'd last seen her mother, or any of her many brothers and sisters.

Perhaps worst of all, she had chosen Dad over every one of her children. Diane's baby would be nearly two years old by now, and she had no idea if it was a boy or a girl. Cheryl had turned up at the front door one day flanked by her fiancé and begged Mum to go to her wedding, but she was given short shrift. As for Davie, she didn't seem to care if he were alive or dead. All this for a man who was now betraying her in the cruellest possible way by abusing her own daughter.

In her eyes, Dad could do no wrong. There was no price she wouldn't pay to keep him happy, and if my life was ruined in the process, it didn't matter. She would let him have his way. I couldn't begin to understand how Mum could love such a man, but I knew she did. Somehow he had her mesmerised, like a snake with its prey. Besides, she would have been too proud ever to admit that she had 'picked a bad 'un', as Nanny used to say. She'd given up everything for Dad and tolerated more than any other woman would, so there wouldn't be any backing out now.

In 1980 the film *The Blue Lagoon* came out, starring a four-teen-year-old Brooke Shields. Pictures of Brooke were splashed all over every newspaper, and I remember reading in Dad's copy of *The Sun* how a debate was raging about whether the film was 'kiddie porn'. Dad became obsessed with the story.

'She's so sensual,' he said. 'She exudes sex.'

He began to liken me to Brooke Shields, even though the only trait we had in common was brown hair. He took a poster of her into the toilet with him and the next time I saw it, it was splattered with his semen. Soon he started to tell me I exuded sex too, but I knew I didn't; he just wanted to blame me for his wicked ways.

Dad's abuse of me gradually started to escalate further. He would grab me at all hours of the day or night and didn't care whether he made a noise or not. Sometimes Mum was in the house, and other times he would send her out on an errand and make the most of the opportunity to enjoy a prolonged session in which he would subject me to the most degrading acts.

Although this was now a way of life, and to a degree I was used to it, there were still some things I resisted doing. Up until this point he had done everything he could to me, except take my virginity, but I would remain passive throughout. Periodically he would grab my hands and try to wrap them around his penis but I would always cry, and although he would get angry, he would always move on to something different. Another time he tried to force himself into my mouth but I gagged and was sick. After slapping and kicking me, he seemed to resign himself to the fact that I wasn't able to do those things, but I knew it was only a matter of time before he forced me with violence because he would always mutter an ominous 'I'll let you off … for now.'

I had developed my own coping mechanisms, which helped me detach from most of the things he did to me – little techniques like reciting poems or times tables in my head. Sometimes I even read a magazine or watched a programme on the television while Dad carried out his depravities.

But I could tell he was losing patience with what he saw as my lack of participation. One day he picked up the magazine I was reading and threw it to the other side of the room. Instinctively I curled into the foetal position and covered my head.

'You make me feel like I'm a fucking necro or something,' he shouted above me. 'You better liven yourself up, girl.'

Only the day before he had made me watch a video nasty with him. It was about a necrophiliac, a man who liked having sex with dead people, so I knew exactly what he meant.

'I'm getting fucking sick of this,' he shouted, pulling me up by the hair and positioning me between his legs, on my knees. 'Put your fucking hand round it,' he ordered, placing his hand over mine on his penis, 'and move it up and down like that.'

My face burned with shame and I felt bile rising in my throat. I knew he'd want me to do this every time now; it was his pattern, the way it worked whenever he introduced something new.

'Don't fucking stop, you silly bitch,' he shouted, slapping the side of my head. 'Go on, that's it.'

Thankfully it was over soon enough. But it wasn't long before he wanted to do it again, and this time he insisted on thrusting himself into my mouth, too.

I wailed and cried, twisting my face away, hoping he would stop, as he always had before when I made a lot of noise, but he held my head firmly in place. I tried to clamp my mouth together but he used his penis as a sort of battering ram, pushing it against my teeth.

'You trying to bite me, you fucking whore? You trying to fucking bite me?'

He kicked me over to the other side of the room, where I pushed myself up against the window. I could hear the sounds of normal life out on the street below as the mechanics from the repair shop next door laughed and joked outside on the pavement, metal clanging as they rifled through their tool boxes, totally oblivious to my terror only a dozen feet above them in our front room.

'Stop snivelling, you snot-nosed little cunt, and get your laughing gear round this. We're going to do a sixty-nine.'

By this time my eyes were so swollen from tears I could barely see. My hair was matted and stuck to my face. I didn't think it was possible for him to hurt me any more than he already had, but then he began to bite, and poke his fingers deep inside me. He was like a depraved animal. Was this a sixty-nine? I had no idea.

I had felt a heavy burden of guilt and shame ever since the first time Dad touched me, but now that he was forcing me to play a more active role, I felt as though it was smothering me. Whereas before I had been completely passive, he now made me do things too and I felt almost complicit in my own abuse. On one level I knew my thinking was wrong – no child wants to be violated in such a way – but still I couldn't stop the demon on my shoulder. What sort of girl must I be to do such things? I felt filthy and totally worthless. I didn't ask him to abuse me. I wanted it to stop. It wasn't my choice, but I had got to a stage where I just accepted it as my lot in life. It had become almost normal.

But I was still aware enough to know it wasn't the kind of normal I wanted. I wanted the kind I imagined the girls at school had; the kind of normal teenage life that was relatively carefree, and involved experimenting with clothes, make-up, music and even boys. I had none of these things. I had never even had a first crush. I might as well have been kept prisoner since I was twelve years old. I would watch *Top of the Pops* on TV and see all the young people dancing and having fun, and I wondered if my life would ever be that way. But somehow I couldn't see it; not with Dad controlling my every waking moment.

One day he announced that we were going on holiday. He was going to take Kat and me to Florida for three weeks.

'What about Mum?' I asked, alarm bells ringing.

'I'll be staying here,' she said. 'Someone's got to work. That building won't clean itself, you know.'

My stomach began to churn at the prospect of being trapped with Dad in one room for three weeks. It didn't matter to me that it would be in Florida; I knew it would be a nightmare, and, what was worse, little Kat would be coming along too, and might witness his sexual abuse of me or maybe he'd even try it on her. Maybe he wouldn't be able to stop himself.

Dad leered at me from his place on the sofa.

'What's the matter?' asked Mum. 'Most kids would be bleedin' happy.'

I bit my lip to stop me saying something I shouldn't. 'I just don't feel well, that's all,' I said.

'You never fucking do,' she replied. 'Moan, whinge, moan fucking moan. That's all she bleedin' does.'

I ran up to my room. Mum was right – most kids would be happy. But I wasn't most kids. And Dad wasn't most dads. The worst thing was, I wouldn't just have myself to worry about, I'd have to try and protect Kat from him as well. As usual, I felt powerless to do anything about it. My only hope was that Mum would see sense and find some last-minute maternal instincts. She knew how quickly he lost his temper and became violent, and by now, I suspected she knew without a shadow of a doubt just what Dad had been doing to me. How could she continue to bury her head in the sand? She was never actually in the room when Dad was violating my body, but most of the time she was in the house while he abused me in his bed upstairs for hours on end. There were many occasions when she had seen him touching me in an inappropriate manner. She was also witness to his overly possessive behaviour. He had to know exactly where I was at any given time, and wouldn't allow me to go out for the evening like other teenagers. She was well aware that he was prone to violent rages and paranoid suspicions, but when she saw me crying, with my hair and clothes in disarray, all she would do was roll her eyes and say, 'You're not boo-hooing again, are you?'

Mum was actually a very bright woman, so pure ignorance didn't work as a defence. She wasn't stupid in the least. She knew Dad was lewd and lecherous and behaved in an overtly sexual manner towards me. She was often present when he demanded I parade in front of him wearing different outfits. On one occasion he bought me a pair of pink candy-striped jeans, which he demanded I wear without knickers on: 'Otherwise you can see the line of your drawers.' I tried my best to refuse in such a way that he wouldn't hit me, but he was insistent. Mum sat on the sofa next to him, drawing deeply on her cigarette, seemingly calm and still except for her foot, which was jiggling up and down.

I went up to my room to put the jeans on. They were so tight I could hardly sit down, which didn't seem to matter to Dad as all he wanted was for me to stand in the corner with my back to him.

'She's got some fucking arse on her, I'll say that,' Dad commented, turning me this way and that so he could study me from all angles.

I blushed beetroot red, conscious that Mum was seething beside him. The jiggling foot was a giveaway. I knew she was angry, but she was angry with me, not him. She saw me as a rival and seemed to believe that I encouraged him to behave like this, instead of understanding that I was the innocent child. What was I supposed to do? Refuse to try on the jeans? Refuse to go up to bed with him every night? Whenever I'd tried, Dad's response was brutal violence.

'You wait till she starts packing on the weight,' said Mum. 'She's already got a spare tyre.'

'With an arse like that, she's sitting on a fucking goldmine,' said Dad. 'We'll have to get you on the game, Lisa.'

A lot of the time he would dress up his disgusting one-liners as a joke, which seemed to make them acceptable to Mum, but they reminded me of the vile things he was doing to me every day and tears would come to my eyes.

'I'm fucking joking, you silly bitch,' he said, and turned to Mum. 'Tell her, Donna.'

Mum gave me a withering look and told me not to be so melodramatic. 'She'd give Liz Taylor a run for her fucking money, that one.'

'Can I take them off now?' I asked in a neutral voice, desperate to kick the candy-striped jeans into the furthest corner of my bedroom and climb back into my comfy cords.

'What, are they cutting you up the minge?' Dad cracked up with laughter. I ignored him and started to leave the room, but he hadn't finished. 'You know where I am if you need any ointment rubbing into it.'

Surely Mum would find his comment a step too far, even for her? But no, as I walked out the door, they were both laughing.

'Oh, you are awful,' she said, echoing Dick Emery's famous catchphrase. 'If your wit was shit you'd have diarrhoea.' This was one of their favourite sayings, something they said to each other all the time.

Sometimes Mum would be irritated when he paid me compliments. Sometimes I felt he did it on purpose to wind her up.

'See how fresh she looks when she gets up in the morning,' was one comment that was always guaranteed to make Mum bristle.

Every time her response was the same: 'Yeah well, she is only fourteen and she doesn't have to get up at 4am every fucking morning, does she?'

At times like that, Mum directed looks of pure hate at me, her brown eyes flashing dangerously. It was as if she was displacing all the anger she felt for him towards me, because I was the easier target. I couldn't have made it any clearer that I hated his attention. I did everything I could to camouflage my body, wearing trousers and long sleeves even in summer. But even that would irritate her because when she realised that I was deliberately trying to make myself unattractive, she didn't like the implications that in itself raised.

I didn't have a lot of clothes. My wardrobe was very basic, filled with practical clothes for cleaning and sitting round the house, and a few bits and pieces for school, where a strict uniform policy was enforced. I had to make do with garments that were nearly or sort of OK. For instance, if policy demanded a grey jumper, a beige one gone muddy in the wash would have to do. I was forever being told off but in the end, the teachers knew I didn't have much control over what my parents bought me and decided to look the other way. They did that quite a lot. In those days the lax school office could barely muster up a letter home about my lengthy and often unexplained absences, let alone things like the dress code.

Everything in my wardrobe had a function. I didn't have party clothes because I didn't go to parties, but one day Dad handed me a rainbow-coloured summer dress and told me to put it on. My heart sank. It was a beautiful dress in a silky material, the sort of thing most girls would look forward to wearing, but it had shoestring straps that ran over bare shoulders. I didn't like wearing clothes that left so much of my flesh exposed, and as I slipped it over my head in the privacy of my bedroom I wanted to cry. I had just bought my first bra from a stall down the market, and I usually wore it under a white vest, desperate to smother a developing body that was only making things worse with Dad. I kept both the bra and the vest on, even though I could see the type of dress demanded nothing underneath.

As I walked into the front room Mum and Dad were waiting for me.

'What the fuck you kept your vest on for?' asked Mum, in such an over-the-top incredulous voice that I knew she had guessed the answer. 'You look ridiculous.'

'Yeah, get it off,' said Dad. 'And the bra and all.'

My stomach was churning, but I knew I didn't have a choice except to do as I was told. I went into the bathroom and removed my vest and bra. Standing there looking in the mirror, I could see the dress was very pretty on me, but I felt almost naked. I had never been a girly girl, probably because I had grown up without lots of frills and luxuries. I stayed in the bathroom for a long time, but eventually Dad became impatient.

'Where's she gone, fucking Timbuktu?' I heard him shout.

I walked back into the front room, holding my arms awkwardly in front of my chest.

Dad whistled. 'Look at that,' he said, drawing out the words as if mocking me. 'I can see your little titties.'

I flashed a look at Mum as if to ask how she could let him talk to me like that.

'Put your arms down, Lisa, and stop being stupid,' she said. 'Who's gonna look at you, anyway?'

I could barely believe she had the gall to ask that question. There was a slight challenge in her voice as if daring me to say something in front of Dad. She must have guessed I wanted to shout 'My dad, your husband, as you well know.' But she knew I was terrified of Dad's anger, and who knew what he would do if we all dropped the pretence and spoke openly about my abuse?

But it was becoming harder for Mum's carefully positioned blinkers to stay in place as Dad grew bolder by the day. She was sharp and didn't miss a trick, but for some reason she chose to accept his perverted behaviour rather than act to protect her child. It wasn't that she lived with her head in the clouds. She knew what was going on but stood by and did nothing. In fact, her negligence actually enabled my abuse to continue and to progress to a life-shattering stage.

One Sunday she actually saw it happening. Dad had me pinned beneath his legs on the sofa while he slept off his Sunday lunch of roast beef and half a bottle of brandy. For once Mum was sitting in the chair opposite with her head in her hand, watching television, instead of in her usual place downstairs.

Dad was snoring, in what seemed like a very deep sleep. He was lying on his side with his feet in my lap. He suddenly snorted, waking himself up momentarily and as he resettled himself he reached down through his legs to rub my genitals. I'm not sure if he realised Mum was in the room or not, but he gave a loud groan of pleasure and muttered 'Lisa's juicy pussy'.

I shifted away quickly, but there was no doubt – Mum had seen it quite clearly. I wasn't sure if I was glad or not. Despite everything, I loved her and didn't want to hurt her. But my overriding emotion was one of fear. I knew that she blamed me for the way Dad behaved, because to blame him would be finally to face the fact she'd thrown away her whole family for nothing. It occurred to me that she had decided to wait out his obsession with me in the hope that I would leave home as soon as I was old enough, just like Cheryl. But it would be another year and a half before I turned sixteen.

She remained sitting as if frozen in the armchair, a twitch in her foot and an angry frown the only signs to betray her feelings. She fixed her eyes on Dad's hand, which now lay in a slightly more acceptable position on my left leg. I stared at her like a frightened rabbit, waiting for her to meet my eyes and confront the truth. Surely she couldn't avoid it now? She had seen and heard it all clearly, and the thing that upset me most was that her face hadn't registered any sense of shock or surprise, only a form of annoyance. A small part of me still clung to the hope that I was wrong, and Mum was living in a blissful cloud of ignorance, but I couldn't delude myself any longer. Not now. The message I took quite clearly from this incident was that she would never stand up to Dad; she had effectively given me to him to do with whatever he wanted, the only condition being that he didn't actually have sex with me in front of her. He could be as verbally rude or as violent as he liked, but anything else had to happen in another room. That was why she would always sit on her own downstairs and tell me to 'Fuck off upstairs to him.'

After a minute or so, she turned back to the TV as if nothing had happened.

A short while after, as I sat pinned under Dad's legs, a programme came on the TV about 'wife-beaters' and how difficult the women found it to break away. The first part of the programme was full of women who reminded me of Mum. They were often totally isolated from their families and even though they sported black eyes and broken ribs, some of them speaking from their hospital beds, they were determined to stand by their man. One of them used the phrase, 'He could charm the birds from the trees', something I'd heard Mum say about Dad.

But there was one woman who was different. She had been jailed for hitting her husband over the head with a frying pan after she found out he'd slept with her sister. I wondered what it would take to make Mum really angry and spur her into some kind of action to save us all?

Chapter Fourteen

I tried not to think too much about the forthcoming holiday to Florida, because the images and possible scenarios I conjured up in my head were too much to bear. When I told Karen about the holiday one day at school, she was incredulous. How on earth was Lisa, with her raggedy clothes and lack of lunch money, suddenly going to America?

I was as surprised as she was, because although Mum earned good money cleaning, Dad usually gambled it away so we always seemed poor. Some weeks Mum struggled to come up with the bus fare to get to work, and that's why there wasn't usually any money for luxuries. Mum didn't give me lunch money because she usually didn't have it, and when she did, we were both so used to me not having it that neither of us remembered. It was torture watching everyone else eat at lunchtime. Most days there was only enough bread in the morning for Kat's toast, so I went without breakfast too. Sometimes when Karen had extra lunch money, she would offer to buy me a roll, but most of the time I didn't like to accept even though my stomach was rumbling.

'You're getting so skinny,' Karen said, concerned. 'Your shoulder blades are sticking out. Why doesn't your Mum give you any lunch money?'

'She's a bit broke at the moment,' I'd reply.

So it seemed strange for me suddenly to be going on a three-week holiday to Florida, a destination that was only just becoming popular. However, Karen was even more surprised when I explained that Mum wouldn't be coming with us.

'How can you go on holiday without your mum?'

'I don't know,' I said, flustered. 'She's got to go to work.'

In fact, Mum and Dad had been arguing about the fact that he was going on holiday and she was expected to stay at home working 'like some fucking mug'. Dad gave in after many rows, during which new dents were put in the walls and doors, and booked a last-minute Easter break in Majorca for Mum, Kat and me. I was astounded when Mum told me I would be going too. I didn't understand why Dad had agreed to it. He usually found a way to keep me with him at all costs, and right up until the last minute when we got on the train to Gatwick Airport, I thought he would change his mind.

Our holiday in Majorca was like a tonic. The minute I waved goodbye to Dad and he secretly cupped my bottom, I put him out of my mind. I think Mum did too. She was like a different person. Gone was the bitterness and the seething anger, which always seemed to be bubbling under the surface at home, and in their place was a woman who looked as though a great weight had been lifted from her shoulders. She liked to sunbathe by the pool or on the beach while I played with Kat in the water. She gave me no unfriendly stares, and treated me almost the same as she did Kat. I even got an occasional hug. It was as if, away from the bad atmosphere of home, she was able to see me as a daughter and not a rival of some sort.

We ate in the hotel's restaurant every night, and afterwards went through to the lounge bar to watch the Spanish dancing for a while. Once or twice the handsome male dancer in tight black trousers pulled Mum up onto the dance floor. I shuddered as I imagined what Dad would do if he found out. Mum was much more outgoing on holiday. She chatted to people as if she didn't have a care in the world, which she could never do at home.

One day we went out on a glass-bottomed boat and sailed to a small island with a beautiful white sandy beach and caves set back in the surrounding hills. I was in seventh heaven. Everything about it was special; even the air smelled different. The captain of our boat cooked a huge vat of paella, which he served on the beach at lunchtime, and it was the most delicious food I had ever tasted.

The holiday was special because there was no fear, but as the week drew to a close, I noticed the familiar weight of oppression beginning to settle again, and Mum started to return to her usual snappy self. I understood why. I knew it was because we would soon be going home to Dad and the anxiety was starting to set in. I felt it myself.

When we arrived back, Mum tried to be jolly to dissipate the thunderclouds that were brewing above Dad's head.

'Who'd you talk to then?' he asked, looking at Mum and me in turn.

'What d'ya mean, who did we talk to?' said Mum, momentarily thrown by his question. 'We didn't talk to anybody.'

'Who'd Mum and Lisa talk to, Kat?' he said, spinning round to my five-year-old sister, who was sitting as unobtrusively as she possibly could in the corner. She looked confused at the question.

Dad asked her again, but louder, and I saw Kat struggle for a satisfactory answer. 'Tony and Linda,' she spluttered.

Tony and Linda had been the couple who sat at the next dining table and occasionally they'd lean over to Mum like the nice sociable couple they were and comment on the weather, or how they missed a nice cup of tea: 'We forgot to bring our PG Tips.'

But Dad made it into something else entirely. 'Who? Who the fuck's Tony and Linda when they're at home?' he demanded, slamming his hand onto the smoked glass and chrome dining table.

'Just people on the next table,' said Mum.

'Couple of fucking swingers, more like,' said Dad. I could see he was working himself up into a frenzy.

Mum gave as good as she got, bolstered perhaps by the fact that Dad hadn't hit her for a couple of years. 'You're bleedin' mad, you are,' she said. 'And I think you've got a right bleedin' cheek an' all, having a go at me. Especially after what you've done …'

Her eyes flickered over to me, and I knew she was talking about me. Feeling scared, I grabbed Kat's hand, and tried to leave the room.

'Where the fuck do you think you're going?' asked Dad, blocking my path.

'Let them go,' shouted Mum, her chest heaving up and down as if she were struggling for breath.

Dad looked into my eyes and said in a low voice, 'I'll talk to you later' before stepping aside. I led Kat up to her bedroom where we started to unpack our suitcase. The happy carefree mood of the week before had been replaced with a sense of dread. The sound of Mum and Dad arguing echoed up the stairs. I tried to busy myself shaking sand from our flip-flops, and I felt like crying as I caught the scent of the sea mixed with coconut suntan lotion. Tears filled my eyes and suddenly Kat was at my side.

'Dad's always angry, isn't he?' she said, grabbing my hand in hers.

'Don't worry, Kat,' I said, feeling so sad that she had to live in this house of hell. 'It'll be alright.' I wished I could protect her, so she could have the normal childhood I had been denied, but the only chance of that happening would be if Mum broke up with Dad, and somehow I couldn't see that happening.

Later the arguing calmed down and was replaced by the noise of the two of them having sex. I turned on the white clock/radio to drown it out, and Kat and I listened to Bucks Fizz singing 'Making Your Mind Up' instead.

In the weeks running up to the Florida holiday in August 1981, I felt a mix of emotions. A part of me was excited at the possibility of visiting Disney World and meeting Mickey Mouse, but my enthusiasm was quickly extinguished by the thought of coping with Dad alone for three whole weeks. I also had the added worry of looking after Kat, and this responsibility weighed heavily on me. I tried to look at the positive side. There were times when Dad could be really nice. Admittedly his happy moods wouldn't last for very long, were few and far between and as fragile as the finest gossamer, but seeing the way that Mum's good side had come out while she was on holiday, I hoped he would be the same.

The night before we were due to leave, Mum looked more subdued than normal. After dinner I made sure we were alone for a few minutes and blurted out my worry: 'What if Dad does something with Kat in the room?' It was as close as I could go without actually saying the words that burned a hole in the tip of my tongue.

'For fuck's sake, Lisa,' said Mum, clapping a hand to her head. 'Just go upstairs, will you? As if I haven't got enough to worry about.'

She didn't want to talk about it. She was probably just hoping for the best, as I was. It wasn't that I worried for myself – to a degree I was used to Dad's behaviour – but I did wonder how Mum could possibly think about letting Kat go on holiday without her. I had never understood the excuse about her having to stay behind to work. Dad's sister Lesley had been working alongside Mum for years and was more than capable of looking after the business for a while.

The day of the holiday came, and I couldn't help feeling a little spark of excitement as we boarded the aeroplane. Things were fine for the first hour or two of the nine-hour flight. Dad was in Dr Jekyll mode, chatting amiably to the man sitting across the aisle. I heard him say that he was divorced and taking his two children on a well-deserved holiday. He almost sounded as if he were a respectable father.

When the stewardess came round with the lunch trays, Dad ordered a large gin and tonic and I noticed him staring down the stewardess's blouse when she leaned over to pour. After a few more drinks he began to tell everyone within earshot how he'd like to 'give her one'. The man he had been chatting with earlier shifted sideways in his seat and turned to look the other way.

When we got to the hotel, I was relieved when Dad left Kat and me to unpack while he went to the bar. We didn't see him again until the next morning, when I woke to find him lying on his bed stark naked. I quickly covered him with a sheet before Kat woke up. It was noon before he stirred. Kat and I had been restlessly pacing the room, waiting to get down to the beach, which lay spread beneath our hotel window. We were hungry and thirsty because we had missed dinner the night before, plus breakfast that morning. I found a packet of crisps in the flight bag and gave them to Kat to tide her over but we didn't dare go downstairs ourselves without Dad's permission.

However, over the next three weeks we had to go out on our own during the day, because once Dad woke up, he just wanted to go straight to the bar. Kat and I would spend our days out by the pool. I took care to protect her from the sun, making her wear a T-shirt or sit under an umbrella, because we didn't have any suntan lotion. My fair skin was burnt to a crisp with huge water blisters across my shoulders and on my forearms. It reminded me of the only other holiday I'd had with Dad, when I was seven. We went for a week to Benidorm in Spain just after he and Mum got married. They spent most of the holiday in bed, leaving Davie and me to play by the pool. By the end of the week my skin was burnt to a crisp, and another guest who was a nurse threatened to report Mum to the authorities for neglect.

The best thing about the Florida holiday was that Kat and I didn't see Dad very much at all. The worst thing was that I would often wake up in the middle of the night to find him masturbating over me. He'd have lifted my nightie up to my waist and put the bedside lamp on to illuminate what was happening, but thankfully Kat always slept through it. So in a way, Dad did modify his behaviour during the holiday because Kat was there, but sometimes I could see what a struggle it was for him.

As the days progressed he became more and more bad-tempered. He would send me out to the diner on the corner to get him a hamburger and fries and despite the fact that I ran all the way back, it was never hot enough for him. He threw the polystyrene box containing his burger at the lemon-painted walls and slapped me from one side of the room to the other while Kat cowered in the corner. He then pinned me down on the bed and I could see that he was fighting the urge to unbutton his flies and force himself into my mouth, as he would have done at home. Thankfully he resisted. But the more he resisted those particular urges, the more violent he became.

Far from being an idyllic family holiday, the envy of all the kids at school, our three-week stay was turning into an absolute nightmare. During the second week I noticed that Dad's back was covered in scratches

'I fucked that tour guide, last night,' he said, twisting to study his back in the mirror. 'She was a right fucking animal. Ripped me back to fucking shreds.'

I could feel him staring at me in the mirror, waiting for a response. I was determined not to look up or react in any way, because by now I was aware he thrived on my humiliation, embarrassment, tears and screams. But when he stumbled off to sit on the loo with a dirty magazine, I felt a solitary tear escape from the corner of my eye.

Kat came in from the balcony where she had been playing with her Sindy doll.

'What's the matter?' she asked.

'Nothing,' I said brushing it away. 'I've got something in my eye.'

Dad made me sick to the pit of my stomach. I was weary of living a life filled with such debasement and degradation, and I wasn't interested in hearing about his lurid encounters. My only wish was that he would go out and 'get laid' when we went home, because maybe then he would leave me alone. But I knew there was little chance of that, because he hardly left the house any more. I began to wonder if Mum didn't prefer him to stay home and abuse me, rather than run off with some other woman and leave her? The thought made me shudder.

A day or two later, I was disappointed to find he had also been with the lovely waitress who served our dinner, and who was really nice to Kat and me. I thought to myself, 'Little do you know who you're dealing with.'

'Now that's what you call a good bunk-up,' was how Dad summed up that particular liaison.

He spent most of the holiday bingeing on alcohol. One morning he told me he had been close to beating up a woman in a bar because he thought she had mocked him when he told her he was a cleaner. Seemingly she'd asked if he had a mop and bucket.

'The ugly cunt came that close to getting my fucking glass in her boat-race.'

Other guests became concerned that we didn't seem to have a responsible adult looking after us, and often had to call reception when they found us shivering in the hall outside our room, wet from the pool and locked out. Once a lady came and unlocked the door and when she pushed it open we saw Dad sprawled on the floor, unconscious, beside a pornographic magazine. I was so humiliated I couldn't look at her.

'Are you alright, honey?' she asked. 'Do you need to call your mommy?'

I couldn't get rid of her fast enough, frightened that Dad would wake up and catch me talking to an 'outsider'. He didn't like us discussing our business with anyone.

It was a relief to go home at the end of the holiday. Dad told me in crude detail what he planned to do to me when we got back, so I knew I only had misery and pain to look forward to, but at least I wouldn't have to worry about Kat any more. Mum would be able to do that.

As was his usual pattern, Dad spent the first few weeks back berating Mum for all the imaginary men she had been sleeping with while he was away. I wished I could find the courage to tell her about all the women he had boasted of sleeping with in Florida, but I realised she wouldn't do anything about it. She was like a broken mustang, all the spirit and fight beaten out of her. If the abuse of her own child didn't move her, some waitress in a Florida diner wouldn't either.

Chapter Fifteen

In the spring of 1982, I was becoming increasingly desperate. Dad's relentless abuse of me made my life a living hell. My world was so narrow that I couldn't see any avenue available to escape. And as if things weren't bad enough, Dad had started to tell me that any day now he planned to ram his penis into me so hard that he would split me in half. He hadn't penetrated me yet, but I knew the next stage in his long-term plan was almost upon me and that full-blown grown-up sex, like Mum had with him, was just around the corner.

As the abuse had progressed over the years, and he had done more and more vile things to me, I came to feel so tainted that I could hardly face going to school. Fear was so ingrained that it didn't even occur to me to bunk off in case Dad found out and beat me up for daring to go anywhere without his consent. I had two choices: go to school and feel odd, dirty and weird amongst my classmates, or stay at home and suffer more abuse. Sometimes I stayed at home simply because I couldn't bear to look at Karen and all the other girls whose lives appeared so pure and simple. I couldn't bear to see what I was missing. It hurt me to listen to them talking about going to the cinema or the youth club or being asked out on a date for the first time. I felt lonely and left out, as though I was a big freak of nature. In those days you didn't hear stories about abuse, so I felt as if I was the only person in the world it was happening to.

When Mum came home from work every day at lunchtime, I could see she was annoyed that I was at home – not because she cared about my education, but because my presence irritated her. I'd hear her arguing with Dad about it.

'Why ain't she at school again?' she said. 'I'm sick of coming home and finding her here every day.'

'It ain't my fucking fault if she don't want to go,' Dad replied.

I'd stand in the bathroom and stare at myself in the mirror as they argued downstairs, and I'd feel so frustrated with the injustice of it all that I'd want to smash my face in the glass until nothing was left where my features used to be. It was getting to the stage where I could barely look at myself any more. After Mum made a fuss, I'd try to make sure I went to school every day for the next week or so. But I was caught between the devil and the deep blue sea, because Dad would often fly into a rage and make me stay at home. I don't know whether he planned this, as he had planned everything else, but he succeeded in driving an even bigger wedge between me and my mother, one that would be virtually impossible to bridge.

In preparation for the day when we would finally have penetrative sex, he began to simulate it, by arranging me into positions where he could place his penis between my legs. I'd have to bend over in front of him and squeeze my legs shut on his penis while he moved back and forth, or he would make me lie on my back on the sofa while he knelt in front of me and hooked my legs over his shoulders. I often used to cry on these occasions, especially when he 'accidentally' penetrated my anus, which was very shocking and painful.

'I bet you've got a nice tight pussy. I'm going to split you in half,' was his favourite turn of phrase, and he made it clear to me that he wasn't prepared to wait much longer for this to happen.

Yet at other times, our relationship remained very much one of strict dad and subservient daughter. Not that he possessed any positive fatherly qualities; it was rather that he liked to be in control and was good at laying down ground rules. I was treated as a child, just as Kat was. No smoking, no swearing, no make-up or grown-up clothes, different food from Mum and Dad because I couldn't possibly handle a hot curry. I was painfully aware that in many ways the girls at school were much more grown-up and worldly-wise than I was. My development had been retarded because I wasn't allowed to grow up normally, and I didn't know what it was to be a normal teenager. So in every way but the vile abuse I suffered on a daily basis, Dad treated me as if I were his daughter, and much younger than I actually was. Perhaps for this reason, I found it hard to believe he would go so far as to take my virginity. Surely that was too drastic a step even for him? I felt the dread and fear overtake me every day, but deep down I always hoped he would stop himself at the last moment. I convinced myself that if he hadn't done it by now, he never would.

But I was wrong. He was simply biding his time. He obviously hoped that all the previous abuses he'd inflicted on me over the years would somehow pave the way and make it easier for him.

I was so shocked when he finally tried to enter me that I became almost hysterical. I uttered a piercing scream and cried and begged him not to, it hurt so much. Of all the pain I had felt in all the years I had been abused by him, this was by far the worst.

For the first time ever I saw a look of doubt pass over his face. My reaction had frightened him. In the past the threat of his violence had meant I hadn't dared to put up too much of a fight, but this time it felt as though he was trying to kill me and I couldn't control my fear. I knew in my head I shouldn't disobey him in case he started hitting me, but I couldn't stop myself writhing in agony and resisting in any way I could. Eventually he stopped trying and zipped his flies back up.

I hoped this meant he had given up on the idea – but no. If anything he became even more determined and tried to enter me every day. He'd send Mum over to the shop or on some other errand, if she wasn't already at work, or he'd take me cleaning with him at the weekend, just the two of us. There he would escort me into a bathroom and lift me up onto a sink to try and lower me down onto his penis, but my body was so tense that he couldn't get it in at all. I was surprised that he wasn't getting angry or lashing out in the way he normally would if I wasn't being compliant. If anything he was being nicer than I'd known him to be in a long time. He told me that he loved me and that I was the most special girl in the world.

He mopped my tears really tenderly and for a moment I thought it was all a bad dream. I fantasised that he was a real and proper dad, someone who didn't want to abuse or rape me, but my reverie was shattered in the next moment as he tried once again to force his penis into my vagina.

Nothing was working and gradually he started reverting to type, his anger and frustration bubbling to the surface. He was used to getting what he wanted and soon he started to hit me again. By this stage I just wanted it to be over. I knew he would get his way eventually, so I tried to relax and escape in my mind the way I used to. But there was no fooling my body, which responded to the revulsion I felt by going into a sort of lockdown spasm. I couldn't pretend to myself that what he was doing was OK, because it wasn't. Instinctively I knew the only thing holding him back from raping me in the swift, brutal way you read about in newspapers was his own fear of being caught. I was barely fifteen, his stepdaughter, and he was worried because my show of resistance had caught him unawares. Could he really be sure I wouldn't run screaming to the police?

He had always been a betting man, and now it was time for him to take the biggest gamble of his life.

'For fuck's sake,' he snapped one day, digging his fingers into the flesh of my hips. 'What's wrong with you?'

'I don't want to,' I whispered. 'I don't want to.'

'What?' he demanded, full of threat and menace, even though I knew he'd heard me clearly. 'What did you fucking say?'

'Nothing. It hurts.'

Suddenly, after keeping his anger contained for the best part of three weeks while he tried and failed to achieve penetration, he exploded into action. 'Don't give me all that, you little fucker,' he shouted, kicking and stamping on my legs and feet where I lay on the front room floor.

He grabbed a fistful of hair and T-shirt in one hand and dragged me upstairs to his bedroom. Mum was out. He threw two towels on the bed, as he normally did whenever he tried to enter me, telling me they were 'for all the blood'. I started to shake so much I could hear my teeth chattering. With one swift movement he removed my skirt, which was bunched up around my waist. I clamped my hands over my T-shirt as if my life depended on it. I couldn't bear him to see me completely naked. It always made everything seem so much worse. Then he produced a paper bag containing a tube of K-Y Jelly and a packet of Durex condoms. He put one of the condoms on and rubbed some K-Y Jelly between my legs, neither of which he had done before. All pretence of gentleness had gone, and I knew this was it. I was rigid with fear and trembling from head to toe.

He put a hand over my mouth, forced my legs open and rammed himself hard against me. The pain was like a hot dagger. It felt as though his promise of 'splitting me in half' was finally happening. I screamed as loudly as I could beneath his big hand, and closed my eyes so I wouldn't have to look at his contorted face as he grunted above me. All I felt was searing pain, and a steady trail of tears running down into my ears.

It had taken him years to get to this point, and although I hated him with every fibre of my being, I also detested myself for letting it happen. I felt dirty right through to the core of my being. I imagined that most girls would throw themselves from the top of a building rather than allowing their own father to rape them. I didn't understand my own powerful instinct for survival – in fact, I felt betrayed by it. I was fifteen years and three months old and my life was a living nightmare. Something had been done that could never be undone. I wasn't a virgin any more, and my virginity had been taken by my own dad.

Now I had been 'broken in', Dad became even more of a sex-crazed animal. Everything I had experienced up to this point had been like a walk in the park compared to the reality of my life now. He raped me at every possible opportunity, many times a day. On the days when I was going to school he would push me into the bathroom and enter me while Kat ate her toast in the kitchen. On one occasion I retched in the gutter on the way to school as I thought of what he had done to me only twenty minutes earlier. A well-spoken lady tutted as she walked past with her sausage dog: 'That's no way to lose weight,' she said. It seemed a bizarre thing to say and I had no idea what she meant by it but humiliation burned my cheeks. I sat on a wall and let her get far enough in front of me that I wouldn't have to pass her again.

From six to nine in the evening I would usually go cleaning with Mum, but Dad would always rape me when I came home, either in the front room or in his bedroom upstairs in front of the portable telly. But at least I wasn't trapped under his legs all evening too.

Then a few months later things got worse for me. The company Mum cleaned for asked if she could sit on the front desk for a few hours every evening to let people in and out. The money was better than for her evening cleaning job, so she gave this up and for the first time in years I was free to stay at home. Unfortunately this meant Dad had even more opportunity to rape me, once Kat had gone to bed.

One evening, while Mum was still at work, Dad gave me some alcohol.

'Get a bit of this down your neck,' he said, filling a tumbler with Liebfraumilch. 'It might loosen you up a bit.'

I hated the taste but drank it down in one or two gulps. I remembered the feeling my surreptitious swig of Babycham had given me on the final night of the school play, the way it made me float and not care about anything very much, and I hoped the glass of warm white wine Dad handed me would recreate that experience. I wanted to float away as far as I could from the horror I lived in every day. As I drank the wine I fought the urge to gag. It didn't taste very nice, but the warmth it spread from the inside of my belly outwards was fairly instantaneous. I felt some of the long-held tension draining out of me, and my shoulders seemed to drop a couple of inches; I was forever bunching them up around my ears as if trying to use them to shield me from hurt.

Lately, Dad had been talking about love a lot. He did it now, pausing only to swallow alternate mouthfuls of gin and wine straight from the bottle.

'I love you. I can't help myself,' he declared, before asking, 'Do you love me?'

I knew that the love he talked about wasn't the kind of love that normal fathers felt for their daughters. It was different to the kind he had spoken about when he told his brother a few years ago that he loved me like his own child and wanted to adopt me. Dad was trying to change the rules to make what he had done seem more acceptable. He was trying to paint himself as my boyfriend. But he had been my dad since I was a tiny girl of four, and even though he now raped me more frequently than he washed or brushed his teeth, that's what he would always remain – my dad. I felt only disgust and revulsion for him.

His eyes watched me as I stared into my empty glass and braced myself for the slap or kick that was only ever a moment away.

'Are you fucking deaf or something? I said, do you love me?'

The wine must have given me courage I had never previously possessed. I took my time to find the right words.

'I love you as a dad,' I muttered not quite brave enough to tell him that I hated him, tears springing to my eyes. 'You're meant to be my dad.'

It was like lighting a fuse.

'You fucking little whore,' he shouted, knocking glasses and bottles flying as he threw himself on top of me and began to slap and punch. 'You like your dad's big cock, don't you?'

I found myself bent over the sofa face down, my nose painfully squashed into the cushions so the only way I could breathe was to open my mouth wide and try to suck warm air through the foam. He released me for a moment and I twisted my head to the side. I felt him rip my knickers sideways, the cotton cutting into me, and then I heard the sound of him undoing his flies.

'I'm going to ram this right up your tight little cunt,' he said, "cos that's what you want, ain't it?'

'No, it's not!' I cried – whether out loud or in my head, I'm not sure.

'You're my fucking girlfriend now,' he snarled, 'not my daughter.'

During the course of this assault, he entered my anus. The sudden pain was overwhelming and I heard myself scream, and scream again.

Dad didn't give me alcohol again until I was much older. He said I couldn't handle it – but maybe it was him who couldn't handle the courage it gave me.

Chapter Sixteen

A couple of months short of my sixteenth birthday, Dad stopped me attending school for good. I didn't even have a chance to sit my mock O' Levels. Karen came to knock for me a few times and she couldn't believe I wasn't going to sit the exams.

'But you're so bright,' she exclaimed. 'How're you going to get a good job without any qualifications?'

I shrugged, aware that Dad was listening to every word. The thought of a job, a life away from Dad, had never entered my mind as a real possibility. I had often dreamed of escaping, but knew that Dad would never let me go. He had told me he would kill me before he let that happen, and I believed him with every fibre of my being.

'You're mine,' he'd say, 'and if you ever try to walk out that door, I'll find ya, fuck ya, and kill ya. Got it?'

Eventually Karen stopped knocking for me. It hurt me to think we'd never laugh together again, but I was skilled at putting painful thoughts into boxes and shutting them away in my mind where they couldn't hurt me, and that's what I did with Karen.

Now that I wasn't attending school and was fast approaching my sixteenth birthday, when I'd be 'legal', Dad's behaviour took a turn for the worse. He started drinking and gambling more than ever, and became more abusive on every level. He would openly touch me in front of Mum, pawing my breasts or bottom and making lewd comments. Despite all that he had done to me, and how defeated and powerless I felt, when he did these things, I always retained the ability to see that it was wrong. This way of living might have become my state of normality, but it was far from normal, and my face would burn in shame and embarrassment to reflect my feelings. Mum continued to turn a blind eye, just leaving the room if Dad started carrying on with me.

Around this time, she began to lose a bit of weight and take more pride in her appearance. One day she came home from a trip down the market, wheeling her pull-along shopping trolley behind her. In amongst the King Edward potatoes and cans of Special Brew lay a small plastic bag. She pulled it out and placed it in the middle of the kitchen table.

''Ere, look at these, Frank,' she said, pulling out a tangle of what looked like black, red and pink netting. 'Got myself some new drawers. What do you think?' She held the flimsy black knickers with red and pink bows against her groin and waited for Dad to comment.

He grunted from behind his copy of *The Sun*, and continued to pick his teeth with a broken matchstick, totally ignoring her.

'That's fucking charming, that is,' she said, stuffing them back into the bag, and flashing me an angry look as she did so.

It was as if she blamed me for all that Dad had done, and the way he treated her. She thought I had stolen her man from her.

In that moment, I realised how much their relationship had changed. Years ago, she wouldn't have dared to buy herself new underwear, or any other clothes, without Dad's permission. If she had, he would have convinced himself she was having an affair and given her a right-hander, or worse. It was as if he had transferred all that obsessive jealousy onto me. Now Mum was free, to a large extent, and it was me who had to account for my every waking moment, every new item of clothing or bottle of deodorant.

'Men can't help acting on Impulse, eh? What the fuck you buying that shit for, you slag.'

At night when I lay in bed, I'd do my best to block out the sound of Mum and Dad having sex. He was insatiable and still wanted his conjugal rights with her despite the three or four times he'd have raped me earlier in the day. Every inch of my body hurt. Only an hour or two before, I was lying in Mum's bed exactly where she was lying now, while Dad pounded into me. When he was finished, he would press the sticky condom into my hand and I'd have to go and flush it down the toilet.

Once Mum went in after me and I heard her shout, 'I wish people would flush the fucking toilet properly in this house.' She must have seen the condom floating on top of the water.

Dad was drinking and gambling heavily every day. There was no escape for me. I was trapped with him all day, every day. I wasn't allowed out on my own, except to run round the corner if Mum or Dad needed something from the shop. I mean run, literally. Dad would time me, and if there was a particularly long queue I'd start to panic. When I got home red-faced and breathless from the run, Dad would be convinced I had been having sex with someone. He'd shout and rant and rage, and take me upstairs to the front room where he'd thrust his fingers between my legs and sniff them.

'I can smell spunk, you cunt.'

'No, Dad,' I'd say, cowering in the corner. 'I haven't done anything. Please, don't.'

One day Dad read a letter on the problem page in *The Sun*. It was about a woman who was fed up with her husband wanting sex several times a day.

'Who's been writing letters about me?' he laughed, looking from me to Mum. There was an awkward silence during which Mum and I carefully avoided each other's eyes.

'Joke,' said Dad, turning to the sports pages to study the horseracing form.

Later, when they weren't looking, I read the letter myself. The man was just like Dad, with an insatiable sexual appetite, and the wife couldn't stand it any more and had started to hope he would have an affair. The agony aunt was of the mind that open relationships were something of a rocky road, and she suggested marriage guidance, as I noticed she did with all the other problems on the page.

I thought about what an 'open' relationship was, and it struck me that Mum and Dad, who were still the best of friends in their own way, had created their own format. Mum allowed Dad to do things to me, as long as he didn't go elsewhere. It would take more than marriage guidance to fix what was wrong with them.

I wondered if Mum was glad Dad only did it to her at night in bed these days? I imagined she must have felt relieved that she didn't have to put up with him wanting sex throughout the day like he used to when they first met, because he had me now. Sometimes he'd wait until Mum was out of the house before bending me over the stairs or the sofa, but other times he'd do it while she was pottering about downstairs. He didn't use condoms on these occasions, which he referred to as 'a quick bunk-up'. There wasn't enough time, so he would simply withdraw at the last moment and leave me to clean up the mess. He was so rough that I often found it painful to sit down afterwards, and suffered increasingly severe bouts of cystitis.

Now that I was a little older, Dad became much more violent. He was still careful not to mark my face, although occasionally he'd make a mistake and I'd be left with a bruise or a bright red hand mark across my cheek. But mostly it was the rest of my body that bore the marks of his increasingly sadistic tendencies.

I'd only have to look at him the wrong way, or use margarine instead of butter on his toast, and he'd be off, pinching and biting my breasts and buttocks. Later I'd look in the mirror and watch the oval teeth-shaped bruises appearing. Over the coming week they'd change colour running through purple, blue, green and yellow, only to be replaced by new ones as soon as they disappeared. Just as one part of me healed, there would be another tender spot to take its place. Now that my pubic hair was growing, he decided there was no better entertainment than dragging me around by it. Once or twice after a loss on the horses, he burnt me with his cigarette, grinding it painfully into my hand. But more often than not, he'd simply smoke his cigarette and instead of putting it out in the ashtray, he'd flick it at me, so I'd have to dodge it or quickly shut my eyes. Then I'd have to find where it had landed before it caused a fire. He'd do this a lot when he'd been drinking, seeming to find it hilarious. If Mum saw, she would just chide him like a naughty child, saying, 'Now, now, Frank, it's time you had a lay down before we go up in bleed-in' flames.'

One night, shortly after my sixteenth birthday, I over-heard a momentous conversation that confirmed one of my worst fears. It must have been around one in the morning and I had been tossing and turning in my bed for at least a couple of hours. My back was grazed where Dad had kicked me earlier that evening, and it hurt no matter what position I tried to lie in. I needed to use the loo but I was frightened I might bump into him again. Usually I could hear him either snoring or having sex with Mum in their bedroom at night, so I was worried he might still be up and roaming around downstairs. But I was desperate, so I decided to take my chances anyway. As I crept down the stairs towards the loo on the first floor, I heard Mum and Dad talking downstairs in the kitchen.

Ordinarily I wouldn't hang about to listen, but something made me stop and what I heard sent a chill down my spine.

They were talking in casual tones, as if discussing nothing more significant than the weather.

'But you were meant to be her father, not her lover,' said Mum, reasonably.

'I know, but I've told you I can't help it,' Dad explained. 'For ages now I've thought of her more as me girlfriend than a daughter. You knew that.'

'You promised you'd stop doing it,' said Mum. 'No other woman would have put up with this for so long.'

I wanted to pass out and throw up all at once. How long had Mum known for sure? They were discussing the situation as if it was an old subject they were revisiting for the hundredth time. There was no shock, anger or surprise on Mum's part. It was final confirmation to me that she had known, if not all along, then for a very long time indeed. How could she let him do this to me, her daughter? How could she tolerate him touching her, knowing what he had done to me?

I had so many questions, I felt dizzy. I crept into the bathroom and stood there in the dark spitting bile into the toilet bowl. My heart pounded as I realised Mum had betrayed me in the worst possible way. She had seen me beaten black and blue, prevented from living a normal life like any other teenage girl. How could she do this to me? The feelings of guilt and shame, of being tainted and dirty, weighed heavily upon me. I knew I hadn't wanted any of what had happened to me, had felt powerless to stop it, but I couldn't help feeling that if Mum wasn't angry with Dad, if she wasn't running screaming to the police or hitting him over the head with a frying pan, then she must be angry with me instead. And I couldn't work out how you could be angry with your own child in such a situation. Had she convinced herself I was a willing participant? I thought back over all the times she had been cold and distant, shooting me hard stares, and I felt terrified. I literally didn't have a friend in the world.

As I lay in bed that night, listening to the usual grunts and groans coming from the bedroom next door, I cried until eventually I drifted off into a merciful sleep. The next morning my heart still hurt, but I made up my mind that I was going to bring it all out in the open with Mum when she came home from work. I was filled with fresh hope that the nightmare would finally come to an end then. Surely she would have to send me off to stay with Diane or Jenny? Once I'd told her that Dad forced me to have sex with him and I hated it, she couldn't let it continue, surely? I knew that this day would mark a turning point, and somehow I hoped that by the end of it I'd have a whole new direction, a new life. The thought of what Dad might do left me petrified, but between the two of us, me and Mum, we could deal with him. Dad had never let us have a phone installed – he preferred us to be totally cut off from the outside world – but if we both screamed loud enough, maybe the neighbours would ring the police.

I stood at the sink and did the washing-up from the night before. I hoped Mum still had that piece of paper with Diane's address on it. If I went there, I could finally meet my little niece or nephew. Or maybe she might be able to remember where Jenny lived in Kent. It would be hard to look my family in the face after all Dad had done to me, but I knew they'd understand that it wasn't my choice. They might even be annoyed with Mum for letting it go on so long. I realised it would take a lot of courage for Mum to face them after everything that had happened, and it was then that all my little dreams of freedom began to waver. If Mum had known for some time, why hadn't she tried to help me before? What would be different now? I began to feel overwhelmed with confusing feelings. I just wanted to be a normal teenager, like Joanie out of *Happy Days*. Was that too much to ask?

By the time Dad slammed into the kitchen and bent down over the stove to light his morning cigarette, my eyes were streaming with tears and my shoulders were heaving.

'What's up with you?' asked Dad, his usual self.

I had planned on being so sensible and grown-up. I had turned sixteen but I felt as if I were six years old again. It was all too much to handle and I could find neither the words nor the courage to express the way I felt.

'She knows, doesn't she?' I wailed, my voice rising in despair. All the emotion I'd suppressed for years was struggling to get out.

Dad looked almost embarrassed. He shrugged his shoulders. 'So what?'

I ran up to my bedroom and sat with my back to the door, my feet braced against the bed in case Dad came storming up the stairs as he normally would. It wasn't until a good half an hour had passed that I felt safe enough to move. It seemed things were changing; he hadn't followed and kicked me round the room for a start. I sat on the edge of my bed and waited for Mum to come home. I tried to rehearse what I would say, but I didn't know where to start. I didn't want to

212

dwell on the fact that she had known and had chosen not to help me. The last thing I wanted was for her to feel bad, because then she would get angry and I needed her now more than ever. She had to get me away from here.

I stared at my clock and watched as each agonising minute ticked by. Periodically I'd look out of the window but I had to sit down again quickly because when I stood up my tummy would do nervous somersaults. I wished I could smoke like Mum did when she was anxious, because it seemed to settle her nerves. I thought about how bizarre it was that I was routinely raped and battered by my dad with my mum's full knowledge and yet both of them had always frowned upon the idea of me taking up smoking. I was just a kid, too young to smoke and swear. Dad always told me that he wanted me to hang on to my innocence for as long as possible.

By the time I heard the gate swing outside and Mum's key turning in the lock, I had worked myself up into another state. My eyes would barely open they were so swollen with tears, and my head was throbbing with pain due to the hours of crying. My whole body was trembling. I was absolutely terrified. Terrified of Mum and what we would both feel when we locked eyes for the first time now that the family's biggest open secret was no longer under wraps. I was terrified of Dad and what damage he would inflict and on whom: Mum and me, or just me, as it had been for the last few years?

I opened the bedroom door and heard them talking downstairs. Dad was saying 'She knows that you know. She heard us talking last night.'

There was more talk in hushed tones, then Mum started coming up the stairs.

When she reached the top flight, she gave a huge, theatrical sigh and exclaimed, 'Oh my Gawd!' as if it were all a big joke. She sounded as though she was doing an impression of Frankie Howerd or one of the *Carry On* team. Surely it was all an act though? She couldn't possibly be dealing with this whole thing in such a light-hearted manner.

I ran back into my bedroom, dreading the moment she'd walk into the room. I was excruciatingly embarrassed and ashamed, as if it was all my fault and I wasn't just a victim of my own dad's perversions. I knew I wasn't thinking rationally. I couldn't, I was so torn up with fear on so many different levels.

As she came through the door, I became almost hysterical. I rushed towards her and threw myself into her arms, my whole body shaking with sobs. As I felt her arms hold me to her for the first time in years, it was as if a dam burst within me. All the grief for my lost family, my childhood, my schooling and my teenage years came flooding out.

'Now don't be silly,' Mum said softly but completely dry-eyed.

And then, even though a voice at the back of my mind urged me to be careful, I began repeating over and over, 'He made me do it. I didn't want to. He made me do it.'

I felt Mum's body stiffen. 'Shush! Shush or he'll hear you.' She was only too aware of the consequences of Dad's anger.

Her next words took my breath away. She spoke as if she hadn't a care in the world. 'Now calm down and come down-

214

stairs for a cup of tea. I don't know about you, but I'm fucking gasping.'

I blinked and dried my snot and tears on the sleeve of my
jumper, not quite sure what she was doing. She seemed to be
behaving as if nothing had happened. Then I got it. I understood that she must be talking in code in case Dad was listening
on the stairs. 'Having a cup of tea' really meant lulling the
dirty violent bastard downstairs into a false sense of security
until we could get away safely. We had to be careful and not
make any sudden moves until we worked out what to do. Dad
probably hadn't wanted a phone in the house because he was
wary of the fact that 999 was all too easy to dial on impulse,
especially if you had a mad man coming at you wanting blood.

As I watched Mum plod her way downstairs, my head was
still reeling from all the emotion, but I felt as if a huge weight
had been lifted from my shoulders. I knew that life would
have to change now. It couldn't go on as it had before, could
it?

I hid in my room for as long as I could, unable to face the
thought of going downstairs. I didn't know how to act. I
wondered if this would be the day when Dad finally lost it and
stabbed me to death, as he had often threatened.

'Lisa, get down here,' Dad shouted up for a second time,
and I didn't dare disobey him any longer. His voice sounded
quite cheerful, under the circumstances, and I thought I'd
better not antagonise him. With a little luck I wouldn't have to
put up with him for much longer, not now that mum couldn't
get away with sticking her head in the sand any longer. I
knew, she knew. There could be no pretence any more.

I walked down the stairs, into the usual choking fug of Benson & Hedges that rose from the ground floor. I stopped outside the kitchen door and listened, expecting to hear them arguing, or at least talking about the situation, but instead they sounded as if it was just like any other day. Dad was saying how his 'guts' were rumbling and he could 'eat a fucking horse', and Mum said, 'I'm gonna make a sandwich in a minute. I got a nice bit of ham over Londis.' It seemed like business as usual, and I almost felt like pinching myself to check I wasn't having a nightmare. How could Mum still talk civilly to him? How could she offer to make him a sandwich, knowing what he had done to her daughter? If someone had done that to a daughter of mine, I thought I wouldn't be able to stop myself from trying to stab them through the heart.

I walked in and when Dad saw me he stopped spooning sugar in his tea for a moment and said, 'Look at the face on that. She looks like a fucking tomato.' He laughed uproariously at his own joke.

Mum cackled and took a last drag of her cigarette before dropping it in a teacup where it made a loud sizzle. 'Mustard or pickle?'

'Mustard, triple-decker please, Donna,' said Dad, without a care in the world.

It was just like any other day. I tried to catch Mum's eye to ask her what was going on, but she wouldn't look at me, just kept layering on the ham she was so pleased with. Gradually it dawned on me that this was it. She wasn't pretending to appease Dad to keep him from getting violent – she wasn't

216

going to do anything. She had simply accepted the situation. It was the ultimate betrayal. She had made her choice a while ago and she was sticking with it. I felt so stupid for believing she would help me. Nothing had changed at all in our weird family set-up, except that the one person who had been living in a state of blind ignorance could finally see the reality. That person was me. It was never Mum – she had known all along. It was me whose eyes were opened at last.

A couple of hours later Dad sent me out to the shop, and when I got back I overheard Mum saying, 'We don't want any accidents. That's all I bleedin' need.'

I wondered what she was talking about, but later in the week it became clear. Far from hatching a plan to get me away from the man who had tortured and abused me for so long, Mum was concerned only that I might get pregnant. Between them they decided I was to go on the Pill.

Dad marched me over to the doctor's surgery. 'You go in, you tell him you want the Pill, bang. Done. No fucking discussion. No chit-chat shit. Nothing. Do you understand?' he said, holding my chin. 'And make sure he don't see any of ... you know, any of those marks.'

'Okay, Dad,' I nodded. I was glad he found it hard to speak about the injuries he gave me: the bruises and scratches all over my back; the lump on my leg where he'd kicked me last week, and which still hadn't gone down. He seemed embarrassed at what he'd done, and in my naivety I thought that meant a small part of him was sorry. I knew that the word wasn't actually in his vocabulary, but I wanted to believe he had at least a little conscience.

He told me he would wait outside by the raised flowerbeds, and added, 'Remember, don't answer him if he starts poking his nose in.'

I pushed open the swing doors to the surgery and was hit by a rush of hot air infused with the smell of disinfectant and antiseptic. I was incredibly nervous. I didn't want to go on the Pill. Neither did I want to be raped by my father any more. But I didn't know how I could help myself, and I had nobody to turn to. I had tried several more times to ask for Mum's help, but she wouldn't have it.

'Mum, please,' I begged, 'I can't believe you're letting him do this to me.'

'Now don't fucking start, Lisa,' she warned. 'I can't stop him. You're sixteen years old, a legal consenting adult.'

'But I'm not consenting!' I shrieked. 'I'm covered in cuts and bruises.'

'As far as I'm concerned, you're his girlfriend, and that's that.'

The truth was that now I was sixteen and 'legal', Mum felt she didn't owe me any duty of care whatsoever. She had been beaten black and blue by this man for years, forced to dump every member of her family, and now she was willing to stand by while he raped and beat her own daughter right under her nose in the family home. I began to realise why she had hidden from the truth for so long. If I were any younger she would have been forced to act in case anyone else found out – like the school, for instance. Now, because Dad wasn't blood-related and I was legally allowed to have sex, they both felt able to brush all the previous years of abuse under the carpet for a fresh start. Clearly they had come to an arrangement between them that I was no longer Dad's daughter – I was his girl-friend instead. Technically Mum may have been the wife who still shared his bed at night, but now she was a sort of mother-in-law as well.

My head spun as I sat in the doctor's waiting room and I realised the light at the end of the tunnel was shrinking to nothing more than a pin prick. I couldn't believe Mum's only response had been to make everything easier in the contraception department, rather than protecting me from harm full stop. What sort of woman was she?

My heart was racing as I waited for my name to be called over the tannoy. I had cauterised my emotions as a matter of survival for so long, but now Mum's betrayal of everything a mother should be overwhelmed me. Unshed tears threatened to spill over, and I was desperate to think about other things. I spotted a pile of well-worn magazines in front of me and was about to reach for one when I saw Dad glaring at me through the plate-glass window and pointing at his watch as if to ask me what was taking so long.

The doctor was obviously running late with his appoint-ments because I should have been called fifteen minutes before. A door opened and a young Indian man emerged. He was very tall and wore a pristine white turban. I presumed he was a doctor as he was carrying some files. As he passed he gave me a smile, showing brilliantly white teeth. 'Okay?' he asked.

I gave a half smile back, and was filled with equal meas-ures of dread and relief as I heard my name called. I made my way along the corridor to Dr Ainsworth's office, practising what I was going to say. It all felt wrong.

'Do your parents know you want to go on the Pill?' he asked, with a slight frown. He was an elderly man and I felt so uncomfortable I could hardly look at him. I was also frightened. Dad said I was to ignore any questions, and I wasn't sure where this was leading.

'No … No, they don't,' I stammered. My face burned as I imagined what he would think of me if he knew he truth: that it was actually my parents who had sent me here, so that my own dad wouldn't make me pregnant. Shame consumed me as the doctor continued to peer at me over the top of his glasses.

'And you are sixteen, aren't you?' He picked up my notes and read out my date of birth to double check.

He looked at me for a moment as if waiting for me to say something, and then chuckled and said, 'Sorry, but you look about the same age as my grand-daughter, and she's only thirteen.'

It was true; I did have a very young face for my age. Some of the girls at school wore make-up, which made them look much older, but Dad wouldn't let me. To me they looked like proper teenagers, as if they might actually have a boyfriend and need the Pill. I could understand the doctor's surprise because I didn't look mature enough to be having sex, and I could see he was a little taken aback, even though he did his best to hide it. I wasn't sure about the procedure and started to worry that he might have to contact my parents. Dad would kill me if that was the case. I could feel prickles of sweat under my armpits.

'Jolly good,' said the doctor, adding a note to my records and reaching for the blood pressure cuff. 'Slip your coat off and we'll just check you over.'

Finally he was satisfied I was in good health and scribbled me a prescription for three months' supply of contraceptive pills. I felt like a criminal, as if I'd got away with hiding the biggest, darkest secret anyone could have. I didn't even think of showing the doctor my injuries and telling him I had been abused for years. Dad was all-powerful, and I knew without a shadow of a doubt that he would kill me if I ever told. I had never seen anyone stand up to him. My whole family had just bowed down and let him walk all over them and I didn't have the courage to break the mould. So when the doctor gave a little wave and said, 'Cheerio, dear,' I was just relieved to get out of there.

But when I saw Dad leaning against the wall outside, I knew something was very wrong. His face was like thunder.

'You took your fucking time. And why are you all red?' He looked me up and down suspiciously.

I was just trying to work out how to answer when he asked, 'Which doctor was it, then? It was that Paki bastard, wasn't it?'

'No, it was Dr Ainsworth, the one with the white hair,' I said, suddenly on high alert, sensitive as ever to Dad's fluctuating moods.

'Don't fucking lie. I saw you smiling at him with his fucking tea cosy on his head.'

The slap connected with the right side of my head and knocked me off balance so that I span away from him. 'No, Dad, it was Dr Ainsworth, the old one.'

'I said don't lie, you little whore.' He grabbed the top of my arm and dug his fingers in through my coat. 'He touched you up, didn't he?'

I felt panic rising. 'Course not, Dad.'

'Do I look like a cunt? I ain't as fucking stupid as you like to think.' His voice rose. 'I bet he had his greasy hand up your fanny faster than a rat up a fucking drainpipe.'

I felt the familiar dread settle over me and prayed he wouldn't keep hitting me because someone might see. I looked over my shoulder to see if anyone was watching from inside the waiting room and was relieved to see the other patients contentedly flicking through their *Reader's Digest*s, or staring into space, totally oblivious to what was happening just outside the swing doors.

He slapped the side of my head again. 'Who you looking for? Gupter?'

'No, Dad. Can we just go home now? I need the toilet.' Fear still made me want to wee, just as it had done all those years ago when I used to wet myself regularly.

'Oh, she needs the fucking toilet,' said Dad, raising his face to talk to the sky for a moment, then pushing his face into mine. 'I bet you fucking do. What, is it to wipe away Gupter's spunk, is it? Like Pakis then, do you?'

He grabbed the back of my neck between vice-like fingers and propelled me along the path that led out onto the pavement. 'We're going home alright, don't you fucking worry about that.'

My stomach was in knots as we walked the short distance home. All the way, Dad kept up his tirade, punctuating his words with sharp digs. People walked by us with their heads down and eyes averted, their body language making it clear they didn't want to get involved.

Dad looked me up and down. 'Do you know how I know what you've been up to?' he bellowed over the rumble of a passing bus. 'It's your fucking coat that's given the game away. It was done up when you went in there and now it's not. Get out of that.'

He looked at me triumphantly, as if he'd proved his point. His argument was so irrational, so weak, that I knew he couldn't possibly believe it himself. He was just looking for an excuse to hurt me. My tears seemed to excite him, so I tried to hold them back for as long as I could, but I was so frightened I couldn't stop them for long.

'Come on, you snivelling bitch, fucking answer me. Did you, or did you not, take that fucking coat off so that he could ram his cock up your arse?'

'But I had to … take my coat off, I mean. He had to do my blood pressure, and then I just didn't button it up again, that's all. I'm sorry.'

'Bollocks!' he shouted, seeming not to care who heard. 'There was no fucking blood test. You're only a kid. You must have me down as a right mug.'

'No, not a blood test … blood pressure,' I garbled. I thought if I could only make him understand then he wouldn't be so angry. I started to drag my feet a little, terrified of arriving home. I reasoned I was relatively safe while we were out in the street, but he grabbed my ear and yanked me over the road: 'Get a move on!' A white van had to screech to a halt and the driver peered angrily at us through the windscreen mouthing the word 'wanker' at Dad. I was surprised when Dad held up a hand in apology. I wasn't used to seeing him back down to anyone.

We continued walking in silence, only a few minutes from home now. I thought his rant had petered out like it did sometimes. But no.

'Don't forget I'm a fucking man, and I know how men think,' he started again as we turned into our road. 'And I know all about you as well, don't I? Fucking slag that you are.'

An old lady passed us, her mouth hanging open in shock.

'And you can fuck off, an' all,' he told her.

As he kicked open our rusty front gate and pushed me ahead of him up the path, I felt pure cold fear. I was only grateful that he was stone cold sober; drunk he would have been worse.

As soon as we were inside the house, he started kicking me and shouting at the top of his voice. 'What, was his curried cock too fucking hot for you, or something? So fucking hot you had to take your bastard coat off while he did you from behind?'

He pushed me through the kitchen door and I landed on my knees in front of Mum, who was sitting at the table.

'What's going on now?' she asked, rolling her eyes and shutting the newspaper.

I scrambled to my feet, aware that Dad was right behind me and desperate to get away. I ran to the recess beside the fridge and pressed myself as far back as I could, absolutely terrified.

Dad came after me, placed one hand round my throat and started banging my head repeatedly against the wall. Urine dribbled down my leg; I couldn't stop it.

'Mum,' I croaked.

'Oi, now calm down,' she said to Dad, putting a hand on his shoulder. 'What's happened?'

'It's her, the cunt,' he said, spittle flying into my face. 'She's just had it off with the doctor.'

Mum laughed. Mum always laughed at times like this. I think it was her way of trying to diffuse the tension but I couldn't help feeling hurt that she found it all so funny.

'I didn't,' I wailed, trying to shake my head.

Dad let me go then and I collapsed coughing onto the floor. He stamped on my hand, leaving the imprint of his heel and a graze that oozed blood. He then tipped a full ashtray over my head. I realised I had got off lightly this time, but my body was wracked with pain, and my hand had started to swell.

'Is there ever a day when she's not boo-hooing?' asked Mum, sitting back down to resume reading the paper, while Dad cracked open a lager.

I sat amongst the cigarette butts, almost motionless for the best part of an hour. I daren't move until Dad said it was OK. Mum sat smoking fag after fag, gradually filling up the ashtray again, her foot jiggling at double speed.

Finally Dad said, 'Oi, piss-arse, go and clean yourself up, you're stinking the place out.'

Mum didn't look at me, but as I went out the door she asked him if we had picked up the pills from the chemist.

'Not with her winding me up like that,' he said.

225

'That's fucking marvellous, that is. I suppose I'll have to go and get 'em,' she said.

And she did.

Chapter Seventeen

Once I had finished school and gone on the Pill, Dad made no effort to conceal his jealous rages. He was free to beat me up in front of Mum in the way a deranged boyfriend would, spouting nonsense about me sleeping with doctors, the newsagent, or the mechanic who worked on the corner in the garage. It was like history repeating itself, except now it was me on the receiving end of his boot rather than Mum. By this time he hadn't hit Mum for years.

Despite everything, Mum and Dad's relationship remained much the same. They worked together, and still shared a bed together at night. The only difference was that Mum had effectively given her blessing to Dad raping me on a regular basis. At night when they had sex, Mum wasn't quite as vocal as she used to be and I noticed that she had become reluctant to join Dad in a 'nap' during the day when he suggested it.

'What, with her here morning, noon and night?' she said, incredulous. 'I tell you what, you must think I'm some fucking mug.'

I realised she must have felt a degree of shame herself, because not only were we all living in some kind of sick *ménage à trois*, but she was actually making an active choice to let the situation continue when she could have ended it with a single phone call. I started to wonder if she was protecting herself in some way. After all, if anybody else found out, what would they think of her? Surely she must wonder this herself.

In the evenings Mum still worked as a receptionist, and Dad would spend this time dishing out what had become nothing short of sexual torture. Once Kat was in bed upstairs, he'd make me kneel naked in front of him until I confessed who I'd been sleeping with. I tried to reason with him, asking where I was meant to have met these men since I was never allowed out, but this seemed to make him angrier. In between drinks, he would kick me in the head or he'd leap on my back, hold me by the hair and shove my face in the carpet until I could hardly breathe and I thought I was going to black out. These sessions would practically always end with my rape.

One night Dad was drinking heavily after losing £700 on a horse. He grabbed an empty bottle and threatened to smash it in my face, before trying to assault my private parts with it. I was in such fear for my life that when he stumbled to the toilet I ran into the street half naked. I had struggled back into the jeans which he had ripped off me earlier but the zip had bust so I couldn't do it up, and I only had slippers on my feet. My top half was completely naked but I managed to grab a thin jacket from the banisters as I ran to the front door. I heard his voice behind me, shouting 'Go on, fuck off, you cunt!'

As I tripped out into the cold night air, I started to run and didn't stop until I was sure Dad wasn't following. I was shivering, and trying my best to cover myself, but I hadn't a clue what to do or where to go. After sitting on a bench for about an hour, reality dawned: I had no money, nowhere to go, and was wearing hardly any clothes. I didn't have a clue how to help myself. It was so ingrained for me to shun contact with others that when a lady passed by and asked if I needed any help, I shook my head. Mum was my only option. I found a call box and reversed the charges to the company where she worked, knowing she would answer the phone at reception.

'Not again,' she moaned as if I was being a great inconvenience. 'You'd better come down here then. I suppose I'll have to send a cab as you've got hardly any bleedin' clothes on. Wait in the phone box.'

When I arrived at the other end, the cabbie said to Mum, 'She alright?'

I caught sight of myself in the mirrored reception and saw I looked a right state. My face was swollen, my hair sticking up all over the place, and I was covered in scratches and bruises. I showed Mum my fresh bite marks, but all she did was roll her eyes as she always did and make a tutting sound.

'Well, you knew what he was like with me,' she said.

Anger suddenly flared in me. 'Do you think I chose to be with him?' I screamed. 'He forced me from when I was little. I've never had a choice, and you've done nothing about it!'

'Don't blame me,' she said, shrugging. 'You're sixteen years old.'

I begged her to find me somewhere to stay. 'Where are the rest of the family living? Surely I could go and stay with them?'

Mum looked shocked and frightened. She didn't want me to contact Jenny and my brother and sisters, because then the truth would come out about what was going on at home and how long she'd known about it.

'I ain't got no addresses,' she insisted, 'so you can get that idea out of your head, do you hear me? They won't want anything to do with you anyway. Not after all this. What do you think Jenny will say when she finds out what you've done?'

'What *I've* done?' I cried, unable to believe my ears. 'I was a child. I'm the victim, Mum!'

'Look, just come home with me. He'll have fallen asleep now.'

'How can you say that?' I asked, tears streaming down my face. 'Look what he's done to me.'

She picked up the *Yellow Pages* and made a half-hearted attempt to find some kind of hostel for me, then closed it again. 'I can't do this, he'll kill me.'

'Please, I can't go back there.'

Mum rang one of the ads and spoke to someone for a few minutes, wrinkling her nose as if it was the most distasteful thing she had ever done. She slammed the phone down.

'Fuck me, you can't go there. They asked if you had your own fucking blanket!'

I couldn't see that was a problem – surely I could get a blanket somewhere? But Mum obviously thought it preferable that I go back to be raped and beaten by Dad. She spent the next half hour pleading with me to return with her, because if I didn't, surely I knew what Dad would do to her?

And then there was Kat. What if he got so mad because of me running away that he turned on her?

The minute she said that, my blood chilled, and I asked her the question I had been worrying about for a long time. 'What if he does to Kat what he's done to me? Would you do anything then?'

I thought she was going to hit me. 'Don't talk fucking stupid. She's his own flesh and blood. What kind of filth is that you're talking?'

'But he's been my dad since I was four.'

'It's not the fucking same thing. She's his blood!'

I wanted to believe her, but there was no way I could. If Dad was capable of doing those things to me, he was capable of doing them to anyone.

I went back home with Mum that night, and luckily the next morning Dad woke up with such a bad hangover and poor recollection of what had happened that I wasn't given an extra punishment for running away.

Bolstered by my taste of rebellion, I tried it again the following week, but this time Dad was sober and ran after me. I had a few minutes' head start down the road before he realised I was gone, and at first I thought I was free. I was just wondering where I should run to, when I looked over my shoulder and saw Dad sprinting after me. It was still daylight and I ran past a boy I'd sat next to in junior school. He stared at me open-mouthed. My hair and clothes were in disarray and I must have looked as though I was running for my life.

'Lisa,' he shouted after me. 'Are you alright?'

Even though I felt as if I was in some kind of horror film being chased by a monster, I felt guilty for ignoring him. But if I had answered, Dad would have heard and a boy I hadn't exchanged a word with in six years would no doubt have been turned into a secret boyfriend in his twisted mind. It didn't take long for Dad to catch up with me, and I got a vicious beating that lasted for several days, making me too scared to attempt to run away again.

I had been paralysed by my own fear and Dad's absolute control over my every movement for so many years that I began to think suicide would be my only way out. Surely he couldn't take it out on Mum and Kat if he were to find me swinging from the banisters? From then on, while he was raping me and I was trying to use the away-in-my-head technique to cope, I'd be thinking of how best to end it all. It looked so easy on the television – a quick slash on both wrists and a warm bath and that was it, sweet release. I'd even broken open one of Dad's Bic razors once and held the blade against my wrist. The reality was that I didn't think I could ever drag the blade across my skin and watch myself bleed. The truth was, I really wanted to live – just not with Dad.

Sometimes when I was pinned under Dad's legs watching television and a music video or travel programme came on, I'd feel a bubble of excitement rise up within me. I was becoming aware that the world was a big place. Most of my time had been spent staring at the same four walls, or the bottom of an office dustbin, and I yearned to see more. I didn't want to end up in a bath of my own blood because that would mean Dad had got away with murder.

Flicking through the paper one day I noticed an abundance of jobs in the back. They all sounded really exciting. Some of them even promised 'a six-figure salary, a new car and holidays abroad' in exchange for commitment and although I knew I would never walk into a job like that straight away, the thought was exciting. An idea came to me. Mum could hardly bear to look at me now because every time she did, I reminded her of what a terrible mother she was. I had heard her bending Dad's ear about me being under her feet in the house all day, and about how she couldn't relax in her own home. I decided to put a flea in her ear about me getting a job. I didn't dare raise the subject with Dad, because I was likely to get a slap.

'It'd be good if I could get a job, wouldn't it, Mum?'

'Yeah, it bloody would,' she said, her eyes widening as if she'd just had a brilliant idea. 'Don't see why it should be just muggins here slaving away.'

Over the next few weeks, Mum kept mentioning the possibility of me getting a job. Dad, of course, was dead set against it. He had waited for years until I was free of school and wouldn't contemplate it at first. He only had to raise his voice and slap a warning fist down on the table for Mum to shut up but she'd bring it up again later and eventually she touched on the one area that made him waver – money.

'She'll be bringing in a wage, Frank,' she said. 'We could do with the extra 'cos you haven't had much luck lately, have you?'

She was referring to the fact that although they earned good money cleaning, there was never enough to fund his gambling addiction and money was always tight. The electricity had been cut off twice in the past year, and we'd had to bump around with candles until they found the money to pay the bill. After that, Dad asked around at the pub over the road and, for a small fee, a bloke came and did something to bypass the meter, so we never got cut off again. But some weeks there was barely enough money for cigarettes and Mum and Dad would buy half an ounce of Old Holborn each to roll their own. When things were really bad, they'd dig through the dustbin and salvage scraps of tobacco from their dog-ends.

So it may have been the prospect of a little more money coming in that finally made Dad change his mind and allow me to get a job. I was dumbstruck but overjoyed when he hit me over the head with the *Evening Standard* one lunchtime and said, 'OK, get a fucking job then.' Suddenly the pinprick of light at the end of the tunnel enlarged, and I had fresh hope of finding a way to escape.

Dad was sceptical I would be able to find one. 'Got no qualifications now, has she?' he laughed spitefully.

But straight away my eyes landed on an ad for a junior secretary at a record company. At first Dad was against it, but when he found out it was only ten minutes' walk away his eyes lit up.

'You can come home for lunch!'

My heart sank, and so did Mum's by the way she rolled her eyes and gave a loud tut.

On the day of the interview my hands were trembling as I dug around in my drawers for something to wear. I couldn't find anything smart enough. I wore jeans when I went cleaning, and they wouldn't do. I ended up putting on my old school uniform, which looked alright because it hadn't been a proper uniform at all – just a light grey skirt and grey blouse, which had started off white.

It was a bright sunny February day, and Dad walked me the short distance to the record company offices. My confidence was at rock bottom because ever since I'd got the interview, Dad had been extra nasty, telling me I was a useless 'spastic' who didn't know my arse from my elbow. He continued now.

'They won't want you anyway,' he said. 'You haven't even got any O' Levels.'

Before I could stop myself I said, 'Yeah, but I would have had some, wouldn't I?'

'What do you mean by that?' he demanded, stopping in his tracks.

Alarm bells began to ring. 'I just meant that if I had stayed on at school, I would have sat them, and I might have got some.'

'So is that what you're gonna tell them, that you weren't allowed to go to school?' he asked. ''Cos' if you're gonna try and land me in any of that shit, I'll knock you out now.'

'No! No …'

''Cos I'll take you back home right now and you can forget all about a poxy fucking job.'

We stood and stared at each other in the street. All I could do was wait and see what happened.

235

'Come on or you'll be late,' he decided at last.

The job I was applying for was to work for the boss's nineteen-year-old son Harry, who was starting an artists' management division, and another guy called Graham who ran the agency that booked bands into gigs. The only typing experience I had ever had was the time I typed 'the cat sat on the mat' while out cleaning, so I didn't reckon my chances much, but the ad hadn't asked for previous experience so I kept my fingers crossed.

My interview was with the financial director Ros Newman, a birdlike, raven-haired woman with the blackest eyes and longest nails I had ever seen. When I filled out the bit on the application form about qualifications, I simply listed the ones I would have taken had Dad let me go to school and left the grades blank.

She gave me a typing test and I seemed to do okay. She asked me whether I took shorthand and I said no, but mentioned I might sign up for a speed-writing course I had seen advertised in the *Standard*. I didn't actually know what speedwriting was, but Ros seemed impressed.

'That shows initiative, Lisa,' she said with a smile. 'This is only a junior position, so we don't expect you to have brilliant skills to start with. You can learn as you go along.'

I smiled, and tried not to think about Dad waiting for me downstairs. Then she said something that made my heart skip a beat.

'Tell me about you, and about your family.'

I opened my mouth and stuttered for a moment, mindful of what Dad had drilled into me for years about not answering questions; the need to keep 'our fucking business, our fucking business.'

Ros's smile faded as she waited for me to speak. What could I say about Mum and Dad and my family set-up that would make anyone want to give me a job? I went for the only positive thing I could think of. 'My parents have worked for a record company in the West End for years.' I named it, and her eyes lit up.

'Oh, yes,' she said, 'I know Saul very well. Jewish family, like us. What do your parents do there?'

She may have been disappointed when I said they were the cleaners, but she positively glowed when I told her Mum always said the Jews were the best people you could possibly work for. I was thinking on my feet and putting a positive slant on Mum's views. What she actually said was 'They're alright, but they work you into the fucking ground for peanuts, tight-fisted bastards.'

When Ros saw me out, she gave me a really warm handshake. I had to suppress a wince because my right hand had been painful since Dad had stamped on it over the Indian doctor thing. Ros asked me to ring her the next morning and she'd let me know.

The first thing Dad wanted to know was how much I would get paid, and whether it was weekly or monthly.

Next morning, he walked me to the phone box under the railway bridge and stood outside while I rang Ros.

'Hello, Lisa,' she said. 'I'm pleased to tell you you've got the job. Can you start next Monday?'

Dad took me up the market so I could buy some work clothes. I got a couple of skirts and jumpers and a new pair of shoes. I was all kitted out, and suddenly the sky looked brighter. I read my horoscope in *The Sun* that day and it said I was about to enter a new cycle. I felt as though I was on the crest of a brand new wave.

Chapter Eighteen

I started work at the record company and suddenly my life went from four walls and Dad's abuse to mixing with a lot of musicians. The rest of the staff there were young and carefree, going to gigs most evenings and socialising with the bands. I'd fill out contracts for the gigs, complete with the bands' requests for vodka and cheese-and-onion crisps in the dressing room. I was always being offered free tickets to concerts but of course I could never go.

Dad liked the fact I brought home a wage every month. He marched me up to the bank to open an account, and every month my salary was paid in. He took most of it, saying it was to pay for my keep, but I got a small allowance for toiletries such as sanitary towels and the odd new skirt.

I wasn't allowed to mix with the other young people who worked at the company and I could tell they thought I was a bit of an oddball. Matters were made worse by the fact that every lunchtime Mum and Dad would meet me at the pub opposite. It used to be very awkward because everybody at the office used the pub too, and they would wonder why I didn't say hello. If I had, Dad would think I was 'having it off' with them, even if it was a woman.

So there I'd be, relatively normal in the office and yet at lunchtime I couldn't even make eye contact with people who only a minute before I'd been chatting with at the photocopier, or making a cup of coffee for. It was especially awkward with Harry and Graham, my bosses. They were only young, and would often flirt with me, flashing smiles and making jokes, as they would with all the other young girls in the office. Over time I think they came to understand that my inhibition was less to do with shyness than something weird.

Sometimes, at five to one, just as I was getting ready to leave and meet Mum and Dad, Harry would ask me to go over to the sandwich shop and get him an egg mayonnaise on brown. My blood would run cold because I knew it would make me late for Dad, and there was no explanation as far as he was concerned other than that I had been having it off behind the filing cabinets.

At home Dad started a new regime. Every day when I got in from work there would be a knicker inspection in which I would have to remove my underwear and let him check it for semen. Some days I'd get an exploratory finger up the vagina too. Even if there was no evidence of sperm, I would be punished if Dad deemed it too moist because according to him that meant I had been fantasising about having it off behind the filing cabinets

I used to wonder why Dad let me go to work. Was it because he wanted time with Mum for 'afternoon naps'? I hoped they might fall in love all over again, but in the meantime I began to plan how I would get away. It was difficult to imagine, because life was like a treadmill, each day running into the next with my every moment accounted for. Dad had timed the walk to work and if I was even a few minutes late home he would hurt me in countless ways. On the days he didn't meet me at lunchtime he would insist I came home, so I never had a moment to myself.

Since Dad had told Mum I was now his girlfriend, they had continued to share a bed, but one day I arrived home from work and found her transferring her possessions into my room. She was doing a swap. Even though things were bad, this was even worse. It seemed to make everything more real.

'What are you doing,' I asked, feeling faint.

'What's it fucking look like?' she snapped. 'This is what his Lordship wants, and what he wants, he gets.'

I looked on, paralysed with shock. I had to find a way out of this. But I didn't have a clue where to turn.

At Christmas 1983, the record company were having a party for employees in the West End. When I told Dad, I expected him to refuse to let me go, but he thought that might appear odd and above all he didn't want me to lose the job. He knew that everyone wondered about my failure to mingle, so decided that if I were to stand any chance of keeping the job, I would have to go to the Christmas party. However, he announced that he would come along – as my boyfriend.

I felt physically sick at the thought of going anywhere in public with Dad, not to mention introducing him to everyone at work, so I was delighted when I found out that partners weren't invited. But Dad was furious. He'd already been down the market together with Mum and chosen a grey suede dress for me to wear. It was really tarty and not me at all. Because it was so clingy, it rode up when I wore tights. I said I didn't want to wear it but for some reason Dad insisted: 'We've paid good money for that.' He told me to put stockings on instead of tights. 'I can look forward to you coming home, then,' he smirked.

My heart sank, because you could see the outline of the suspenders through the fabric.

I couldn't work out what was going on. What was he doing pushing me to go to a Christmas party in a tarty dress with stockings showing through?

'I feel sick,' I said, trying to find a way to get out of it because I knew it would only mean trouble.

'You're fucking going,' he said.

On the night, I met the receptionist, a girl called Susie, because we had planned to travel there together in a taxi.

'You should come out more often,' she said. 'Get to know everyone.'

I tried not to look happy because I knew Dad was watching from the corner and I didn't want to make him angry. When we arrived at the restaurant, the first thing I did before checking in my coat in was go to the loo and remove the stockings Dad had told me to wear. I put them in my coat pocket.

When I walked into the restaurant I could see all my colleagues were taken aback by my transformation. Usually I wore frumpy clothes but tonight the dress was what would be considered quite sexy. I felt very uncomfortable and tried to slink into the background and not draw attention to myself. I grabbed a glass of champagne from a tray that was being handed round to try and ease my nerves. I wasn't used to alcohol and it went straight to my head, but thanks to that champagne I was able to get through the evening without worrying too much about what would happen when I got home.

After the meal, everyone said they were going on to another club, but I knew I had to get back. I remember standing in the queue for the coats and when I got mine, Susie noticed the stockings poking out of my coat and pointed them out to Graham, my boss. They had a little laugh about it, to my great embarrassment. Outside, Susie and someone else I worked with called Neville put me in a black taxi.

When I got home, I jumped out and paid the cab. It pulled off. As I approached the front door to let myself in, Dad flung it open and dragged me in by the hair. I had never seen him in more of a rage. He beat me senseless, kicking me all over the room. Much of it's a blur but he was shouting that I had come home in a white Rover car instead of a black taxi and he wanted to know who was in the car. I was the biggest cunt, the biggest slut in the world. Look I'd even taken the stockings off. He pulled my hair and bit me all over. He stripped me of my clothes and raped me anally. Usually he tried not to mark my face but the next day I had a big bruise down one side of it. He interrogated me mercilessly all night long, while drinking vodka and flicking lit cigarettes at my eyes.

All the while Mum was upstairs. She couldn't possibly have slept through it because he was screaming and raging like a madman. I remember at one point he made me drink neat vodka. I was choking and a part of me just wanted to die. I was sick immediately afterwards, and for that he beat me even more. By the end of it all I was delirious with confusion and I was even starting to wonder whose white Rover I had come home in and who I had had sex with in the back.

For days and days the interrogations and beatings continued. I had to go over everything about the evening in minute detail. He kept asking me about the white Rover but I didn't know anything about a white Rover. He even dragged me down to the restaurant in the West End to check on the road configuration and the flow of traffic in the place where I said I had got the taxi. The whole time I had been at the record company I had never flirted with anybody, even though there was plenty of opportunity since everyone I worked with was young and there were lots of bands in all the time. I just knew it was more than my life was worth to flirt with anyone, and I got upset if any of the guys were playful with me. I didn't know how to handle normal social interactions like that.

Christmas was terrible, with Dad's violence continuing as viciously as ever. I was a nervous wreck. On my seventeenth birthday, just before New Year, Dad's sister Lesley turned up unexpectedly with her two sons Charlie and George and another relative I hadn't met before.

Nobody apart from Mum knew what Dad had done to me. As far as they were concerned, I was still the daughter. I ran and hid in the bathroom because I didn't know how to behave in front of them – it was all too much. I found it hard not to scream and blurt out what was happening to me. Dad followed, and told me through gritted teeth to get that grey dress on as we were all going over the pub.

Now that I was older, Dad allowed me to drink wine and I took refuge in that, standing alone at the end of the bar as Dad chatted to his nephew in the corner. At one stage I went to the toilet and when I came back everyone had gone. Just like that. I walked over the road home and it was obvious there had been a row of some sort. Everyone was being cagey and because I was still treated as a 'child' nobody explained anything. In fact, nobody spoke to me. Lesley and her boys had gone but the female relative I had never met before was still there.

Suddenly there was a bang at the door. A few voices said 'There they are' and Dad got up to go to the door, looking strangely reluctant.

There were a few raised voices then I heard some crashing sounds. We all ran out to see what was going on and found Dad face down on the pathway with blood pooling at the side of his head.

I knew that the fight was about me because everyone turned to look at me, and I started crying hysterically. After the sustained beatings I had taken over the mystery white Rover during the past couple of weeks, I knew Dad would blame me. He might even kill me, as he was always saying he would.

I couldn't take any more. In bare feet and the stupid skimpy dress, I ran out of the door, past where Dad lay on the ground, and across to the pub. The barman who had been serving us all night was leaving because it was after closing time. 'What's happened?' he asked but I didn't answer, just kept running.

I came to a phone box and realised that if Dad was dead, I should tell the police, and if he wasn't, he would be mad as hell that I didn't get an ambulance and save his life. I stopped at the phone and called both the police and an ambulance. The lady on the switchboard told me to go back home so I did.

As I got there, a squad car was just pulling up. I noticed Dad was no longer lying on the ground. The front door opened and Mum pulled me in quickly. I could hear somebody explaining to the police that it had all been a misunderstanding. Dad was sitting on a chair holding a cloth to his head. At that moment I just wanted it to all come out, I wanted the police to know what had been going on, and I started screaming. But the front door had been closed by that time and the police were driving off. The relative I didn't know came over and gave me a hard slap.

'Calm down, darlin',' she said. 'Your Dad's alright – look.'

Like everything else, the incident was never mentioned again but Dad let something slip, which was to confirm to me that Lesley and her family now knew about the 'secret'. He said that when I went off to the toilet that night he could see his nephew Charlie following me with his eyes. Because Dad was drunk and careless he said to him, 'Too late. I've had her, she's mine.'

I like to think that a sense of decency prompted one of them to knock him out, but I don't know the full truth.

Some time early in the New Year, Dad's elder brother Keith came to the house. I remember my mum saying to Dad 'Keith's here' and Dad saying 'You've told him, haven't you, you cunt?'

I ran upstairs, mortified and frightened. I crouched on the landing outside my bedroom from where I could hear Keith saying to Dad 'But she's almost the same age as my Alison.' That was his own daughter, who was only a few months younger than me. 'How could you do this? You said you wanted to adopt her when she was little.'

Dad replied, 'I love her.'

Keith said, 'What about her? Bring her down here. I want to hear it for myself.'

Dad came up the first flight of stairs and said, 'Come down here and tell him.'

I could see the warning in his eyes and hear it underlying his tone of voice but there was no way I was going to go down and tell Keith what Dad wanted me to say, which was that I loved him too and it was a dream come true. It was all a lie. All I could do was cry like a baby and say I didn't want to. Keith must have heard that, at least. In my confused head, I even thought this would be the end of it. Perhaps Keith would take me home. I wondered if they'd let me live in their caravan?

But just like everyone else who found out that this brute of a man was sleeping with the stepdaughter he had brought up since she was four, Keith accepted it. As if a young girl like me, with the rest of her life in front of her, would make that ludicrous choice. As if one day after my sixteenth birthday I'd looked at Dad over the oven chips and decided, without any coercion or grooming, that yes, he was the violent drunken bully for me. He was the one. None of them insisted on getting to the truth. None of them tried to speak to me without Dad's looming presence. I had no one to help me, and I didn't have a clue how to help myself. My isolation was total.

Chapter Nineteen

As well as insisting on seeing me at lunchtime, Dad took to ringing me at work during the day and screaming obscenities down the phone. Susie the receptionist asked me who the man was that kept calling me. I had to tell her it was a boyfriend because he certainly wasn't acting like a dad. It became a standing joke with the office girls that I was seeing an 'old bloke' who was a bit of a jealous nutter. So whenever Dad rang, Susie the receptionist recognised his voice and she would say to me 'It's your mad boyfriend'. I'd have to dart into a spare office or an empty corner where nobody could over-hear the screaming coming from the phone. He would rant that he was going to storm in and kill me and everybody else there.

One day he called in the middle of the afternoon from the phone box in the street downstairs, demanding that I leave the building. He said that if I didn't come down in the next five minutes, he would come up and get me. At that time, I thought that he was the most powerful man on earth. Totally fearless. I thought that if I didn't go out to him, someone might get hurt. I don't know why, but clearly upset I asked to see Ros Newman, the woman who had originally given me the job. In a garbled fashion I explained that I had to go home early. I told her that I had a very jealous boyfriend who had become convinced I was having an affair with someone who drove a white Rover and it had all started after the office party. I didn't tell her that the boyfriend was my Dad and that he was effectively keeping me prisoner. She seemed concerned about me but gave me permission to leave.

As I got down the office stairs I could see Dad waiting for me, and my legs were shaking with fear. He seemed wild with rage. Without seeming to care who saw, he dragged me into the office car park and pulled me by the hair over to a white car. I was petrified.

'What the fuck's that then?' he screamed. 'It's a white fucking Rover, you whore.'

I was in the worst nightmare imaginable. After kicking me about the place and screaming in my face for answers he pinned me by the throat to the back windscreen and started choking me. Just when I thought I was going to pass out, he threw me aside on the ground and shouted 'fucking cunts' at the top of his voice. With that he brought both fists down on the back window of the car and it shattered into smithereens. There was a shocked stillness for a moment or two. I think he was surprised at his own strength.

As I lay sprawled on the ground sobbing and Dad stood motionless by the car, the company accountant happened to be passing with some paperwork.

He squinted into the gloom, took everything in and said hesitantly, 'What are you doing in there? That's Stuart King's car.'

At that point a whole crowd of people emerged from the studio to see what was causing all the noise. There were murmurings about the police being called so Dad grabbed my arm and dragged me off. All the way home he kept pushing me into shop doorways to hit and kick me.

'Who the fuck's Stuart King?' he kept spitting in my face.

I tried to tell the truth, that I had barely spoken to him the whole time I'd been at the company, but Dad wasn't in a mood to listen. When he got me home he raped me sadistically and covered me with bites all over.

As I had told Ros Newman about a raving boyfriend and a white Rover, and the next minute a member of staff had witnessed me sobbing on the ground next to a smashed-up white Rover, I wondered if perhaps the police might pay us a visit, but they never came. I think Ros took pity on me and didn't want to cause me any trouble, but it was another lost opportunity for the abuse to come out.

I couldn't go back to work after that. A few days later Dad decided that they had diddled me out of some pay I was due and marched me down to the phone box to call and ask for it. He stood with the door open as I spoke, poking me in the ribs if I didn't say the right thing.

First I spoke to the managing director's secretary. 'I don't want to be awkward,' I said, trying to explain to her telepathically what was going on.

'But you are being, aren't you?' she replied. 'I'll put you through to Ros.'

Ros, who was older and wiser, said 'I don't think this is you, Lisa. I think someone is making you do this.'

What could I say with Dad's foot holding the door open to listen? I was relieved she didn't mention the car or what had happened in the car park.

'You're a good worker,' she said. 'Don't let that boyfriend ruin any more chances for you. Take care.'

I was jobless now but Dad was keen for me to get more work as he missed my wages. Since I didn't have any qualifications my options were limited, but I got a job at a fashionable tanning salon in Mayfair. At first I was an assistant to the controller who operated the machines and took the money, but I quickly proved myself and was promoted to a more responsible position. I even had to cash up, lock up and take the takings to the night-safe round the corner when I was on evening shifts.

One good thing was that it wasn't so easy for Dad to meet me all the time as it had been when I worked at the record company. He still phoned me at work at least once every day and he would pick me up after my evening shifts. If nobody else was around he would ransack the reception, scattering leaflets and spilling bottles all over the place. He'd grab the keys to old lockers where lost clothing was kept, convinced that this was where the 'kinky' outfits were kept. I'd be petrified that the owners would pop by on their way home from dinner, as they sometimes used to do.

There was a girl called Bridget who also worked there. She was very worldly-wise and had previously lived in New York, where she had owned a boutique. She liked me and took me under her wing. I think she could tell that something wasn't quite right with the 'boyfriend' who she saw picking me up a couple of times. As we worked more shifts together, she began telling me about her violent first marriage and explaining how she escaped from it, but I was so guarded that I gave nothing away about my own circumstances. I was still riddled with guilt and shame that Dad was my 'boyfriend'.

Meanwhile, out of the blue one Wednesday, Dad awkwardly announced that he and my mum had been granted a divorce. This was the first I'd known of it. Neither of them had mentioned it was happening, but then we were far from a normal family where such a discussion might take place. My spirits soared and I was careful to hide my jubilation in case Dad gave me a back-hander. Mum was finally taking action and was going to kick Dad out of our lives. I had hoped and prayed she would come through in the end.

Later, when Dad was out of earshot upstairs, engrossed in the racing on television, I had a word with Mum in the kitchen.

'I hear you're getting a divorce,' I said grinning and doing a little hop of elation.

Mum frowned as she dunked a teabag in Dad's mug before dumping it into a sink full of greasy plates. She turned slowly, her face set in a sneer.

'We didn't want to, but we've been forced into it now that Lesley's lot have found out about you,' she said pointedly. 'They've been asking questions and we can't have that, can we?'

A ripple of dread ran through me. This wasn't going as I'd hoped. I felt my face fall as Mum went on.

'It'd look mighty fucking odd if we all continued living here together forever,' she hissed.

The rollercoaster of emotion I was on took an upwards turn. 'You mean Dad's moving out?'

Mum nodded. 'Yeah, he is, and you're going with him.'

'No!' I shouted, unable to contain my horror.

'Shush,' she said urgently. 'He don't want you to know until the last minute. Don't you tell him I've told you.'

This couldn't be happening. I spent the next few days in turmoil, wondering how I could save myself but I couldn't think of anything. Dad had spent years making me believe that I was useless, worthless and powerless. I had no money because Dad took almost all my wages every month, no friends, and no family other than Mum. I was so beaten down I couldn't see any options for a way out. Running into a police station and screaming for help didn't even occur to me. It was a Wednesday morning when Dad officially broke the news.

'Get your bags packed. We're moving out on Saturday,' he told me. 'I've got us a flat up the road.'

'But why …?' I started to ask, but before I had time to finish, Dad had thrown his 'World's Best Husband' mug in my lap. Scalding tea soaked through my skirt, running in rivulets into my knickers. I jumped up in pain, and the mug rolled off my lap and bounced on the floor, breaking the handle.

Dad leapt up from the sofa and scooped it up. 'Look what you've fucking done, you good-for-nothing cunt.'

'Sorry, Dad,' I said automatically, backing away.

'Stop calling me Dad! My name's Frank. Call me Frank, for fuck's sake.'

'OK, but why do we have to move?'

'I'm sick of you, with your "Why this? Why fucking that?"' he shouted, slapping my face with the back of his hand. A dribble of blood ran from my nose. 'Just do as you're fucking told, got it?'

'Yes, Dad.' I said, cowering.

He slapped me again. 'It's Frank, remember? I'm not your fucking Dad.'

Over the next few days I stopped eating, unable to keep anything down.

'You're so fucking vain,' said Mum, insinuating I was trying to lose weight. 'He don't care what you look like as long as you've got a hole he can poke.'

I broke down then, sliding down the wall in the dining room, until I lay curled up on the floor.

'What a fucking actress,' Mum jeered. 'I tell you what, you should get a fucking Oscar.'

'I can't go, I can't,' I sobbed.

'Tell him that, not me,' Mum said coldly, an unlit cigarette clamped between her lips. 'This is what you wanted, isn't it?'

'No, it's not!' I bellowed so loudly that Mum jumped and I felt my temples bulge.

'Keep your fucking voice down,' she said, removing her cigarette temporarily. 'He'll be back in a minute and he'll fucking scalp you if he hears.'

'Where do Jenny and Diane live?' I demanded.

'I don't fucking know,' Mum insisted, 'and you should be fucking grateful I don't. Nanny'd be turning in her fucking grave, she would.'

I blocked my ears against Mum's spite and ran up to my room. Not for the first time I lay on my bed and wondered if any of this was my fault. My mind strayed back to the days when Dad first came to live with us. I remembered his lewd and crude ways, the nudity and the surreptitious touching and I understood for the first time that Dad had a vile plan right from the very start. That much was clear to me; what I continued to struggle with was how to get out of it.

On the day of the move, Mum helped, laughing and joking with Dad, all chummy as usual – still the best of friends. When Dad said goodbye, he gave her a lingering kiss and pinched her bum.

'See you later, Donna,' said Dad. 'About four o'clock should do it. Means I get a lay in.'

'Jammy bastard,' laughed Mum.

The plan was that every morning Mum would stop off in a taxi and pick Dad up so they could go to work together as usual. Nothing seemed to have changed between them. This whole move to the flat was a smoke screen, designed to make it look as though Dad and I were in a relationship. This scenario was hard enough for the family to swallow, bearing in mind how long he had been my father, but the alternative – that he had been abusing me since I was very young, and he and Mum were still very much together – would have been even harder and would have stirred up all sorts of problems.

The flat was very small, on the first floor of a converted house, and about ten minutes away from Mum's place. There was a tiny kitchen and bathroom, a cramped living room at the front and a dark bedroom at the back. There was no furniture, but Mum and Dad had thought about that.

A few days later, they marched me into various furniture shops, picked out what they wanted, and told the salesman that it was for their daughter's first flat. I was made to sign credit agreements in my name for everything. I felt sick with fear the whole time but too terrorised to object to the new arrangement.

Once Dad had me alone in the flat, things went from bad to worse. Now there were no constraints, he was free to be as violent and sadistic as he wanted. He was drinking more and more and remained convinced that I was sleeping with all sorts of other men the minute his back was turned. I tried to explain that this would be impossible even if I wanted to, because he knew where I was at every minute of the day.

'Oh, so you want to fuck every Tom, Dick and Harry, do you?' he'd shout, his face twisted in fury. 'You just don't have the fucking time, is that it?'

There was no reasoning with him, ever.

He didn't seem to worry about marking my face now. His new thing was to headbutt me in the face, giving me a nosebleed or a big lump on my forehead.

On quite a few occasions I thought he was going to kill me and I ran all the way home to Mum's house, hoping that she would finally listen and try to help me. What mother wouldn't help her daughter in a situation like this?

Once I arrived with a swollen eye and a cut lip, naked apart from my underwear and a coat. I knocked at the front door, and rang the bell for ages before she bothered to answer it. I could see the television flickering through the drawn curtains.

'What do you keep coming round here for?' she cried as she opened the door and I stumbled inside. 'I've told you, he only gets the fucking hump with me.'

'Please, Mum, he's getting worse. You've got to help me.'

'I ain't got to do nothing,' she snarled in my face. 'Now why don't you fuck off back to him. Or do you want him to wake Kat when he comes round and starts screaming blue murder?'

I felt I had no choice but to turn around and go back then. I didn't want Kat to wake up frightened. The only good thing about us being in the flat was that Kat didn't have to witness Dad's rampages quite so much any more. Mum was right. What was the point? Dad always knew where I was, and always came to get me. I was seventeen now and the only thing I could think to do was to walk back to my abuser.

We hardly ever went out, which was how I preferred it because I imagined everybody could see the 'secret' and I was too ashamed. Dad was twenty years older than me, but years of smoking, drinking and unhealthy food had left him looking as though he was due his bus pass. His hair was thinning, and his eyes, like currants, were almost lost in the puffy bags that sat beneath them. The fact he hardly bothered to wash didn't help matters. He looked unkempt, old and raddled compared to my baby-faced looks and the contrast between us was startling enough to provoke double-takes. Most people would think I was with my dad until he came out with a lewd comment or made a grab for me.

Despite his ageing appearance, Dad remained very strong and fast. Once I watched as he knocked down two young lads who were looking at me, so I always used to dread it when he insisted on an outing because I knew it would end in disaster. One day he took me to France on the ferry because he wanted to stock up on duty-free cigarettes. When we reached the port, it took two stewards and some other passengers to rouse him from his drunken stupor. All the way home he interrogated me about what I'd been up to with an imagined man while he was asleep. Inevitably he beat me when we got home, throwing glasses and ashtrays at the wall behind my head.

Once he took me to a disco off Oxford Street. I'd try to drink as much as possible because it helped me to cope with the shame of being with him, and this went some way to anaesthetise the pain. But unfortunately, it made me make mistakes. If he said jump, I had to jump – and fast. If he said lie down in the gutter, I'd have to do it without question. When I had been drinking my reaction times weren't always quick enough to respond to his commands, or I would lack the power of logic needed to talk my way out of danger, as I'd had to do so many times. Inside the club that night he took a bite out of my lip. It wouldn't stop bleeding and my clothes were covered in blood. A group of girls took me into the toilet and offered to get me home to my mum. How could I explain that she would be totally useless and there was no way I could escape from the pig outside? All the way home that night he beat me – in the street, in the cab – and no one helped. When we got inside he really went to town before once again raping me anally, which he did whenever he wanted to punish me. Luckily I passed out for most of it.

When Mum turned up at four in the morning to pick him up for work, I buzzed her up to the flat. For once, she had the good grace to look worried. My face was swollen, my lips cut and double their normal size, with caked-on blood; the dress I had been wearing was hanging in shreds from my waist and beneath it my whole body was covered in bruises, scratches and bite marks.

After tutting that she'd have to go to work on her own, she told me to be sure to come round to her place the next day when I got up. I wondered what protection she thought she was suddenly going to offer me? As it happened, I fell asleep again, only to wake up with Dad screaming that I'd managed to lose one of my earrings.

I was so petrified that I jumped out of bed and ran out of the flat and all the way back to Mum's as passersby stared after me. She let me stay for a couple of days because I was in such a state and on this occasion Dad didn't come for me immediately, as he usually would. When I tried to start a conversation about Dad's violence, she didn't want to know.

'Change the bleedin' record, will ya?' she'd say. 'What's this got to do with me? It's your fucking problem, not mine any more, thank fuck.'

Two days later, when Dad came round to fetch me, she ushered me out the door: 'Off you go – and try not to upset him again 'cos I won't open the door next time.'

One day, I got a cab home from the day shift at the tanning salon because I'd missed the bus and Dad had insisted I be home at a certain time. As I got out of the cab I noticed a brown envelope on the seat next to my bag and without thinking I picked it up. I could see Dad watching me out of the window.

After he'd inspected my knickers for semen and my body for love bites, I showed him the envelope. I could hardly believe my eyes when I saw that it contained about £5,000 in used notes. He was ecstatic.

'Shouldn't we hand it in to the police?' I asked.

'Don't be so fucking stupid,' he said, throwing handfuls of it in the air. 'It's a gift from fucking God, isn't it?'

It's very telling that at the time, I was so conditioned and beaten down that it never occurred to me that I could have hidden that money from Dad and used it to rent a flat and start a new life of my own. Dad was all-powerful and no matter where I went, I believed he would always get me in the end.

He lost most of that money at the bookies, and spent some on drink, but a hundred pounds went on buying me a fake diamond solitaire, which was his idea of an engagement ring. It made me sick to wear it and I used to 'forget' to put it on, but that made him mad. Usually I'd slip it in my pocket when I got to the tanning salon, but once Bridget saw it and asked me where it was from. I burned with shame as I told her my boyfriend had given it to me, and tried to ignore the worried look in her eyes.

I always thought people could see the truth and that they knew he was really my abusive dad, and I felt ashamed, as though it was my fault. I didn't realise that what Bridget saw was someone stuck in a violent relationship, as she had once been, and too lacking in confidence and self-esteem to take action to end the situation. She could spot that a mile off.

Chapter Twenty

Just before Christmas 1984, the owner of the tanning salon announced he was taking all the staff out for dinner and then on to Tramp, the famous nightclub – and what's more, partners were welcome to join us after dinner. On the night, I tried to feign illness but Dad pushed me into the cab to go to the restaurant, giving me a secret dig in the ribs. He slammed the taxi door on one of my legs, hissing that he'd see me later. The times when he was nice were few and far between now.

All evening I was frozen with fear, anticipating the moment Dad would arrive. When he did turn up, I could tell he had already been drinking heavily. He was totally out of his depth in the sophisticated environment and company. Later on I heard that my boss had warned everyone to watch out for him as he looked like trouble. People tried to make conversation but he would just glare at me and we ended up sitting in a corner while everyone else danced and celebrated the festive season.

I noticed Bridget watching me a lot, as did Dad.

'What the fuck's she keep looking at, fat-arsed cunt?' he demanded.

He led me to the dance floor for a slow dance, so that he could get me on my own to give me a painful squeeze and a warning whisper.

'What the fuck have you been saying to that slag? I can see her looking at us.'

He spat into my ear and dug his nails into my back through the soft material of my dress, so hard that they drew blood. The pain must have registered on my face, no matter how hard I tried to look impassive, because at the end of the dance, Bridget came over and asked me to go to the loo with her.

I could see Dad was absolutely furious but I went anyway, not knowing how to refuse.

'Are you alright?' Bridget asked once we were on our own.

'Yes, I'm fine,' I insisted, trying to hold back the tears.

'Are you sure?' She obviously didn't believe me so I tried to muster a weak smile.

'I'm sure,' I said quietly.

When I got back outside, Dad announced we were leaving. As he marched me up the stairs of the club, hissing and spitting in my face, I suddenly felt in fear of my life. He had promised to kill me so many times and I really felt this was the night. I knew if I left the club with him, I might end up dead. He was completely beyond reason, consumed by rage.

I stopped suddenly, shrugged my arm loose and pressed myself into the wall, whimpering with fear. All I knew was that I didn't dare leave this place where there were people who could restrain him. If I was on my own with him, I didn't think I'd live through the night.

He went berserk, kicking and stamping on my feet and legs, shredding my tights and causing a bleeding gash on my shin.

Somehow I managed to pull away, limping badly, and ran into the ladies' loo for safety. It was very surreal. A girl was applying her lipstick and she looked up, surprised at the sight of me. Suddenly the door burst open and Dad made a final lunge for me. Fortunately, the club's bouncers were on him in seconds and they dragged him out. I slumped down on a chair, trembling, unable to speak.

Bridget appeared and crouched beside me. 'It's alright, he's gone. They've chucked him out.'

'But he'll be waiting outside for me,' I whispered. 'I've got nowhere to go.' I couldn't risk going back to Mum's because that's the first place he would look for me.

'Don't worry,' Bridget said firmly. 'You're coming home with me tonight.'

Her kindness made my tears well up and spill over. I don't know if she realised it, but she had probably saved my life.

That night, Bridget tucked me into her spare bed as if I were a small child. 'Try and get some sleep,' she urged.

I was exhausted, and after tossing and turning for a while, I fell into a deep sleep. I woke with a start the following morning, my heart racing in panic as I struggled to orientate myself to my new surroundings. Where was I – and, more importantly, where was Dad? My stomach clenched in knots as panic rose within me.

I heard the bustle of the West End traffic coming from the street below, and someone stirring a cup in the kitchen. It was

265

Bridget. Memories of last night and how I had refused to leave the club with Dad came flooding back and I knew it was over. There was no way I was ever going back. It was as if a spell had been broken. I realised I would rather be dead than suffer his abuse any more. I pulled back the sheets and looked at my shins. They were bruised and bloodied, but somehow I could barely feel any pain. My mind was whirling with so many thoughts and emotions that my body felt curiously numb.

There was a little tap at the bedroom door, and Bridget appeared with a cup of tea for me. 'How'd you sleep?' she asked. 'Alright?'

I pulled the sheet back over my legs, and sat up in bed. 'Thanks,' I said, taking the steaming cup of tea. 'I'm really sorry …'

'Hey, listen,' she said, 'You've got nothing to be sorry for. It's that pig who should be sorry, not you. I know about men like him, trust me … and you don't have to put up with it any more.'

For a moment I thought she meant she knew about dads like him and I felt myself starting to colour with shame, but then she asked, 'Is there anyone I can call? What about your parents? We should let them know you're safe.'

'I don't have a dad,' I said, dropping my eyes, 'and … and Frank's really friendly with Mum. She'll think it's my fault.'

I burst into tears, upset that I didn't have the courage to be honest with Bridget when she was being so kind. She didn't have to help me. It wasn't as if we were friends. I was just the oddball who worked some shifts with her at the tanning salon.

She owed me nothing, but she was a good person, reaching out to a virtual stranger.

'I've rung work and told them you won't be in today,' she said, patting my hand. 'I'll run you a nice bath, OK? Try not to worry.'

By lunchtime, the tight knot in my stomach had eased slightly to be replaced with the tentative flutter of butterflies as I began to realise that life without Dad was actually a real possibility. For now, at least, I was safe from the sort of violence and degradation that had become my normality over many years. I was grateful for the liveried doorman downstairs, who Bridget assured me was paid to keep undesirables out of the building.

Her flat was so luxurious that I was almost frightened to touch anything. The sofas were made of the softest leather, and the pile of the white carpet was deep and springy beneath my battered feet. I was reminded of the places I used to clean with Mum when I was very young. I couldn't help but think the marbled bathroom, as well-equipped as any spa, would be a nightmare to polish. Even the air was sweet, a mixture of expensive leather and bowls of exotically fragranced pot pourri. I was more accustomed to the stench of overflowing ashtrays, alcohol and rancid bacon fat. Bridget laughed when she caught me taking deep lungful after lungful.

'You're such a funny little thing,' she said.

'It's just so lovely here. You're so lucky.'

'Oh, it's not mine,' she explained. 'I flat-sit for a company. They use it as a *pied à terre*.'

I didn't know what she meant at first.

'Saves them paying for hotels. Problem is, they could need it at any minute and I'd have to go and stay with my mum for a few days. I'm not really allowed to have anyone staying here.'

The last thing I wanted to do was get Bridget in trouble, so I assured her I would start looking around for a place straight away. How I would go about that, I didn't know, so I was more than a little relieved when she said she had heard through a friend about the possibility of a room in Shepherd's Bush. 'If it was up to me you could stay here – but it's not, unfortunately.'

The tanning salon was only a fifteen-minute walk from the flat, but I was too scared to walk there on my own the next day so Bridget came with me all the way, reassuring me that nobody could hurt me any more. I wanted to believe her, but I knew what Dad was like. I tried not to think what he would do to me if he found me. I kept looking over my shoulder, convinced that he would grab me by the hair at any minute.

'You're a nervous wreck,' Bridget commented with concern in her eyes.

When we arrived at work, I had other things to worry about because everyone crowded around me in reception, eager to hear about my violent boyfriend. They all said they could tell what type he was the minute they saw him, and they were surprised I was seeing someone so old.

'He looked old enough to be your dad,' said one girl, causing me to jump in alarm.

I felt so ashamed of my past that I was determined none of them would find out the real truth, but it was difficult to fend off their questions. Where had I met him? What did my family think? Had he hit me in the past? I didn't know how to answer. All I felt was the familiar sense of guilt enveloping me and I wondered if I would ever be able to shrug it off. How could I even begin to articulate what had been happening to me since I was a little girl? I was convinced that if they knew, they would feel nothing but disgust for me. The most important thing was to hide the truth inside – bury it away as far and as deep in my mind as I possibly could.

But still the questions kept coming.

'Surely you could move back in with your parents?' suggested the manageress. 'He wouldn't dare turn up there, would he?'

Everyone around me nodded. 'Yeah, they could call the police.'

At that moment, I caught Bridget's eye. She knew I wasn't ready to talk. 'Let's just give her a break, shall we?' she said. 'The best thing she can do is carry on as normal. Help take her mind off it.'

It was during that first shift back at work that the telephone calls began. Mum had recently moved into a new flat, and for the first time ever she had installed a phone line. Seemingly she had been ringing non-stop asking where I was the day before.

'Here, Lisa,' someone handed me the phone. 'She must be mad with worry.'

My heart lifted at the thought that maybe Mum cared about me after all.

'Mum, it's OK, I'm alright,' I said into the phone.

Seconds later, I had to lift the phone away from my ear as she screamed down the line. 'Oh, so that's alright then. As long as you're fucking alright, sod the fucking rest of us.'

I stood rooted to the spot in shock.

'Now listen to me, you little fucker. You get yourself home, do you bleedin' hear me? He's going fucking mad here.'

I could hear Dad in the background, ranting and raving as usual. 'Fucking whore. You tell her to come home. Fucking shit-cunt.'

The manageress stared at me with her mouth open and a look of confusion on her face, obviously able to hear the shouting. 'Who is it, Lisa?' she asked, obviously unable to believe it was my mother on the phone.

'I'm not coming back,' I said, my legs trembling beneath me.

'You're a fucking selfish bitch, always have been. Do you know that?' she shouted. 'You've left me right fucking in it. Can you hear him? He's doing his nut here. But as long as you're alright, eh?'

I was angry then. 'You don't have to put up with him either, Mum,' I cried. 'You've always had a choice, which is more than any of us kids had.'

Dad snatched the phone then. 'Listen, you bitch, you get your fucking arse back here before I have to come and get you.'

At that point, the manageress took the phone from me and slammed it down.

'He's coming, he's coming,' I panicked.

'Quite frankly, I hope he does. Then we can call the police and let them deal with him.' She had real anger in her voice. 'He should be ashamed of himself, beating up a young girl.'

'What on earth is he doing at your mother's?' asked Bridget, incredulous. 'Why would she want you to go back to him?'

I was wondering how to answer when the phone rang again. The manageress snatched up the receiver to be greeted by a barrage of abuse that Bridget and I could hear, too.

'If either of you call here again, I'll ring the police,' she said, a distinct tremble in her voice. Suddenly the shouting stopped, and she calmly replaced the handset. 'That's got them worried. They hung up.'

I spent the rest of my shift jumping every time the door opened. After work, Bridget hailed a taxi to take us the short distance back to the sanctuary of the flat, as she could see that the phone calls had terrified me. She couldn't have been kinder to me during the few days I stayed there.

Then on the 23rd of December, she drove me over to Shepherd's Bush to look at the room for rent that her friends had told her about. Although the area wasn't the best, the room itself was fresh and clean, the landlord was friendly and the rent was cheap.

'Can I move in now?' I asked.

'But what about all your stuff?' the landlord asked.

'Here it is,' I said, holding up a carrier bag. I only had the clothes I stood up in and a few bits and pieces Bridget had given me until I could afford to buy some new things of my own.

As I waved Bridget off that evening, I felt a confusing mix of two very distinct emotions: both excitement and fear. On the one hand I was ecstatic finally to have my own place and no longer be a burden to Bridget, but on the other hand, I still worried about Dad finding me and I wasn't sure how I would cope with life on my own. For so many years my every moment had been controlled and every decision made for me, that the freedom seemed vast and unsettling.

I wondered if I could hire a private eye from the *Yellow Pages* to find the rest of my family? But then I felt sick as I imagined them finding out about what had happened with Dad. I couldn't let that happen, so resolved to continue as I had done for the last ten years or so, and pretend that Jenny, Diane, Cheryl and Davie didn't exist. It was a matter of survival.

The next day was Christmas Eve. I was on the early shift at work. Just before I was due to finish, I picked up the phone and felt my stomach flip as I heard Mum's voice. But something was different this time. She wasn't shouting at me any more. She was being nice, and I felt tears spring to my eyes. For so many years I had wanted to hear just a trace of tenderness in her voice, and here it was.

'Now listen, Lisa,' she said, 'It's not right to be on your own on Christmas Day. I want you to come round here.'

'But I've told you …'

'Don't worry about him,' she interrupted me. 'He won't be here. He's bought a ticket to Spain.'

I could barely believe my ears. 'Spain?'

'He's shitting himself,' she said. 'Thinks you're going to get him into trouble with the law.'

Relief spread through me. Perhaps the nightmare was well and truly over. With Dad gone, I didn't have to worry about Kat any more and whether he would turn his attentions on her.

'Go on, Lisa, come home. Just for Christmas,' Mum went on, and finally I agreed

Things would be different now. I was amazed at how life had changed in the space of a week. That afternoon I pushed my way through the thronging Christmas Eve crowds on Oxford Street and spent most of my bonus money on presents for Mum and Kat. I bought Mum a bottle of Shalimar perfume from Selfridge's, as well as a porcelain dove – a 'dove of peace', which seemed symbolic. I thought she might like to put it on a shelf in her new flat. Living with Dad for so many years had left her without any ornaments whatsoever, and I thought it might signify a new beginning of sorts. For Kat I bought some toys, and a new outfit. I wrapped everything up before I went to bed that night, but found it difficult to sleep.

The next day I had to ring for a minicab. I hadn't realised that the buses and tubes wouldn't be running on Christmas Day and I had only just enough for the fare. As I stepped out of the minicab and paid the driver, I thought I saw the net curtains in Mum's upstairs bedroom twitch. I waved, thinking Kat must be watching, and walked up the front path trailing my bags behind me. I didn't have time to knock before Kat opened the door.

'Merry Christmas,' I smiled, giving her a hug.

As I walked into the kitchen, Mum was smoking at the table and smirking. 'The wanderer returns,' she said sarcastically, her eyes focussed on something behind me.

The hairs rose on the back of my neck as I realised she was looking at Dad. He hadn't gone to Spain at all. She had lied to me. I didn't have time to turn before he grabbed my hair and swung me hard against the wall. I dropped the presents I was carrying and heard something break as Dad kicked them against the wall in a frenzy. I thought it was going to be my turn next, but for some reason he stopped, standing before me clenching his fists and trying to catch his breath. My heart was beating twenty to the dozen.

'Bolt the door, Donna,' he said, 'or she might go galavanting again. You know what slags are like.'

Mum slid two heavy bolts at the top and bottom of the front door. 'I hope you're not gonna start again today,' she said to me, ''cos I'm not having it. Not today. It's meant to be fucking Christmas.'

I was so hurt and angry I could barely look at Mum after that. In the past I had tried to find excuses for her betrayal, but this was blatant. She had purposefully lied and lured me back, even though she knew what would happen to me.

After the initial beating, Dad made an effort not to hit me for the rest of the day – after all, it was Christmas – but I knew he was struggling to contain himself. I could see his jaw flexing and tightening, and I was dreading the moment Mum decided to leave me alone with him, as I knew she would.

'So what's the address then?' asked Dad, opening another can of Special Brew. 'Where is this knocking shop you've been staying?'

'In Stepney,' I lied, trying to throw him off the scent.

'Well, you won't be going back there again,' he said ominously. 'We'll be in Spain this time next week.'

A jolt of shock passed through me. Could he somehow force me to get on a plane? But deep down I knew I wouldn't be going anywhere except out the door the minute I got the chance. Things were different now. I knew there was life outside, and I knew that Dad understood that, too.

After dinner, Mum found her presents out in the hall. The dove of peace was shattered. 'What a load of rubbish,' she said, hurling it in the bin. She then handed me a joint present from her and Dad. Dad was chewing a matchstick at the table, a sly grin spreading over his face.

'Go on, open it,' he said. 'You'll like it.'

I did as I was told and slowly peeled the paper off to reveal a red and black baby doll nightdress. I was revolted and shot Mum a look of ill-disguised disgust. Why was she encouraging me to be Dad's sex object? What kind of mother would do that?

Later that night, once Mum and Kat had gone up to bed, Dad raped me for the last time. I endured it as I had endured it so many times. He was especially brutal but I blocked out the pain as best I could. This time I had hope. I knew it couldn't last forever, and that soon I would be free of him for good.

The next day, as soon as Dad went to the pub, I grabbed my opportunity to escape.

'You're not going,' shouted Mum, trying to block my way. 'He'll blame me!'

'What is *wrong* with you, Mum?' I asked. 'You've thrown away your whole family for him. Maybe I should let the people at work ring the police after all.'

I knew I'd touched a nerve, and I could see the fear in her eyes as she stepped aside to let me pass.

'It's no good trying to blame me. You should have kept your fucking legs shut.'

'I was a child,' I said. 'I didn't stand a chance, as you well knew.'

'Yeah, and it ain't exactly been a bed of fucking roses for me either, has it?' she replied. 'I'm warning you, Lisa, don't you go doing anything stupid, cos' the only person you'll hurt is Kat.'

'How do you work that out?'

'What do you think's gonna happen if social services start poking their nose in?' Then she softened a little. 'He'll be gone to Spain soon anyway. He's bought his ticket and everything.'

We had all suffered so much, and I was glad the nightmare was coming to an end for us all. The sooner Dad got on that plane, the better.

'Bye, Mum,' I said.

'And Lisa,' said Mum, in the hard tone I was used to, 'I don't wanna see you here again. Just do us a favour and make someone else's life a misery for a change. You've been nothing but trouble since the day you were born.'

Although I hadn't expected a loving goodbye hug, Mum's words still hurt. It was Boxing Day, 1984. In a few days I would be eighteen years old. My whole life stretched ahead of me and I ran towards it without looking back.

Chapter Twenty-one

I lived in Shepherd's Bush for a few weeks, until I discovered a family of mice living behind the wardrobe, and then I found a place in Chiswick, sharing with two other girls. The rent was more expensive and money became a problem. I had to find a better paid job. I signed up to a few temping agencies and began working at various media companies around London. It paid well and the nomadic nature of the work suited me perfectly because it meant I never got too close to anyone. I would make friends at one job, and then move on to another a few months later. I tended not to keep in touch. This left me feeling rootless and very lonely at times, but I was desperate to hide my past and I thought it was a price worth paying.

I also took a job as a waitress at a well-known casino on Park Lane. All I had to do was serve coffee and sandwiches to high-rollers and they would throw a hefty tip on my tray. The waitresses earned more money that the croupiers, and some weeks I was taking home hundreds of pounds in tips. During this time I had quite a few good-looking, wealthy boyfriends but the sticking point always came when they asked questions about my past, because I just didn't want to talk about it. One or two relationships progressed to a more serious level, and I found myself travelling round the world as a guest on private planes and yachts, but along with words of love came more probing questions about my past.

'Why can't I meet your parents, Lisa? I'd like to ask your father's permission to marry you.' Or 'What are you hiding?'

When this happened, I knew it was time to move on.

I found intimacy difficult and often used alcohol as a prop, but I had very little tolerance for it and invariably I would become over-emotional. All the pent-up anguish and pain would come flooding out, leaving me a sobbing wreck. Since I wouldn't explain what was wrong, boyfriends quickly lost patience and I became known as 'an enigma'.

I found Christmas particularly depressing. My housemates went home for the festivities but I would stay in the house alone. To avoid awkward questions I'd pretend I was going home too, and once or twice I even bought my own Christmas presents to put under the tree because I couldn't bear the thought of anyone feeling sorry for me.

On the morning of my twenty-first birthday, I was alone in the house with no plans to celebrate when there was a knock at the front door. I opened it and was astonished to find my sister Diane and Aunt Jenny standing there. I couldn't believe it. How had they found me?

'Is Lisa in?' asked Diane, narrowing her eyes. She obviously wasn't sure whether it was me or not because we hadn't seen each other for ten years.

'It's you, isn't it, Lisa?' said Jenny recognising me at once, with tears in her eyes.

I was so overcome that I almost collapsed. 'Yes, it's me, Jen. It's me, Di,' I stammered, choked with emotion.

It turned out Diane had used a contact at the tax office to trace me through my employment records and date of birth. After we'd all recovered from the shock of seeing one another again, I hurriedly packed a bag and set off in the car to Diane's house. She was having a big party for New Year's Eve and the whole family would be there. I was overwhelmed and it was on the journey there that I began to worry. I didn't know how I could tell them about what had happened with Dad, but I knew it had to be done. I couldn't lie to my own family.

'Have you seen anything of Mum?' I asked Diane.

I detected a slight hesitation before she said, 'No, not since the last time I saw you when I was pregnant. I had a little boy – he's nine now and I just had another one four months ago.'

That night we stayed up until the early hours. Cheryl and Davie turned up and both gave me the biggest hugs. We were all so happy to see one another again. Like Diane, Cheryl now had two young children, and Davie had been living with Aunt Jenny since he left home. Many tears were shed as we remembered old times, all of us careful to avoid any mention of Mum and Dad. Once or twice I entered a room and got the impression they had been talking about things they didn't want me to hear but I was so happy I brushed it off as my paranoia.

The next night was New Year's Eve and while friends and family did the conga round the room, I sat with Cheryl in the corner. I had always loved Cheryl. Although she was nine years older than me, she had looked out for me as best she could back in the days when we shared a bedroom. I remembered the times she used to sing me songs such as 'There's a Tiny House' and I felt a fresh wave of love for her. I couldn't bear the fact that I hadn't told her about what had happened to me after she left. It was now or never. I took a deep breath and said 'Things went wrong after you left. Dad … Dad … did things he shouldn't. He touched …'

Cheryl flinched. 'Don't, Lisa,' she said urgently, slurring her words slightly. What she said next literally took my breath away. 'We know all about it. Mum told us. We saw the washing machine in that flat.'

Saw the washing machine? I stared at her, trying to decipher what she'd said to me as a young boy in front of us attempted to break dance to 'Pump Up The Volume'.

'What do you mean?' was all I managed to say.

'Mum showed us that flat. But it doesn't matter. We still love you, Lisa. We love you.'

I dropped my drink in shock and watched as the red wine soaked into the carpet. But Cheryl wasn't finished.

'It doesn't matter,' she said gripping my arm and shouting above the music. 'We still love you.'

The words 'still love you' echoed through my head. She was saying that no matter what *I'd done* they were prepared to forgive me. What had Mum been saying? How could they possibly believe I'd wanted to sleep with my own dad?

'Honestly, Lisa,' she went on, 'I understand 'cos it nearly happened to me.'

Things were becoming more confusing, and by this time I was nearly hysterical. I had to make her understand.

'No, Cheryl,' I shouted above the music. 'He abused me. I was raped for years.'

I could hardly see through my tears. The injustice of it was too much. People were starting to stare, and suddenly Diane appeared and marched me out of the room with Cheryl staggering along behind.

'You're showing us right up,' she hissed, echoes of Mum coming through. 'What's it all about?'

'Dad abused me,' I hiccoughed through my sobs. The word 'abused' sounded odd because at that time nobody spoke about it. It was still hidden, rarely reported in the press.

'Don't give us all that,' said Diane. 'Mum's told us all about it.'

'We don't blame you,' offered Cheryl. 'You were only young.'

I started to get angry then. 'What is it with you people?' I screamed. 'How can you think that one day out of the blue, I looked at Dad and thought "Yes, I'll have him!"'

Cheryl and Diane stared at me with their mouths open.

'He was my dad since I was a baby, for god's sake,' I went on. 'I wasn't some hormonal teenager taking a fancy to Mum's new boyfriend.'

Cheryl reddened as if I was implying that about her, but I wasn't. I knew she hadn't invited Dad's perverted behaviour, any more than I had. I watched as her face crumpled and felt sad that I'd brought back such horrible memories for her. I thought back to all the tensions at home when Cheryl was

281

around. It was clear Dad had tried it on with her too, except she wasn't a defenceless child, manipulated and beaten into submission over years like me. Cheryl was older, with a network of support, and was able to get away just in time. I hadn't had anyone to turn to. Diane was looking at me as if she hated me, in complete contrast to the way she'd kept hugging me in the car the day before. 'Mum would never let that happen. You were a consenting adult.'

'Are you mad?' I demanded. 'The only consenting adults in this were Mum and Dad. I was a child. I can't believe you didn't bother to hear my side of the story at the time.'

'What, and risk going near him again?' she exclaimed. 'We had our own lives.'

'Well, thanks a lot, Diane,' I sobbed. 'I'm lucky I had the help of a virtual stranger because my own family couldn't have cared less, by the sounds of it.'

I became desperate to get away but Cheryl blocked my way, sobbing as if her heart would break. 'Please stay,' she begged me. 'Don't go off like this.'

There was one more thing I had to know. 'Mum swore to me she didn't know where any of you lived. Were you really in contact all the time?'

I could see Diane's eyes well up with tears then. 'No. She always had the address but we only heard from her that once, when she told us that you and Dad had moved in together.'

'We couldn't believe it,' chipped in Cheryl. 'So she offered to show us the flat as proof while you were out.'

'And that was enough for you, was it?' I said. 'You didn't think it was weird?'

'Course we did,' said Diane, 'but Mum looked us all in the eyes and told us it was what you wanted. So we believed her.'

'And do you see her now?'

'No,' said Diane sadly. 'She hasn't see any of her grandchildren. But we love her and she knows where we are.'

There were more tears as I told them all about how Mum had known I was being abused for years and had simply let it happen. I could see from Diane and Cheryl's eyes that they knew I was telling the truth but they just couldn't face it. I agreed to stay the night, and when I left the next day Diane hugged me and told me to put the past behind me. 'He's in Spain now,' she said. 'Just leave it, eh?'

But as I sat on the Tube home, I felt as though I had come to the end. My life was a mess. I had no real friends and now I didn't even have a family to fantasise about. I knew I would never be able to visit any of them again. There was no way I could sit and have tea and cake with them, knowing they had all been convinced I had seduced Dad for the hell of it. I didn't want their 'forgiveness'; I wanted their understanding, and sadly it wasn't there.

When I got home, the house was empty. My housemates were still away visiting their families. I sat in the middle of the living room floor and wailed. I knew I shouldn't sink into self-pity, and most of the time I didn't, but at that moment I felt that everybody I had ever loved had betrayed me in the most vile way. I had been abused by my dad and, on many levels, Mum too, but nobody thought my pain was worth acknowledging because that might involve them in actually having to do something. I didn't matter. They didn't love me.

I found a bottle of Bacardi in the cupboard under the stairs and proceeded to drink myself into a stupor. Then, feeling totally distraught, I decided the only solution was to kill myself. I broke open a disposable razor and held the blade in my trembling hand. At that point I truly wanted to die, and if it was a case of simply pushing a button, I would have done it without question, but as it was, I lacked the courage to pull the blade across my wrists. Instead I slashed my right arm deeply three times near the elbow. The cuts gaped like mouths and blood began to pour down my arm. The blade became slippery but I hadn't finished yet. I made a final slash on the back of my hand, exposing veins and tendons beneath the skin.

It was as if I had been in a trance, and suddenly the sight of my wounds bleeding copiously brought me round. I sobered up immediately and was horrified at what I'd done. I used towels to try and stem the flow of blood which pooled on the carpet, but the wounds were so deep that I realised I would have to go to the hospital for stitches. I called a cab, feeling dizzy and sick.

When I reached A&E it was clear they were used to dealing with people like me.

'Not another one,' muttered a nurse to her colleague.

A kindly doctor stitched my wounds – fifty stitches in my arm, and fifteen in my hand. I cried throughout the process, not because of the pain but because of the hurt I felt inside. Hurt for the loss of a life I could have had without Dad, hurt for the loss of every person I had ever loved, and hurt for the overwhelming disappointment I felt. I couldn't even kill myself properly.

The hospital staff were concerned about my mental state, and it was only because the duty psychiatrist was already occupied with someone else in crisis that I managed to slip away without them insisting I stay in for observation. I spent the whole of the next day desperately trying to scrub spots of blood from the carpet and the sofa before my housemates came back.

Once I'd sobered up, I was horrified at what I'd done to myself. When it was time for the stiches to come out, I was too embarrassed to go back to hospital so I locked myself in the bathroom and removed them myself instead.

I didn't visit my family again but sometimes, especially when I'd been drinking, I would ring Cheryl or Jenny and simply cry on the phone. Sometimes Davie would answer the phone at Jenny's because he was still living with her, and it became clear that he didn't have a clue what was wrong with me. Diane, Cheryl and Jenny had decided he must never know, because they feared it might make him confront Dad, and he would get hurt or else end up in trouble with the law.

'I don't understand what's wrong, Lisa,' he said. 'We lose touch for years, and then get back in touch and you're crying down the phone. Why aren't you happy? I don't get it.'

Usually Jenny, the woman I'd idolised as a child, would snatch the phone from him at this point in case I told Davie what was wrong. 'Put the past behind you, Lisa,' she always advised.

If only it were that easy.

Chapter Twenty-two

When I was twenty-five, the landlord announced that he was selling the house I lived in so I would have to move. I scoured the small ads looking for somewhere suitable and went to view a flat in Fulham. A guy called Neil, who was already a tenant there, showed me round. I wasn't too keen on the room but Neil was another matter. Straight away we started chatting as if we'd been friends for years. It all felt completely effortless and natural. I knew I wanted to see him again, and could tell he felt the same way. He was completely different to the men I'd met in the past, who tended to be highly successful workaholics who liked having a pretty young girl on their arm in restaurants. Neil was around my own age and worked with his family in their building firm. He was funny and kind and I recognised something special in him. He was like nobody I'd ever met before. I took the room, and almost immediately we became an item.

We connected on many levels, which was surprising because we'd had vastly different life experiences. Our sense of humour was the same, and we spent hours laughing together, but beneath that we understood each other on a deeper level. I found it easy to open up with him. There was none of the inhibition I'd felt with previous boyfriends – and it didn't take long for Neil to discover everything there was to know about me.

Naturally he was horrified when I told him about my upbringing, and he helped me see for the first time ever how crazy it was for me to feel any sense of shame about it. With his help, I was finally able to shed the burdens of guilt and shame I had carried for so long, and truly move on in my life. But there was still something niggling.

'I want to report him to the police,' I said, 'but I don't feel strong enough. I don't know whether I'd be able to stand in a courtroom full of strangers and talk about it.'

We debated the subject for hours, but in the end I still felt too raw to seek justice. All I wanted to do at that stage was forget the past and forge a new life.

Within a year, Neil and I were married. We had a registry office wedding followed by a small party for a handful of friends and Neil's relatives.

We spent our honeymoon doing up a cottage we'd bought in a village on the north-east coast of England. It was a fresh start and we were blissfully happy. Within a couple of years I was expecting our first child and, with my hormones all over the place, the past came back to haunt me once more. At the ante-natal clinic I'd see girls surrounded by their sisters and mums. Neil was great but I really wished I had a family to lean on. I began having nightmares about Mum and Dad again, and all the old feelings of shame came flooding back, but this time I felt anger as well. I became outraged that my parents had shattered our family and not only robbed me of my childhood, but taken away the rest of my family too.

Neil spent hours reassuring me that everything would be alright, and when the baby came, I was consumed with love for her. I was determined not to dwell on the past any more; life was about the future now.

I surprised myself by taking to motherhood quite naturally. Throughout the pregnancy I had been worried about how I would cope, especially when I had been set such an appalling example of motherhood, but it turned out to be easy. I just did everything Mum never did and threw myself into being the kind of mother I'd always wished I'd had.

Both Neil and I wanted a large family. For my part, I couldn't bear the thought of our children ever being alone in the world. There would be strength in numbers. I wanted them to always have one another for support. I had experienced first-hand how lonely the world could be without a soul to call on in times of need. Things would be different with our family. Over the next few years I had five more children before we decided our family was complete.

As I held our sixth child in my arms, I started to wonder about Kat. She had been nine years old when I left home, and even though I hadn't been able to contact her since, she had never been far from my mind.

'I just want to know she's alright,' I said. 'I should have got in touch before.'

'Please don't beat yourself up about the past,' Neil urged. 'You've always done the best you can. And at least she didn't have to grow up with that monster around.'

'Maybe we could try to find her?'

I couldn't remember Mum's address, but within half an hour Neil had found it on the Internet. 'It looks as though Kat's still living with your mum. She's on the electoral roll there.'

The next day I paced up and down, unsure whether I wanted to bring the past back into my life. But I had spent so many hours looking after Kat when she was a baby that every time I looked at my own children I was reminded of her. At the same time, I was worried about stirring up the emotional silt. It had taken me years to get to a point where I was happy. I had my own family, untainted by abuse and rape.

In the end, I knew I would never be able to rest if I didn't find out if Kat was OK. I sat down and spent hours writing and rewriting a letter. I addressed it to both Mum and Kat, and included photos of my children. As soon as I posted it I wanted to reach into the postbox and pull it out again, because suddenly I couldn't bear the thought of Mum looking at or touching photos of my children. But it was too late; it had gone.

Neil told me I had done the right thing.

A few days later the phone rang. I picked it up and when there was silence at the other end, I knew it was Kat.

'It's me,' she said at last. 'Mum told me to ring and tell you never to write again.'

'It's you I care about. I've never stopped thinking about you,' I said. 'I just have to know you're alright.'

Kat was quiet on the other end of the phone.

'Are you there?' I asked. 'So you're still living with Mum, are you?'

'Mum, yeah,' she said. 'Mum and Dad.'

I almost dropped the phone in shock, and my heart pounded in my ears.

'What do you mean – he's there?' I asked, thinking I'd misunderstood somehow. 'Mum said he went to Spain. Everyone said he went to Spain.'

'He never went,' she said.

For the next three hours we stayed on the phone talking. She told me that after I had left, Dad gave up the flat immediately, and moved in with her and Mum. Mum and Dad were back together and lived as man and wife. Kat said my name was never mentioned in the house, and neither was the divorce. It was as if it had never happened.

I was mortified to realise that in the fifteen years since I escaped, Dad had been there all the time. It was the final confirmation that Mum had a massive screw loose. How on earth could she stay with a man like that? I had long understood and accepted that she had never cared about me, but how could she put Kat at risk like that?

Kat insisted that he had never touched her in a sexual way, but told me some hair-raising stories about his violence. There were other disturbing echoes of my experience too. He routinely spat in her food, and if she ever went out she had to account for every minute she was gone. He would even inspect her till receipts to check the times tallied. Also, Mum and Dad would meet her at lunchtimes, just as they used to do with me. It sounded as though he controlled her every movement and she told me she was desperate to get away.

'Don't worry,' I told her. 'You don't have to put up with it any more.' I told her about the way I finally managed to escape and helped her to make her plans.

She was calling from work, where she had very understanding bosses. They arranged a police escort to meet her at Mum and Dad's flat so she could gather her belongings, and a girl she worked with offered her a place to stay. I wanted her to join me as soon as she could. I wanted to look into her eyes, and ask her again if he'd ever touched her because I knew how difficult it was to discuss such things and I suspected she wasn't telling the truth.

When we spoke later that night, she was in the safety of her friend's flat and elated to be free from fear and violence. 'Thank God you got in touch, Lisa. There's no way I would have been able to get out on my own.'

We arranged that she would come up to see me the following weekend and I hung up the phone with my customary mix of emotions: pleased that Kat was free, but heart-sick I hadn't contacted her earlier. As usual, Neil reassured me that I could only do my best at any one time.

Kat said she would ring to let me know which train she was catching so we could pick her up from the station, but instead she called to cancel the trip. Things had changed. After she had left with the police, Mum and Dad had a blazing row. Mum walked out and set off to Diane's house, the sanctuary she had denied me all those years ago when I was bruised and bleeding. At last she was free, and Kat said she was going to stay with her now. So I didn't get my little sister back, but at least she was out of danger. That was the main thing.

Chapter Twenty-three

Thirty years too late, Mum had finally left Dad. It was easy in the end – she just upped and went. Kat told me they were both going to stay at Diane's for a while, and then they would get a flat together. I knew at that moment that Mum would never let me develop a relationship with Kat. She would be lost to me forever, just like my other sisters and my brother.

The irony was that by writing the letter, I had reunited Mum with her family. Apparently everyone was overjoyed to have her back in the fold. Very quickly Kat stopped returning my calls. I spoke to Mum a couple of times, even sending presents for her new flat. I was pleased she had finally left Dad. No matter how badly she had hurt and betrayed me in the past, I wanted her to be happy.

However, writing the letter had a disastrous effect on me. I became depressed and unable to sleep properly. I'd look at my young daughters and think about Dad and the vile things he did to me at the same age. It was becoming clear that I had to do something. It had got to the stage where I couldn't bury the past any more. Motherhood and contact with people from my childhood had brought it all back.

I decided to report my abuse to the police. I looked at my own innocent children and realised that Dad could hurt anyone. He could infiltrate another unsuspecting family and target another child, just as he had done with me. Guilt was back, but this time I didn't feel guilty about what had happened to me – that was old thinking; now I felt guilty that I had let him get away with it. For the first time ever, I realised that I had a duty to report him. Too many people kept silent about their abuse, thinking that because they had 'survived', it was over. I knew from my own experience that an abuser could go on to abuse other children and I had to make sure that didn't happen.

I made a statement to the police, detailing everything that had happened, and in liaison with the Crown Prosecution Service, they decided that Mum had a case to answer too. It was never my intention to report her, but in recounting events it became clear that she had acted in a highly negligent way.

One early morning in August 2005, both Mum and Dad were arrested and taken to separate police stations for questioning. When I spoke to the detective later that day, I noticed a change in her tone. Earlier she had been completely sympathetic and supportive, but now she said that Mum's and Dad's stories were completely different from mine. They claimed there had been no abuse. Dad had admitted he had a sexual relationship with me when I was sixteen but he insisted I was a fully consenting adult and even said he had tried his best to push me away. Mum had told the same story.

'But they're lying. Who on earth would consent to sex with their dad?' I cried. 'And don't forget they've had years to come up with the same story. They were worried I was going to report them back when I first left.'

'But he's not your blood father, is he?' said the probationary detective constable who had been assigned to my case.

I felt as if my whole world was crashing down. This was madness. Dad was claiming I had willingly entered into a relationship with him a few days after my sixteenth birthday. It seemed that the only person who could back me up was Mum, and apparently she was outraged at her arrest and desperately telling defensive lies in order to wriggle out of the charges of neglect. It became clear that in order to save herself she was proving to be Dad's biggest asset. As long as she stuck to the story that I had fallen dramatically in love with Dad a couple of days after my sixteenth birthday she would be alright, and so would he. The only way the police had a chance of proceeding against Mum would be if Dad admitted everything, and there was no way he was going to do that. Mum had done wrong – there was no doubt in my mind – but the person I really wanted to bring to justice was Dad.

I gave the police every detail I could think of, including the names of people who could confirm my stories of missing school and violent attacks in public. But a few weeks later I received the phone call I had been dreading. The CPS had decided there was insufficient evidence to proceed against Dad. I was devastated.

I tried to move on for the sake of my young family, but I couldn't let such a massive injustice rest. Not after what Dad had done. Now that I was older and a mother, I began to worry he could infiltrate another family and do the same to someone else. I couldn't let that happen.

I insisted on speaking to a senior officer and he assured me they had no intention of letting the matter drop. They would continue their investigations in the hope of gathering enough evidence to re-submit the case to the CPS for further consideration.

I replaced the telephone receiver with shaking hands and braced myself to walk downstairs where I could hear my children playing, thankfully oblivious to the turmoil I was feeling inside. I couldn't understand why this wasn't being treated as an open and shut case, especially as Dad had made a partial admission. It should be obvious to any right-minded person that no child ever wants to enter into a sexual relationship with a parent of their own free will. Surely they could see that there must have been a substantial period of prior abuse and grooming? All I could do now was wait and see what would happen but by this stage my faith in the justice system was starting to crack.

In desperation I trawled the Internet in the hope of finding some help and support. I quickly came across The Phoenix Chief Advocates, a group who act on behalf of victims of child sexual abuse. I sent an email outlining my situation and asked if they could help. Shortly after, I received a telephone call from Shy Keenan, the founder of Phoenix and an award-winning children's champion and campaigner. We spoke for nearly two hours, during which time I was enveloped in what felt like Shy's protective Phoenix wings. I sobbed as I explained what had happened so far with the police investigation. She was outraged at the way I had been treated by the police, and immediately phoned the detective I'd been dealing with to tell him so. I no longer felt so frightened and alone. Not now I had Shy and Phoenix on my side. In contrast to how I felt earlier that morning after speaking to the police, I replaced the phone having said goodbye to Shy, feeling strong and inspired to fight for what I knew was right.

Shy and I kept in regular contact as I waited to hear back from the detective. I knew that she was highly regarded by both the police and the media for her campaigning work, and I hoped the fact that she was behind me would make all the difference. But, ever professional, she was at pains to point out there was no magic wand. We were very much dependent on the officer in charge of the case to do his job properly, and gather all available evidence before the case stood a chance of proceeding.

This turned out to be painfully true when a few weeks later I received a letter from the police informing me they had taken the investigation as far as they could. With Mum and the rest of the family refusing to offer valuable corroborative evidence, they felt the case was no longer viable. I was distraught as I stared at the letter and was very upset to be told in such a cold manner. It was as if I was being told that what Dad had done to me didn't matter. Sickening memories of his abuse and violence played in my head and I imagined his arrogant smile when the police told him they were dropping the case. It was then I started to feel a burning sense of injustice.

I re-read the letter and it became clear the police hadn't bothered to investigate my case properly. Leads hadn't been followed up. No attempts had been made to trace important witnesses, and according to Shy, strict procedures laid down by the Metropolitan Police themselves were not adhered to. I had very good grounds to register a complaint and ask for the case to be reinvestigated by another team.

I wrote lengthy letters outlining my case to the head of the Child Abuse Investigation Unit and the Sector Director of the Crown Prosecution Service. I mentioned I had the full support of Shy Keenan at Phoenix, and the end result was that I received a very quick apology, and a high-ranking specialist officer was assigned to review my case formally. However, it took a further two years and many more letters before finally they were able to gather the evidence needed by the Crown Prosecution Service to press charges against Dad. Apparently it is quite usual for historical abuse cases to take this long due to the sheer length of time that has passed since the crimes were committed, and the fact that important witnesses may have moved to another area and be nigh on impossible to find. Shy remained a tower of strength throughout what was a very draining process, and without her bolstering support I'm sure I might have given up like so many other people do.

Finally, in the autumn of 2007 Dad was charged with four sample counts of indecent assault. The officer who had fought so hard over the past two years was over the moon when she told me.

'It's what we've been fighting for, Lisa,' she smiled.

'How long before it goes to court?' I asked, elated at the news.

'It'll take about a year,' she said. 'Hopefully I can talk to your family again and see if any of them are willing to come forward to back you up about how violent he was.'

A few weeks later I called and asked if there was any news. I didn't expect Mum to come forward because that would implicate her for charges of neglect, but surely Jenny, Diane, Cheryl and Davie wouldn't let me down?

'Sorry, Lisa,' my officer said. 'They don't want to say anything that might get your Mum in trouble.'

I was distraught. What chance did I have if my own family couldn't be bothered to come forward and confirm the simplest fact, like Dad's violence. If only Cheryl would speak about what nearly happened to her, it would make such a difference.

'Maybe I can talk to them,' I suggested.

'You're not allowed to approach them. Otherwise you could be accused by the other side of coercing witnesses.'

So there it was. Although my testimony was rock solid, I had little in the way of support. Mum had refused to give evidence for either Dad or me, frightened that the prosecution would rip her to shreds. And not one member of my family was prepared to stand up and tell the court how violent or lecherous Dad was.

'I can't believe it,' I complained to Neil later. 'All I want is for them to tell the truth – nothing more, nothing less. I don't know how they can live with themselves.'

'Think about it, Lisa,' he said. 'If they told the truth, it could land your Mum in trouble. They're petrified they'll lose her again.'

I knew Neil was right. Diane, Cheryl, Davie and Jenny couldn't face the truth. Kat was too young to remember much, but even if she did, I knew that her first loyalty would be to Mum, not some sister she hadn't seen for nearly two decades. The only people I could rely on were Bridget from the tanning salon and Karen, my old school friend, who the police had managed to trace after much searching. I hoped that both of them would be able to remember the events I mentioned in my statement but I had no way of knowing because we weren't allowed any contact before the trial. So much time had passed since it all happened, I could only hope that Karen would remember how I was kept off school, unable to take any exams, and never allowed out to play. Bridget had seen my cut and bruised legs the night she offered me a place to stay, and I was pretty sure she would testify given her own past history.

Their testimonies were small components of my whole case, but very important nevertheless. The crucial thing was going to be how well I came across in the witness box. I had to be very clear and certain in giving my evidence. Dad's defence barrister specialised in defending all manner of sexual assault cases. He was nicknamed 'the Rottweiler' and, as I was to find out, he employed a particularly aggressive cross-examination technique.

The months leading up to the case passed slowly, and then time went into free fall. I tried to concentrate on normal family life, and used my old survival technique of placing things I found particularly stressful in a separate box in my mind.

Finally the day of the court case arrived. The defence had tried numerous times to get the whole case thrown out, using legal technicalities and points of law which left me reeling in confusion and fear. There were so many pre-trial hearings that I spent the final run-up to the trial on perpetual tenter-hooks, waiting for my police officer to ring with news. In fact, the case was a day late in starting, because right up to the last minute the Rottweiler was arguing against it, but the judge was having none of it.

I was to be the first witness. Before I went in, my barrister introduced himself briefly and told me to speak the truth clearly. He was a middle-aged man with sparkling blue eyes and, according to my officer, was highly regarded. I was taken aback by the brevity of our meeting, though, because I expected we would talk through strategies.

'You've been watching too much TV,' my police officer laughed, trying to relieve the tension. 'It's only the defence barristers who get to talk to their clients like that.'

I imagined the Rottweiler ensconced with Dad, priming him on what to say and how to say it. It all seemed so unfair. Even my officer wasn't allowed to stay to settle me in the witness suite, or contact me throughout the trial, or she might have compromised her own evidence. I was left alone.

I waited all day until finally I was called into court. I'll never forget the fear that gripped me, making me want to throw up. I walked into a small modern courtroom, with Formica benches that looked as though they were straight off the set of *Crossroads*, the old 1970s soap opera that was notorious for its wonky walls. Every pair of eyes in the court-room turned towards me. Including Dad's.

He sat slouched in the dock, a look of pure hatred on his face, which was puffy and lined, with huge black bags under his eyes. He was wearing an ill-fitting suit and his sparse head of hair looked as though he had dyed it with a tin of black boot polish only that morning. I could see the skin on his scalp was stained black. I felt ill to look at him, and dragged my eyes away.

The judge seemed like a kindly old man and made sure I had access to water and tissues, which would come in very handy. My barrister started to take me through my statement. There was no room for skirting round the issue. Everything was detailed in the most graphic manner so there could be no misunderstanding. I felt as though I was being raped all over again, and this was the prosecution. He kept motioning me to direct my answers to the jury but it was hard to look directly into the faces of twelve strangers and talk about the most lurid acts imaginable.

A couple of times I heard Dad snort with derision, his familiar gravelly tones roughened further by many more years of drinking and smoking. His barrister shot him a warning look, and the judge told me to ignore him.

I had promised myself I wouldn't cry but after ten minutes, the dam burst. The strain of waiting years, months and days for this moment was too much. I let it out and sobbed so much that we had to pause while I pulled myself together. From that point on, I gave my evidence clearly and concisely. I looked at each jury member in turn, no longer frightened to tell them the truth, no matter how unpleasant. I could see by subtle shakes of the head and the odd tear-filled eye that most of them were moved.

At five o'clock the judge sent us home. I was staying in a hotel nearby because the case had to be heard in London, where the crimes had been committed. I spent a long and troubled night thinking over my statement, and hoping I wouldn't forget things, get dates wrong, or make any other innocent mistake the defence would leap on.

I finished giving my evidence at the end of day two and the judge had just dismissed me from the witness box when the Rottweiler jumped to his feet and barked, 'Your honour, I would just like to take this opportunity to remind Mrs James that she is only part way through giving her evidence, and she is absolutely forbidden to discuss this case with anyone.'

I knew it was all part of his bravado, his way of telling me that I might have had an easy time with the prosecution, but tomorrow he would be the one calling the shots.

That night I was more scared than I had ever been. I had come so far, fought so hard against the justice system to get my day in court, and now if I said the wrong thing it could all be over.

As I walked into court the next morning, my hand shook as I took a glass of water from the usher. The Rottweiler noticed and I thought I detected a hint of a smirk.

When his questioning started, he managed to unsettle me straight away. His tone was unnecessarily harsh and aggressive, and he repeatedly asked me the same question in different ways. I suspected he was trying to throw me off balance, but the judge became impatient and stepped in to remind him that he had already asked me that question several times and furthermore his line of questioning didn't seem to be leading anywhere.

'Now, can we move along, Mr Farmer?'

I realised quickly that much of the Rottweiler's abrasive style was bravado. I was able to answer every question he asked me in a manner consistent with my statement. I also complained to the judge on at least two occasions when I felt he was purposefully trying to mislead the jury. He was forced to apologise before moving on.

I began to realise he had his work cut out in defending a man who had already admitted taking his stepdaughter's virginity. Surely it would be hard for the jury to accept there had been no prior abuse or grooming? After all, it wasn't natural for a girl to decide of her own free will to jump into bed with her dad as soon as she turned sixteen.

In total I spent four further days under cross-examination, which by all accounts is something of a record. Many times the defence barrister would say something and I'd point out he had made a mistake. The judge would then have to clear the court while the barristers engaged in legal argument. This was pushing the court time to the limit and there was a danger we would run out of time, which would result in the case being classed as a mis-trial.

Once, after a lunch break, the usher showed me into the ante-room beside the court to wait until I was called. I nearly threw up. I could tell my dad had been in there before me from the stench of stale cigarettes, body odour and alcohol. I couldn't stay there. After taking a whiff herself, the usher understood completely and moved me outside.

'Yes, he's just been in there with his barrister,' she confirmed.

Just when I was starting to flag, and thought I couldn't go on for much longer, the Rottweiler announced he'd finished with me. I gave a sigh of relief. It was nearly over. I could do no more. Before the judge could dismiss me, my barrister was given the opportunity to question me again but he only needed to ask me one further question, which I am told was very good going. It indicated I had done an excellent job at delivering my evidence, so we didn't have a long list of clarifications to make.

'Thank you, Mrs James. You are free to go,' said the judge over the top of his spectacles.

But the trial was far from over. I was told Bridget and Karen would be going in next, and then it would be the defence's turn to bring forward any supporting witnesses. Everybody was conscious that the trial had over-run quite considerably, and it was fingers crossed we wouldn't run out of time.

Now that I had been dismissed, I had a choice whether to stay and listen to the rest of the case or not. But it would have meant staying in the hotel for a few more days, and by this time I was desperate to go home to my husband and children, who I hadn't seen in nearly a week. My police officer advised that no purpose could be served by me staying.

'In my experience, it'll only upset you,' she explained.

I agreed. I knew that if I had to sit and listen to the Rottweiler trying to defend the indefensible for a moment longer I might spontaneously combust. No, my work was done. I was going home.

As I left the court I felt as if a huge burden had been lifted. I told myself it didn't matter what the outcome was, although maybe this was just my mind in self-preservation mode. I knew I had fought a long hard battle, and even if the foreman of the court announced a not guilty verdict, I had done my very best to secure justice. I could finally hold my head up high and know I had done everything possible to rid the streets of a very evil man.

The detective promised to call as soon as there was any news. I spent the next few days trying to keep myself occupied but both Neil and I jumped every time the phone rang.

Eventually the verdict was in. The jury found Dad guilty of four counts of indecent assault.

My police officer reported that Dad hardly reacted when the verdict was delivered, just slumping forward slightly with a look of resignation on his face.

'Sentencing won't be for a couple of weeks while reports are prepared.'

'What sort of reports?' I asked.

'Just his general health, that sort of thing,' she said. 'But I want to warn you not to expect too much.'

She had already explained that because the offences were committed while I was growing up in the 1970s and 80s, he would be sentenced with the tariffs in place at the time. 'If he'd done the same these days, he'd be looking at ten years,' she said. 'But it won't be anything near that.'

A few weeks later, the detective rang with news of the sentence. 'He got four terms of twenty-one months,' she said. 'It doesn't sound much, and he'll probably be out in half that, but don't lose sight of your victory, Lisa. You overcame great odds to present your case in front of the judiciary and they believed beyond all reasonable doubt that he abused you while you grew up. He'll also be placed on the Sex Offender's Register for ten years.'

The sentence didn't sound much in comparison to what Dad had done to me, but I had learned enough over the past months to know that only a minuscule percentage of cases reach as far as the court room. I was one of the lucky ones. Besides, it had never been about the length of time Dad served. I cared only that a judge and jury of 'twelve good men and true' made it clear that civilised society will not tolerate Dad's kind of depravity.

I wanted justice done to enable me to shake off the shackles of guilt, shame and fear that had held me down for most of my life.

I wanted justice for the little girl I used to be. I knew I would never truly find peace unless I had stood up for that small, frightened child.

Mummy knew but she didn't care, and when my family found out, they didn't care either. But I did. I am different to them. It took a while but through experiencing the wonder of my own children, witnessing their joy, beauty and innocence, I finally learned to care enough about myself to do what was right by the little Lisa within me.

And I know that when my children are old enough to hear my story, they will be proud I did.

Acknowledgements

I t's fair to say that writing this book has taken me on a white-knuckle rollercoaster ride of emotion. I have relived the highs and lows of my childhood and somehow managed to roll out of the dark tunnel and into the light of the future, wearing a smile – albeit looking a little windswept!

It has been such a privilege to share my story, and I owe a debt of gratitude to Judith Chilcote for introducing me to Susanna Abbott and Sally Annett at HarperCollins, who trusted me to write this book in my own words. Thank you all for giving me the opportunity to finally draw a line under my past. Thanks also to the brilliant Gill Paul, whose help and encouragement is greatly appreciated.

A special thanks to Shy Keenan and Sara Payne of The Phoenix Chief Advocates for keeping me safe and warm under those huge Phoenix wings. Keep up the good work!

I will also be eternally grateful to my old friends and saviours, Bridget and Karen, for showing such courage in stepping forward to give evidence when it would have been so much easier for them to turn away like all the others did. The world would be a much better place if there were more people like you.

Huge hugs and kisses to my amazing friend Shaz up in bonnie Scotland for all the warmth, wit and incredible wisdom she's given me over the years. I would have been lost without you.

Lastly, I owe my wonderful husband and children more than I could ever attempt to fit into a sentence. Suffice it to say, my heart swells with love and pride as I write. Thank you for filling my life with such love and happiness, showing me what a real family is and allowing me to be the kind of mother I never knew myself.

Further information

To find out more about the author, visit www.lisa-james.com.

For more information about The Phoenix Chief Advocates and the work they do please visit www.tpcauk.com.